To Cousin Kathy —
And to the three days we spend together at 50 — It was a good year for me — hope it is the same for you.
With fond memories of the good times we've had together.

Susan Cooke Soderberg
July 4, 1995

"LEST WE FORGET"

A GUIDE TO
CIVIL WAR MONUMENTS IN MARYLAND

by
Susan Cooke Soderberg

WHITE MANE PUBLISHING CO., INC.

This White Mane Publishing Company, Inc. publication was printed by:
Beidel Printing House, Inc.
63 West Burd Street
Shippensburg, PA 17257 USA

The acid-free paper used in this book meets the guidelines for permanence and durability of the Committee on Production Guidelines for Book Longevity of the Council on Library Resources.

For a complete list of available publications please write:
White Mane Publishing Company, Inc.
P.O. Box 152
Shippensburg, PA 17257 USA

Library of Congress Cataloging-in-Publication-Data

Soderberg, Susan Cooke, 1944-
      Lest we forget : a guide to Civil War monuments in Maryland / by
Susan Cooke Soderberg.
          p.   cm.
      Includes bibliographical references and index.
      ISBN 0-942597-76-1 (alk. paper) : $29.95
      1. Maryland--History--Civil War, 1861-1865--Monuments--Guidebooks.
   2. United States--History--Civil War, 1861-1865--Monuments-
   -Guidebooks. 3. Soldiers' monuments--Maryland--Guidebooks.
   I. Title.
   E512.9.S65 1995
   973.7'6'09752--dc20   94-37410
                                                              CIP

PRINTED IN THE UNITED STATES OF AMERICA

ACKNOWLEDGEMENTS

I could not have written this book without the help of my family. I would like to thank my husband, Bill, for his editing of the manuscript, my daughter, Jenny, for her secretarial skills in helping to make the maps, and my daughter, Anna, and son, Keir, for their support and help in the many tasks and trips involved in the research and writing of the book.

My sincere appreciation goes out to Patrick Griffin III for all of his help and the use of his impressive library, and to Phillip Sauerlender for his inestimable aid in identifying monument sculptures and their various origins.

A book which covers an entire state and as much primary research as this necessarily needed the aid of many people in local historical societies, county libraries, government organizations, and Civil War organizations. My heartfelt appreciation goes out especially to: Gregg Stiverson, Assistant State Archivist at the Maryland State Archives; Ted Alexander, Historian for Antietam National Battlefield Park; Nancy Kurtz of the Maryland Historical Trust; James Aguirre of the Maryland Civil War Heritage Commission; Martha Dory of the Maryland Office of Arts and Culture; Jane Sween of the Montgomery County Historical Society; Samuel Pruett of the Washington Cemetery Commission; Dennis Frye of the Hagerstown Library; Anita Cushing of the Howard County Historical Society; Jean Kelly and Judge Marvin Smith of the Caroline County Historical Society; Hank Griffith of the National Building Museum; John Potts of the Dorchester County Historical Society; Nancy Nunn of the Kent County Historical Society; Marian Jacobs of the Montgomery County Historical Society; Michael Ribikowsky, Gerald Bayer, Robert Doss, and Charles Goolsby of the Sons of Confederate Veterans; George Brigham of the Central Maryland Heritage League; Scotti Oliver of the Talbot County Library; and Ed Taylor, Jr. of the Cumberland Historic Cemetery Organization.

Much welcome aid was also received from my friends at the Montgomery County Civil War Round Table, especially Vicky Hielig, Greg Clemmer, and Charles Jacobs. Thanks also to the sharing of resources and findings by Ross Kimmel, Steven Stotelmyer, Dan Hartzler, Daniel Toomey and Paul McDermott.

This book began as a master's thesis and I received excellent guidance and valuable advice on organization and research for that thesis from my advisors Dr. Clarence Mondale and Dr. Bernard Mergen of George Washington University. I would like to thank them for giving me useful tools which will last throughout my writing career.

TABLE OF CONTENTS

PREFACE

This is a book for Civil War students, people interested in Maryland and in architectural history, and social historians. I have discussed not only the historical significance of Civil War monuments, but also their interpretation so that all interested in learning from and about the monuments concerning our Civil War will gain knowledge and, I hope, insight.

My research covered aspects of Maryland history, Civil War and post-Civil War history, cultural history, art history, sociology, folklore, and Greek and Roman mythology — as well as the individual history of each monument.

Because of the lack of published sources on this topic much of my research has concentrated on primary sources such as archival records, association minutes and reports, newspapers, and ceremony programs. The most helpful information came from newspaper reports of the dedication ceremonies of the monuments. These often published entire speeches as well as detailed descriptions of the monuments, the officials, the programs and the processions. The local nature of many of the monuments required that research be carried out at county libraries and historical societies which involved traveling to many areas of the state.

The result is this comprehensive list of Civil War monuments in Maryland and their messages to us, both literally and as cultural signposts.

The monuments discussed in the text are all in Maryland and erected by Maryland groups or individuals, the state of Maryland, or the federal government. They are all dedicated to events, groups, or individuals of the Civil War. My only exceptions are the Reno, Garland, and Meade monuments not erected by Marylanders, but included because they have a special significance to the tours, and are off the beaten track. My definition of a monument includes all types and sizes of construction in a variety of materials. Not included are roadside markers, plaques not in or on public buildings, historic houses, and cemetery monuments to individuals which were not erected by a group. The only plaque which has been included as a major monument is the Civil War Centennial Plaque in the State House in Annapolis. That plaque is a monument to the work of the Maryland Civil War Centennial Commission and states its philosophy and objectives, making it a guideline for all Civil War commemorations to follow.

I have tried to be exhaustive in my research on the monuments, but it is possible that I may have missed some. Please report any additional findings to your local historical society.

Most of the monuments under the care of a city, state, or federal government are in excellent condition. Sadly, that is not true of many of the monuments under private care. I found monuments with pieces knocked off or stolen, monuments on which the inscription is no longer readable because of deterioration, and monuments on the verge of crumbling. I have discovered monuments of which people were unaware, even when they were situated near the center of their town.

If you are interested in helping to preserve these monuments, there is a national organization that has just such a goal. It is *Save Outdoor Sculpture!* (S.O.S.) and is based in Washington, D.C. Its main sponsor is the Smithsonian Institution, but it has affiliations with many state preservation commissions. To find out more about that organization and its work at the national and local levels write or call:

Save Outdoor Sculpture!
c/o Nat. Inst. for the Conservation of Cultural Property
3299 K Street, NW
Suite 403
Washington, D.C. 20007
(800) 421-1381, (202) 625-1495

NOTES TO THE READER

Those following these tours will find themselves on busy surface and limited access roads. They should observe extra caution on those roads and not let this book distract them from exercising all due caution on the roads and highways.

Many Union and Confederate veterans' organizations had the custom of giving the title of "general" to their senior elected officials. Where those groups used the title general for their officers in the ceremonies and organizations described herein, the author followed their custom. The title general as used in this book does not automatically refer to a valid Civil War or Army grade.

The illustrations at the end of the descriptions of some of the monuments are depictions of symbols found on Civil War monuments, pertaining to, but not necessarily on, the monument being described.

HOW TO USE THIS BOOK

This book is both a guidebook and a historical reference work. It is divided into five tours that cover Civil War monuments in different areas of the state with maps showing each tour. In addition, a sixth chapter covers monuments in four areas of the state that did not fit into the major tours. Detailed directions are given for each monument on the tours as well as for the gravesites, minor monuments and monuments in chapter six.

The major monuments are identified by a numerical prefix referring to the chapter number and the number of the monument on that tour — for example, 5.2. The Civil War gravesites and minor monuments are identified by a number for the chapter and a lower-case letter prefix for the site — for example, 2.a. An attempt has been made to place the descriptions of the gravesites and minor monuments in appropriate places on the tours so that they may be visited as a side trip from that tour.

All of the monuments are on public property or public cemetery grounds.

KEY MAP

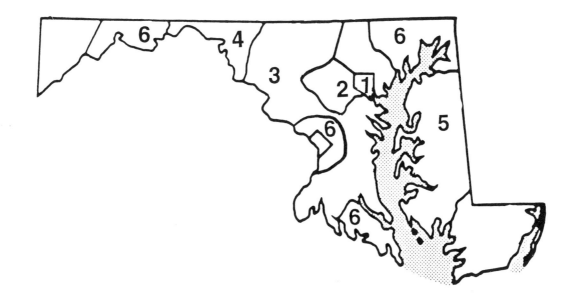

MARYLAND CIVIL WAR MONUMENT FACTS

EARLIEST — Gleeson Union, 1866

LARGEST — War Correspondents

TALLEST — Point Lookout Prisoners of War, Federal

SMALLEST — Cecil County Union

MOST EXPENSIVE — Lee/Jackson, Baltimore, $100,000

LEAST EXPENSIVE — Clara Barton, Antietam Battlefield

MOST RECENT — Gen. Garland Confederate, 1993

SMALLEST NATIONAL CEMETERY — Tulip, St. Inigoes, Maryland

MONUMENTS FINANCED ALL OR IN PART BY THE STATE OF MARYLAND

Gov. Hicks, Cambridge, 1868
Chief Justice Taney, 1870
Point Lookout Confederate Prisoners of War, Maryland, 1876
Washington Cemetery Confederate, 1877
Union statue, Antietam National Cemetery, 1880
5th Maryland Union, Antietam, 1890
Maryland Monument & markers, Antietam Battlefield, 1900
Confederate Prisoners of War, Loudon Park National Cemetery, 1908
Union Soldiers & Sailors, Baltimore, 1909
Confederate Women, Baltimore, 1918
Clara Barton, Antietam Battlefield, 1962
Monocacy Battlefield, 1964
Annapolis Plaque, 1964

MONUMENTS FINANCED ALL OR IN PART BY THE FEDERAL GOVERNMENT

Point Lookout Confederate Prisoners of War, Federal, 1911
Cumberland Confederate Prisoners of War, 1912
Loudon Park Confederate Prisoners of War, 1912
Tulip, St. Inigoes, 1937

NUMBER OF UNION MONUMENTS IN MARYLAND

Cemetery 16   Town Square 1   Battlefield 9   Total 26

NUMBER OF CONFEDERATE MONUMENTS IN MARYLAND

Cemetery 17   Town Square 8   Battlefield 4   Total 29

NUMBER OF MONUMENTS TO BOTH SIDES

Cemetery 0   Town Square 2   Battlefield 2   Total 4

NUMBER OF MONUMENTS NOT ASSOCIATED WITH A SIDE

Cemetery 1   Town Square 3   Battlefield 2   Total 6

Total 65

Introduction

INTERPRETATION OF THE MONUMENTS

THE MEANING

Monuments are all around us in the big cities and small towns of America, in cemeteries and battlefields, along country lanes and major highways. Sometimes they are beautiful works of art, sometimes they are ugly piles of stone which don't fit in with their surroundings. Often they can be found as the centerpiece of a town, but sometimes they are inconspicuous and hard to find. Whether they are prominent or not, we tend to view monuments as just part of the landscape we live in, souvenirs of the past.

But a monument is not just a work of art, a sign-post, or a landmark. It is a message, a message infused with emotion and tinged with deep-seated values. The word "monument" comes from the Latin "monumentum," meaning "a recollection which may also be a warning." When we look at a monument we are supposed to be reminded of something. This is what sets a monument apart from other man-made structures: its significance and its sanctity to the people who erected it lie not in its beauty or usefulness, but in its message. Monuments are unique because they are designed to send a message to the future. They are surrounded by an aura of the past, by the ghosts of the people who built them.

Monuments are testaments to the important events and people of our national past and how we interpret them affects our national identity. Their stone and bronze can teach us about the people of the past if we know how to interpret them, and the more we learn about them, the more we learn about ourselves. The message that most of the Civil War monuments in Maryland are sending to us has to do with the people's feelings about the war that they had experienced. It has to do with sorrow and regret and with reconciliation of Northern and Southern values, as well as with pride and honor.

In order to interpret those monuments one must know the symbolic language of the monument. A person viewing a monument in a later age may receive a different message than that which was sent by its builders because signs and symbols which were well-known at the time of the monument's erection may have become obsolete, time may have blurred the memories supposed to be evoked by the visualization, or the society may have changed structurally or politically so that values held by a later viewer may be incompatible with the values of the people who erected the monument. To discover the message of those monuments we have to try to see them through the eyes of the people who built them. We have to know what the symbols and words on the monument mean, and how the ceremonies surrounding the monument reinforced their symbolic meaning.

Perhaps even more important than the intended messages on monuments are the underlying messages about the society in which they were erected. We can find those underlying messages by looking at who erected the monuments, their funding, and the reasons for their erection. The historical context of monuments — the social and political atmosphere, the commonly held values and beliefs, and the common view of history at the time — is extremely important to their meaning.

A monument is erected by a group of people and thus represents a collective memory of history. A collective memory may or may not be in accord with individual memories. Its main purpose is not to reflect individual memories, but to shape them — to mold a certain collective view of history which will unite and give order to a community. The individual can then verify his personal memory through the group memory, but, at the same time, his personal memory is affected and shaped by the group memory. Collective memories are often constructed in a time of change and upheaval in order to bring order and harmony to a society in transition. They can be constructed purposefully by a group or by a government in order to promote a particular view. Governments have often been known to invent traditions in order to aid in the acceptance and support of their policies. They do this by modifying an existing tradition, or by adding new symbols or suggestive oratory to an existing traditional ceremony. When we discover how a certain collective view of history was molded, and who molded it, we can discover more about the culture and values of the past than if we were to just look at the intended message.*

When a monument makes visible a certain view, it alters the concept of the past held by future generations like a written history does. But it is different from the written word because it is a concrete thing — an artifact. An artifact is an attempt to re-create an actual experience. Through symbolism and its existence as a physical object in space, it is able to evoke individual memories and emotions that mere written words cannot.

A modern example of how a monument can evoke emotions through visual symbolism is the Vietnam Veterans Memorial in Washington, D.C. It is similar to Confederate monuments in that it is a memorial to a war that does not represent victory to those erecting the monument, but was tremendously disruptive to society, and a war whose losing participants were vilified by the rest of the society. It demonstrates the power of monuments by the way that it attempts to legitimize the action taken by superimposing one narrative of the war over another. The incommunicability of the actual experience of the war, along with feelings of guilt, futility, and ambivalence, is submerged in the official narrative. Thus the monument or memorial can serve as a unifying as well as a healing factor, evoking painful memories, but at the same time presenting an official and acceptable communal memory. Instead of glorifying the war, the memorial projects an image of individual sacrifice. With its emphasis on the individual, it can affect a variety of people in a deeply personal way. The emotional pain evoked by the remembering is a part of the healing process, and there would be no healing without it, either for the individual or for the nation. In order to forget, one first needs to remember.

---

* For more on collective memory and the manipulation of tradition see John Bodnar, *The Remaking of America.*

THE CEREMONY

The message of a monument — as well as the emotions evoked by that message — is reinforced through formal ritual. The ritual is a solemn, structured ceremony carried out by a group of people and designed to demonstrate a shared belief and create cultural unity through the practice of a common tradition. Ceremonies make visible a collective connection with some common symbol and can bring together dissimilar people. Without the ceremony the monument ceases to exist as a meaningful symbol.

A ritual always involves many signs and symbols, the meanings of which are supposed to be self-evident to the participants. But the self-evident meanings of the symbols and of the entire ceremony can be manipulated and changed. A meaning can be changed simply by adding signs to an already-conceived symbol — which subtly changes the message. Sometimes the ritual is used to communicate those things that are in doubt by displaying the opposite message. This type of symbol manipulation is called "reversal" and would be reinforced by other symbolic reversals in the ceremony. Examples of such reversals in a Civil War monument ceremony would be a child carrying a battle flag, Confederate symbols being combined with Union symbols, or flowers being placed by a Confederate on a Union grave. Those kinds of reversals would not change the ultimate meaning of the ritual: they would only subtly change the meaning of the symbols. The meaning of the symbols can change and keep their power as long as the ceremony continues to give unity and order to the society.

The symbolism of the ritual reflects the symbolism of the monument and helps to place that monument in historical context. There are two types of reinforcing ceremonies for the Civil War monuments: the dedication or unveiling ceremony, which is a one-time event; and the Memorial Day or Decoration Day ceremony, which is an annual event. The Confederate annual event, Decoration Day, began soon after the Civil War as a day set aside, usually in the spring, to clean and repair the graveyards and lay flowers on the graves of soldiers killed in the war. Many different associations claim to have celebrated the first Decoration Day (1864-1865) and many different dates were used for the occasion. It involved a formal ceremony and a social gathering, sometimes including a picnic. In later years the Decoration Day ceremony may also have been held at a monument in the town; usually it included the town monument, with a procession beginning at the monument and ending at the cemetery. In Maryland the most common days for the Decoration Day ceremony were June 3, the birthdate of Jefferson Davis, or June 6, the date of the defeat of the Pennsylvania "Buck Tail" regiment by the 1st Maryland regiment, CSA, at Harrisonburg which was a major event in that regiment's Civil War service. The practice of the celebration of Decoration Day has nearly died out as its rival, Memorial Day, became an official national holiday and the primary symbols of Decoration Day, the Confederate veterans, all passed away.

Memorial Day had a more formal beginning. On May 5, 1868 Major General John A. Logan, national head of the Grand Army of the Republic (G.A.R.), issued General Order Number 1 which begins: "The 30th of May, 1868, is designated for the purpose of strewing with flowers, or otherwise decorating the graves of comrades who died in defense of their country during the late rebellion...." Thus he proclaimed a unified date for this annual ritual which began as a very solemn and sacred affair of which the cemetery was a central part. Today Memorial Day pays tribute to the veterans of all our wars and has become secularized. By contrast with the Confederate Decoration Day, Memorial Day has survived and flourished.

THE STAGES

There are three stages to the war memorial movement after the Civil War: the funereal stage, the reconciliation stage, and the commemoration stage. They are essentially the same for both Union and Confederate monuments and often overlap. The dedication ceremony for the monument links that monument with a certain stage more than its date or locale.

The Funereal Stage

The funereal stage was part of the natural process of the burial and honoring of the dead after the end of the War. It was a time of mourning, and the ceremonies and monuments were usually located in cemeteries. The participants in that stage of memorializing had actually been affected, either directly or indirectly, by the war and coping with their bereavement was an integral part of the ceremony.

The cemetery dedication or the monument unveiling ceremony took place when the bodies were re-interred or the monument completed. That sometimes coincided with the Decoration Day or Memorial Day, but often another, more convenient or locally significant day was chosen which required a more elaborate, more structured, and less social ceremony. Churches were usually involved in some way with that stage, since the burial ground had to be sanctified and the bodies blessed.

Both types of funereal ceremonies usually were structured in this sequence: procession, invocation by a religious leader, music, introductory address, poetry reading, music,

Unveiling of the Confederate Soldiers & Sailors Monument in Baltimore
Courtesy of the Maryland Historical Society

featured orator, music, and a benediction by a religious leader. The introductory speaker would be a member of the committee of preparation, or, if the committee was made up of women, a man chosen by them. The poetry could be a well-known poem or one made up for the occasion. The featured orator had to be a man who was

A Gathering of Confederate Veterans at Loudon Park Cemetery
Courtesy of the Maryland Historical Society

well-known and respected by the entire society, not just the community represented in the ceremony. The ceremonies had religious overtones with long prayers, ministers as orators, and choirs singing hymns. Children were almost always involved in some way, either unveiling a monument, laying flowers, or leading a procession. Flowers played a central part in this stage as they represented rebirth and were traditionally laid on graves. Because of the use of flowers these ceremonies were usually held in the spring or early summer. The monuments displayed funereal symbolism such as angels and wreaths and were often inscribed with sentimental poetry.

The Reconciliation Stage

The second stage of the memorial movement, the reconciliation stage, gradually grew out of the first, but was different from it in many ways. It involved an active reconciliation between the Union and Confederate soldiers and their supporters that marked an end to the hostilities of war. After the dead were all buried, the emphasis of the ceremonies changed to the survivors. That second stage took place in town squares, city parks and battlefields more often than in cemeteries. The monuments themselves looked similar to the first-stage monuments, but more attention was paid to the visual image, and the inscriptions were less romantic.

The ceremonies were longer and more complex, with the emphasis more on speeches than on prayer. Congressmen or former generals were usually the featured speakers. Bands replaced choirs, patriotic and sentimental songs* sung by a woman replaced hymns, and poetry was sometimes omitted altogether. There were still flowers — but not as many — and children — but only a select few. The Union monuments were usually unveiled by little boys, and the Confederate monuments by little girls — the use of girls being a "reversal" emphasizing the down-play of the military symbolism of the monument. Clergymen were still participants, but only for the opening prayer and closing benediction. The old veterans of the war were primary symbols, leading the parade and sitting in front of the monument facing the spectators. Flags and military regalia were also prominent symbols.

The Commemorative Stage

The third stage is the one we are in today. It is the stage of commemoration, where, because there are no longer any survivors of the ordeal, the emphasis is now on history and education. The monuments and ceremonies began to be commemorative after the First World War when, although there were still a few Civil War veterans alive, another war had taken the place of the Civil War in the active memories of the society. The monuments have lost their immediate emotional impact and are looked on more as works of art or museum pieces. The inscriptions on the new monuments are geared more toward teaching a historical perspective than on evoking an emotional response. The commemorative ceremonies are lacking in the intense passion and emotion of the previous ceremonies. They put more emphasis on historical interpretation than on patriotic rhetoric. The symbols used in the commemorative ceremonies are usually the same as those in the reconciliation ceremonies — the flags, the flowers, the songs, the children, the military regalia, the parades — but the speeches sound more like history lessons than emotional appeals, and the ceremony more like a play than a living ritual.

Modern Ceremony

---

*Examples of these songs can be heard on the audio tape "All Quiet Along the Potomac" by Coleen Mastrangelo.

THE POLITICAL ENVIRONMENT

The Civil War monuments of Maryland are especially significant because the middle placement and "Middle Temperament" of the people of Maryland make it a kind of America in miniature. Maryland was a state with Southern traditions and ideals, but Northern ambitions. It was a Southern, slave state which never seceded from the Union — bound to the South by its traditions, agricultural economy, and history, yet bound to the North by its increasing commercialization and industrialization. Politically, since the time of the Revolutionary War, it had been staunchly conservative and staunchly Union. After the Civil War it was increasingly progressive, business-oriented, and nationalist.

The Southern leaning of Maryland before the war was demonstrated dramatically in the 1860 election in which Lincoln received only 2,294 out of Maryland's 91,841 popular votes. Southern Rights Democrat John Breckenridge won the state with 42,482 votes. The votes for Lincoln came primarily from Baltimore city and the far northwestern "tail" of Maryland, which was populated by fairly recent settlers who came mainly from Pennsylvania.

Maryland definitely had a "split personality" when it came to politics, the predominant slave-owning counties on the eastern shore and southern and central areas being very different culturally and politically than the northern and western counties. For a while before the war the governor of Maryland was elected alternately from three separate regions, a practice that emphasized that sectionalism.

The Baltimore riot on April 19, 1861, in which Union troops marching through Baltimore were attacked by citizens, demonstrated the Southern sympathies of the people of Baltimore. Several soldiers and civilians were killed in this riot, and the city was in turmoil. Mayor George W. Brown had the railroad bridges north of Baltimore burned to prevent further troops from coming through the city, in an effort to calm the residents. President Abraham Lincoln needed that railroad line and gave full authority to then Brigadier General Benjamin F. Butler to gain control of Baltimore and reopen the train lines. The night of May 13, during a storm, Butler brought in his soldiers and set up cannons on Federal Hill, which overlooks the harbor and city. When the unruly citizens of Baltimore woke up the next morning, they were under military rule — which lasted the duration of the war.

Maryland teetered on the brink of secession, but Governor Thomas H. Hicks refused to call a special session of the General Assembly. Because of Maryland's strategic position north of the capital city, Lincoln fought the secessionists by suspending the writ of *habeas corpus* and essentially declaring martial law in all of Maryland — to the consternation of both unionist and secessionist citizens. When the General Assembly finally did meet, all of the South-leaning delegates were arrested, as were many other prominent citizens including Baltimore's chief of police. Before the arrests took place the General Assembly was split evenly on the question of secession, but the members were able to draft a proclamation that called for peace and, at the same time, supported the right of the Southern states to secede. That official support of the South sealed the fate of the state, and for the rest of the war political power in Maryland was held by the Radical Union party supported by the military.

In 1864 a constitutional convention was called by Governor Augustus Bradford (1862-1866) and a new state constitution drafted. This constitution freed the slaves, making Maryland the first state to do so. It also imposed an "ironclad" oath of allegiance to be taken by anyone voting or running for office. Among the questions asked a prospective voter in accordance with that Registration Law were: "Have you ever in any manner adhered to the enemies of the United States...? Have you ever on any occasion directly or indirectly...given any aid [to the enemy]?"

This oath effectively disfranchised Confederate sympathizers as well as those who fought for the South. This state constitution was passed by administering the oath to those voting as well as by allowing occupying soldiers to vote. The Union party had been split prior to this vote into conservatives and radicals. The Radical or Unconditional Union party had been instrumental in devising the new State Constitution, but the party essentially collapsed after their triumph and the Conservative Union party began to gain control with the election of Thomas Swann as governor at the end of 1864.

Men from Maryland fought on both sides of the conflict. According to the latest count from the Maryland State Archives, 46,638 Marylanders joined the Union forces and 12,000 to 16,000 joined the Confederate forces. (Those figures are different from the information on the Centennial plaque at the State House in Annapolis, but are based on more recent research.) Many Confederate sympathizers who stayed at home aided the South in other ways such as sending money, clothing and medicine south, misdirecting federal troops, and aiding Confederate troops when they passed through the state. Spying was rampant in the state. Many Southern sympathizers were arrested and imprisoned without trial. Often, all it took for an arrest was an anonymous note to a federal officer. The society was in turmoil. No one knew whom they could trust.

The end of the war was a relief for most Marylanders. Whether they were torn by sympathies for the South or not, it meant the end of military rule and the return of their Constitutional freedoms.*

With the freeing of the slaves and the subsequent end of the war, the primary question in Maryland became the re-enfranchising of the rebels and the fear of the Black vote. Maryland had rejected the 15th Amendment, which guaranteed the Blacks the right to vote, but the Republican states held the power and eventual ratification of the amendment seemed to be inevitable. Many former Unionists now went over to the Democratic party in order to fight the Registration Law requiring the strict "oath," which continued to keep many of Maryland's white citizens from voting. The most famous was Montgomery Blair, previously a staunch Unionist. Blair was elected president of the Anti-Registration Convention held in January, 1866. He called for a union of the people of Maryland "for the honor, glory and prosperity of our good old Commonwealth" to fight the takeover of the government by the Republicans. "They will hold power over us and other Southern states by present appliances until the blacks are inducted to be managed by the Freedman's Bureau, and absolutely controlling the whole of the states in which slavery has existed, and so the Union," Blair stated. He also dismissed the appropriateness of the Black vote by referring to the Blacks as a "separate caste" which was "subject to despotism."

But the Maryland legislature was still under the control of the Radical Unionists. They held staunchly to the oath as their only means of survival. The governor, however, was a Conservative Unionist. Governor Swann was an ambitious man who wanted his next office to be that of U.S. senator. Since senators were elected by the General Assembly, he did not have much choice but to ensure that the next election would place Conservative Unionists and Democrats in the General Assembly. There was no way to do this with the iron-clad oath preventing the Southern sympathizers from voting. But Swann had an ace up his sleeve — since the registrars who administered the oaths to prospective voters were appointed by the governor, he replaced all the registrars with men from lists provided by the Southern sympathizers.

---

*For more on Maryland in the Civil War see Robert J. Brugger, *Maryland: A Middle Temperament.*

So the old rebels and Southern sympathizers were allowed to vote in the 1867 election. Although the oath was still technically in effect, it was not administered by the registrars. The Democrats took political power in 1867, devised a new state constitution that did away with the hated oath, and reapportioned the state in order to give more delegates to the former slave counties and take power away from Baltimore and the northern counties. Past support of the Confederate cause now became part of the credentials for those seeking appointed posts, and many Confederate veterans were elected to public office.

Even though Blacks eventually did gain the vote (1870), so many Unionists went over to the Democratic party that the Union party collapsed. The emerging Republican party, to which most of the new Black voters belonged, remained small but still a force. The Democrats remained in political power in the state, except for a few years in the 1890s, until the First World War.

Economically, the Civil War had not hurt Maryland. After an initial depression, business readjusted and benefited from federal contracts. After the war Maryland began to industrialize in earnest and Baltimore resumed its position as a competitive port in foreign trade. More railroads were built and factories seemed to pop up everywhere. Banks prospered and there was heavy investment from Maryland in Southern economic development. Agriculture declined as industrialization increased and there was a steady movement of the population to urban areas. By 1900 there were more people working in manufacture than in agriculture. This change in work patterns in turn affected the population distribution and by 1910 the population of Maryland was more urban than rural.

Maryland definitely had a stake in the progress and prosperity of the nation. Without national support the state could not move forward with its industrialization and trade expansion. It was also of utmost importance that the state achieve a unity of its people, for without this unity economic progress would be stymied by internal conflict.

The radical economic changes, coming on the heels of the division of loyalties during the war, greatly affected Maryland society, creating instability and a high degree of anxiety. Old communities and social networks were disintegrating and new ones were being created. The upper classes grasped the ideal of Progressivism, and gathered in mutual support groups to create public schools, health care centers, welfare institutions, universities and hospitals. The lower classes gathered into work groups that substituted for their former town communities and gradually embraced the idea of labor unions and protective labor legislation. For all classes associations became a way of centering their disintegrating communities, and all kinds of associations, both social and political, came into being in the latter part of the 19th century. The associations that built Civil War monuments were a part of this new social and political configuration, but were different from most volunteer organizations because of their political involvement and public displays.

THE PEOPLE

The message a monument displays depends on who is in control of the process of erecting the monument and creating the ceremony. That control was usually exercised by a central body within the larger group. That smaller group was made up of highly respected members of the community, represented by the association, who were supposed to have an expertise or a special relationship to the event being celebrated — although their social standing was usually more important than their expertise. Because of that respectability and expertise, practically any ceremony the committee devised, as long as it was well ordered and fit into a traditional structural pattern, would be acceptable to the larger group.

The first associations were the local Memorial Associations that were organized to help reinter the remains of soldiers so that they could be properly honored, and so that relatives would be able to locate the graves more easily. Those associations arranged for the burial of the dead soldiers in common plots, sometimes bringing bodies from remote areas for reburial in "home ground." They raised money for the burials and the erection of individual markers and monuments, and then organized the ceremonies. They were usually headed and governed by men, but women did most of the organizational work and fund raising. Many of the women had already been organized during the war into groups that had raised money for the war effort, made bandages and clothing for the soldiers, or cared for the sick and wounded in hospitals. Actually the women were good organizers and fundraisers. The men later recognized their talents, and, in later organizations, gave them more leadership positions.

Clergymen were often members of these memorial associations and were always involved in the ceremonies because of the need to sanctify the burial ground. For a clergyman to head an association was rare, but it sometimes occurred when a churchyard was used for the burial — as with the Silver Spring reinterment.

Those local memorial associations were often replaced by associations that had affiliations with national organizations, especially after the bodies were reinterred and there was not much left for the local association to do but sponsor an annual Decoration Day ceremony. For example in 1871, the Society of the Army and Navy of the Confederate States in the State of Maryland (S.A.N.C.), a division of the Association of the Army of Northern Virginia, replaced the Loudon Park Memorial Association. The objectives of that society were "to preserve material for a truthful history of the war, to honor the memory of the dead, to cherish ties with comrades, and to give charity to those in need."

The S.A.N.C. held annual banquets and sponsored funerals for members. The Baltimore Division had much power and influence because it had as its first president Brigadier General Bradley T. Johnson, a local heroic figure, and it also had as members many men who were successful in business and politics. The fact that one didn't have to be a veteran to be a member of the association made it more popular than the United Confederate Veterans in Maryland because of the number of Southern sympathizers in Maryland who could now let their previous allegiances show. Those Southern sympathizers who had been imprisoned considered themselves veterans even though they never joined the Confederate army. Because of the avid support of both the hidden and the open ex-Confederates, that association was able to achieve state governmental funding for the reinterment of Confederate soldiers and raise enormous amounts of money for monuments. The S.A.N.C. formed an affiliate organization, The Association of the Maryland Line, made up of veterans, and was able to convince the state to donate the old Pikesville Armory for use as a Confederate veterans home for that association.

Another example of the generosity of the Baltimoreans towards the South was the Baltimore Agricultural Aid Society formed immediately after the surrender at Appomattox in order to send stock, farm tools, seed, and money to the defeated states. The railroads and bay steamers out of Baltimore carried those contributions free of charge. Many other Southern aid associations were formed in the city, the most prominent of which was the Southern Relief Association, made up of women. This society held a Bazaar at the 5th Regiment Armory in April, 1866, which raised $164,570. In 1877 the Maryland legislature appropriated $100,000 for Southern aid and appointed commissioners for its distribution. After the South was back on its feet, those women's organizations continued to hold their bazaars and fairs, but put the proceeds towards aiding in the building of the monuments and the helping of veterans.

Maryland Line Confederate Soldiers' Home, Pikesville
Courtesy of the Maryland Historical Society

The United Confederate Veterans (U.C.V.) national organization did not form until 1889. In the Southern states, that new organization drew many members away from the Association of the Army and Navy of Virginia and the Southern Historical Society, sapping the latter organizations' power. The U.C.V., however, never gathered much support in Maryland. Perhaps this was because its membership was limited to actual veterans who had served in the Confederate forces. The Sons of Confederate Veterans (S.C.V.), an offshoot of the U.C.V., did not have any more success in attracting Maryland members at the time.

The United Daughters of the Confederacy (U.D.C.) had much more success, both in the South and in Maryland, than either the U.C.V. or the S.C.V. It grew out of the Ladies Auxiliaries of the U.C.V. organizations and was formed in Nashville, Tennessee in 1894. Not only descendants of veterans, but any woman who sympathized with the Southern cause, could join the U.D.C. The main goal of the organization was to promote the Southern view of the war, "the true history," which they did through sponsoring Decoration Day ceremonies, raising funds for monuments, maintaining museums and relic rooms, and educating children by providing materials for schools and starting the Children of the Confederacy organization in 1896. They even offered scholarships for needy sons and daughters of Confederate veterans. These kinds of activities had a special appeal to reform-minded women. By 1912 the U.D.C. boasted 45,000 members.

Men were not allowed as members of the U.D.C., but the state division usually had an official chaplain. The Maryland U.D.C. chaplain was Reverend William Dame, a very influential man who was also chaplain for the 5th Regiment and had been called on to give invocations at most Confederate ceremonies between 1877 and 1918, as well as for the dedication of the Maryland Monument at Antietam.

Because the Daughters welcomed a wide variety of women into its membership, its scope began to widen with the various interests and objectives of its members. In just a few years, the organization added patriotic services in addition to the preservation of Confederate history and aiding veterans of all wars. It is still active, but now limits its membership to women descended from Confederate veterans.

The Grand Army of the Republic (G.A.R) was the Union veterans group. It was founded in 1866 "to provide fellowship among men who fought to preserve the Union, to honor those killed in the war, to provide care for their dependents, and to uphold the Constitution." Membership was limited to veterans of the war. By 1890 the organization had over 400,000 members, and the last member died in 1955. The organization was the primary force in achieving federal pensions for veterans.

In Maryland the G.A.R. disappeared in the early 1870s, but was revived in 1878. It peaked at 3,578 members in 1892. Baltimore had the largest contingent with 13 posts and almost 2,000 members. The "mystic tie" that bound members together was the experience of the war, but, unlike S.A.N.C., they excluded most working class veterans. They also excluded Black veterans. Their activities were much like those of S.A.N.C. and U.C.V. — sponsoring Memorial Day ceremonies and funerals for members, erecting monuments, lobbying state and federal governments, and holding banquets. Like the U.C.V., they were very much involved in national reunions; they participated in the first joint reunion of Confederate and Union veterans at Gettysburg in 1882 and in many subsequent Blue-Gray reunions.

Grand Army of the Republic Badge

The Women's Relief Corps (W.R.C.) began in 1883 as an auxiliary of the G.A.R. It is the oldest women's patriotic organization in the U.S. Like the U.D.C. its membership was open to any woman in the beginning, and it is still active. Its original purpose was to aid the Union veterans and to honor Union soldiers who died in the war. It later expanded to promoting patriotism, aiding veterans of all wars, and doing child welfare work.

As the veterans of the Civil War died, their organizations died with them. After the First World War, the commemoration of the Civil War didn't seem as important, and Civil War organizations suffered in membership. Because they were responsible for the annual ceremony, in many towns and cities those ceremonies faded away entirely, cutting the monuments adrift from the people.

Women's Relief Corps Badge

THE PROCESS

The typical Civil War monument that was sponsored by a group originated in a motion approved by the group. A committee was then appointed or a separate organization was formed to raise the necessary funds. Usually men's groups, who needed women to raise the money, formed the separate structures. The men of that time considered fund raising to be women's work. They would not admit that the women were actually better at raising money than the men because the women were good organizers and had a vast social network to draw from which crossed class lines.

When enough money had been raised the same committee or, less often, a different committee, would arrange a contract for the monument. They would do this either by sending away for monument catalogues or advertising for bids. A monument and inscription was then chosen by the committee, usually subject to approval by the organization as a whole.

If the state was sponsoring a monument, the state legislature or the governor appointed a commission to plan the monument. The state-sponsored monument contractors were chosen by sealed bids, the artists by submitting anonymous models.

The culmination of the process was the dedication or unveiling ceremony, which was usually planned by the same committee.

THE MONUMENT AS ART

Because they could evoke such emotions and also could be aesthetically pleasing, monuments were especially appealing to people of the late 19th century society, immersed as the people were in the Victorian ideals of beauty and sentiment. The great period of monument-building was from about the middle of the 19th century until after World War I, and the majority of those monuments were war memorials.

That period also marked the rise of the park type of cemetery in America. Those two phenomena reinforced each other for, although not all war memorials were built in cemeteries, they both portrayed society's movement toward a separation of death from life, and toward a rationalization of death. Both the park cemetery and the war memorial, were based on a Renaissance aesthetic of beauty — classical yet natural, romantic yet spiritual and imparting a sense of timelessness. Also, the rural park cemetery allowed much more space for sculptures than the city cemetery had, and sepulchers, mausoleums, and large individual monuments proliferated and made the cemetery more like a woodland sculpture garden than a burying ground.*

The most popular forms for the Civil War monuments were the obelisk and the solitary private soldier statue, both usually embellished with classical and romantic inscriptions. The obelisk style of monument represented the extreme of simplification, fashionable because it reflected classical Egyptian structures. The private soldier statue demonstrated the ideal of classical beauty through his relaxed stance and intent expression. It was also a symbol of the individual rights of man, of equality, of democracy over tyranny. Previous secular sculpture in Europe since Medieval times had been dedicated to leaders or great victories. Not since the

---

*For more on cemeteries of the era see David Charles Sloane, *The Last Great Necessity.*

time of the Greeks, with their democratic ideals, had monuments been built to the common soldier. It was this idea that every man was equally important no matter what his rank or wealth, combined with the Victorian preoccupation with death, that made it important to the society that all men who fell in battle should be commemorated, not just the great heroes. Thus the period of the Civil War was the first war in modern times where there was an attempt to mark every grave regardless of loyalties or rank.

Although utilitarian, or living, memorials such as libraries and hospitals were not unknown, they were rare during that period, for only with a recognizable monument could the community reinforce its group identity and communal memory through ritual.

The larger and more intricate sculptures, commissioned from an artist, were only affordable by large groups, or groups with wealthy (or government) patrons, and were usually found in conjunction with the city beautification projects dominant in the early twentieth century. Those large monuments were dedicated to ideals such as patriotism, loyalty, and liberty. In keeping with that idealism they consisted of predominantly allegorical figures loosely based on classical mythology and surrounded by symbols. Small town monuments and monuments sponsored by small groups were much simpler and usually were commercially produced.

That emphasis on monuments gave new life to artistic sculpture in America, which previously had been limited to tombstones and building decorations. Artists went to Italy or Paris to learn the classical art of sculpture, or to Germany to learn the techniques of bronze casting. Some of the more famous American sculptors of that time were August St. Gaudins, William Rhinehart, Olin Warner, and Daniel Chester French.

The standard prototype private-soldier-at-parade-rest statue was created by artisan sculptors who worked for marble or granite quarries or bronze casting companies. The New England artisans John Rogers and Martin Milmore have been credited with the creation of that standard form, but individual forms grew out of popular demand to which different artisans responded by creating their own version of the common soldier type.

Far from being produced on an assembly line, those statues were individually made, usually using a standard model,

which could be changed in minor ways to suit the organization's committee. The models were made in clay by the company's artist in residence. When ready, the model was sent to the artisan who transposed the measurements of the model, using calipers, to the re-

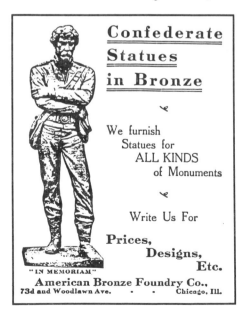

quired measurements of the requested statue and then chipped those measurements out of a marble or granite block. The process was similar with bronze except the artisan transferred the clay model into a plaster model which was then cast into bronze using the lost-wax process. Both the artists and artisans freely exchanged or pirated models and sketches from other companies. American sculpture was still much influenced by European art and so those models, though clothed in modern uniforms, had cloaks and long-coats which accentuated the flowing lines, and stood in the classical Greek pose of "contrapposto."

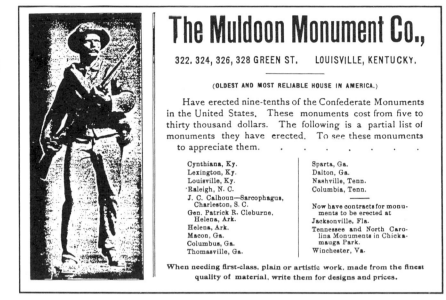

The Muldoon Monument Co.,

322, 324, 326, 328 GREEN ST.   LOUISVILLE, KENTUCKY.

(OLDEST AND MOST RELIABLE HOUSE IN AMERICA.)

Have erected nine-tenths of the Confederate Monuments in the United States. These monuments cost from five to thirty thousand dollars. The following is a partial list of monuments they have erected. To see these monuments to appreciate them.   .   .   .   .   .   .

Cynthiana, Ky.	Sparta, Ga.
Lexington, Ky.	Dalton, Ga.
Louisville, Ky.	Nashville, Tenn.
Raleigh, N. C.	Columbia, Tenn.
J. C. Calhoun—Sarcophagus, Charleston, S. C.	
Gen. Patrick R. Cleburne. Helena, Ark.	Now have contracts for monuments to be erected at
Helena, Ark.	Jacksonville, Fla.
Macon, Ga.	Tennessee and North Carolina Monuments in Chickamauga Park.
Columbus, Ga.	
Thomasville, Ga.	Winchester, Va.

When needing first-class, plain or artistic work, made from the finest quality of material, write them for designs and prices.

All of the companies made both Confederate and Union soldiers, just changing the uniform details, but the Confederate soldiers usually had a large-brimmed hat, and the Union, unless depicting an officer, had a private's hat.

Because of the popularity of Civil War monuments, existing quarry companies and bronze foundries quickly adapted to make them. New companies appeared as well. Before the Civil War there were only four companies making statuary in the U.S. and by 1915 there were 63. One of the biggest was the Van Amridge Granite Company of Boston which made the Point Lookout Federal Monument. The companies sent out catalogues and design sheets on request and stressed that combinations and special additions could be arranged. One company had over 1,000 designs for military monuments. There were also several public books of designs. Sometimes a salesman would come to an organization's committee meeting to sell his company's design.

Often a committee would work through a local cemetery monument dealer who had purchased stock monuments from a wholesaler. Many of those dealers were established before the war in importing statuary from Europe. One of the dealers who became wealthy selling monuments was James Batterson whose sales included the Maryland Monument at Antietam and the Mt. Olivet Confederate Monument.

Sometimes a committee would hire a local artisan to make the monument. Those locally created statues were usually lacking in artistic detail and finesse, but were often charming and always individual.

Local companies were usually favored in Maryland. Granite quarries were in Granite, Maryland, on the Patuxent River southeast of Baltimore, and in western Maryland. There was a quarry for a rare green marble in Cardiff, Maryland north of Baltimore, and a quarry for white marble in the central/western part of the state. If a particular monument could not be purchased locally, the Maryland committee usually chose a northern company or imported a monument from Europe.

THE SYMBOLS

The Cross Bottony

Maryland had no official flag during the Civil War. Troops of both sides usually carried a regimental flag into battle. Maryland did, however, have an official state seal, adopted in 1854.

It bears the heraldic coat-of-arms of Lord Baltimore flanked by figures of a farmer and a fisherman. The shield is divided into four quadrants — two showing the black and yellow checker pattern of the Calvert family and two showing the cross bottony (French botonée) in red and white of the Crossland, Lord Baltimore's mother's, family. The black-and-yellow checker pattern had been used before the Civil War, especially by the city of Baltimore, on flags representing Maryland. Because of that traditional use of the black-and-gold checker pattern, the Southern sympathizing Marylanders adopted the other quadrant of the shield on the state seal — the red-and-white cross. Especially in Baltimore, red and white became known as "secession colors" and were worn on articles of clothing to indicate allegiance to the Southern cause. Major General John A. Dix, commanding the Department of Annapolis in the summer of 1861, forbade the displaying of those red-and-white symbols of resistance. Many Maryland Confederate soldiers wore a small cross bottony pin of brass or tin on their uniform to signify they were from Maryland. For example, Confederate General Johnson used the red-and-white cross bottony on his headquarters flag.

The Maryland Flag

The current Maryland flag, adopted in 1904, is a combination of the black-and-white checker pattern of the Calvert family — the symbol of the Union Marylanders — and the white cross on a red field of the Crossland family — the symbol of the Confederate Marylanders. It is not known who brought together the two emblems, but the first recorded public display of this flag was at the parade for celebration of Baltimore's 150th birthday in October, 1880. It was next seen at the dedication of the Maryland Monument at the Gettysburg battlefield in 1888. In 1889 the 5th Regiment, Maryland National Guard, adopted the flag as its regimental color and carried it in all of the Civil War monument ceremonies, as well as all other parades and special occasions, in which it participated.

NOTE
The "Cross Bottony" is affixed on the top of the Maryland flagpole as prescribed by Maryland Law.

The 5th Regiment

The 5th Regiment participated in almost all of the monument dedication ceremonies in Maryland. The history of the 5th Regiment made it one of the symbols of the ceremony, along with the flag it carried. The Maryland Guard, a successor of the Maryland Line of the Revolutionary War, was formed in 1857, but dissolved when most of its members went South when the war started. Most of those refugees joined the Confederacy's 1st Regiment, Infantry, which became known as the "Maryland Line." When the war was over many of those men returned to Maryland and rejoined the 5th Regiment, National Guard. It soon became known as the "Rebel Brigade," or the "Dandy Fifth" because so many men from wealthy families belonged to it. When the state revoked funding for state militias in 1869 the other units dissolved, but the 5th persevered through private funding. The uniform of the 5th was of grey cloth, symbolizing its Confederate past. The 5th consciously tried to heal the wounds of the war by holding its summer camp in northern states, by eventually admitting former Union men, and by adopting the combination flag. The 5th Regiment went on to serve in the Spanish-American War, and was part of the 29th, or Blue and Gray, Division in World War II.

By its association with the Maryland Line, the 5th Regiment reawakened people's nationalist feelings about the Revolutionary War; by its association with the lost cause, the 5th Regiment engendered visions of heroism, honor and loyalty. The reconciling of those nationalist and lost cause feelings is symbolized in the Maryland flag.

XI OCTOBER MDCCCLXXX.

Illustration by Frank B. Mayer of the first units in the parade in *An Account of the Municipal Celebration of the 150th Anniversary of the Settlement of Baltimore: October 11-19, 1880*

"Maryland, My Maryland"

The one song that was sung at all of the second stage ceremonies, but not many of the first stage, was "Maryland, My Maryland," which was written in response to the Baltimore riot of April, 1861 by James Ryder Randall, a Marylander living in Louisiana at the time. This song, which refers to Lincoln as "a despot," is a call to the citizens of the state to arm for a fight to "spurn the Northern scum," for "Virginia should not call in vain."* It became very popular with both Maryland Confederate soldiers, and the Southern sympathizers at home, during the war. When Lee's army crossed Montgomery County, Maryland, on the way to Antietam in September, 1862, regimental bands played "Maryland, My Maryland" to cheering crowds of local citizens. It was unique in that it was the only original song of the patriotic war-song type to survive after the war. After the war the song was sung at so many popular events that it was finally adopted as the official state song by the General Assembly in 1939.

The "Star-Spangled Banner"

The "Star-Spangled Banner," written by Francis Scott Key during the War of 1812 and set to the tune of "Anachreon in Heaven," became immediately popular because it was published in a Baltimore newspaper and individual copies of it sold in the streets. It was not, however, a military song, could not be marched to, and was difficult to sing, so it waned in popularity after that war. Its rise to fame after the Civil War accompanied the increasing non-military use of the flag, since the song is a tribute to the flag. It was not often played or sung at dedication ceremonies until after 1900.

The United States Flag

The United States Flag, designed in 1777, was primarily used for the navy since ships had to have a way of identifying each other from a distance. The army in the Revolutionary War, the War of 1812 and the Civil War carried regimental flags which gave each regiment its own special identity and had reference to their home area, symbolizing hearth and home to the men. During the Civil War the poem "Barbara Fritchie" by John Greenleaf Whittier, sparked a popular response to the public display of the American flag and its significance.

It wasn't until the 1890s, however, that the American flag began to be flown over buildings that were not military and used in non-military ceremonies. This transformation was mainly due to the efforts of the Women's Relief Corps and the Daughters of the American Revolution, founded in 1890. They zealously pursued what they felt was their patriotic duty to promote the teaching of patriotism and good citizenship in the schools and the veneration of the flag as the symbol of our united country. As a result the government started making special rules about the use of the flag – legislating tradition. That new universal use of the American flag represented the change from local allegiances to a national allegiance.

1861 U.S. Flag

The U.S. flag changed frequently between 1861 and 1912. As states were added to the Union, the number of stars increased from 37 to 48. The 1912 flag was used until 1959 when Alaska and Hawaii became states, making 50 stars.

1912 U.S. Flag

---

* See Appendix E.

The Confederate Flag

Several different Confederate flag designs were used during the Civil War, but all were banned from public display after the war. The flag used most often in the Confederate monument ceremonies was an elongated version of the battle flag, the elongation making it a differ-

ent flag than that used during the war, but the familiar colors and crossed stars making it a fitting symbol for the soldiers who had once carried a similar emblem into battle. The thirteen stars stood for the eleven Confederate states and the two secession governments of Missouri and Kentucky.

Confederate Battle Flag

After the First World War, when the ceremonies became more commemorative and historical in nature, the 1865 Confederate flag was often used.

1865 Confederate Flag

The Veterans

The veterans themselves were the primary symbols of the ceremonies. They led the procession and were given places of honor facing the spectators during the ceremony. They were usually dressed in full military regalia, or at least adorned with their badges and ribbons. At every important ceremony and reunion the veterans were given special badges made for the occasion which identified them as honored veterans. The Grand Army of the Republic had their own special badge which was worn at those events and almost every monument that they erected had an image of this badge on it.

Newspaper reports of the ceremonies were always pointing out the emotional response of those venerable old heroes. No ceremony seemed a success unless it brought "tears to the eyes" of the veterans.

When the Civil War veterans died out, the Memorial Day Committee transferred that emotional symbol to the veterans of other wars. The Confederate ceremonies had no real-life substitutes for their beloved heroes, and so Decoration Day faded away with the old soldiers. Modern Confederate ceremonies rely on re-enactors to supply that emotional focus.

Regimental Insignia

Regimental flags and insignia were important to the veterans as a symbol of the "mystic tie" of the common experience of the war which bound them together. Union regimental flags, the same ones that had been carried into battle, if they were available, were always on display at ceremonies and parades. The Confederate regimental flags, when they were available, were carried furled as a sign of defeat. Beginning in the 1890s there were ceremonial returnings of flags captured in the war to their original owners. Both Union

II Corps

and Confederate monuments erected by or to a particular regiment or regimental leader most often displayed regimental symbols — such as the anchor on the Reno Monument, the shamrock on the 5th Regiment (Union) Monument at Antietam, and the cap and bugle on the Monument to Meade.

IX Corps

Flowers

Flowers were an integral part of the early ceremonies because of their association with cemeteries and with rebirth and regeneration. Women would spend all year tending their gardens to grow beautiful and exotic varieties of flowers which they would then arrange in elaborate symbolic designs such as crosses within circles, anchors, flags, shields, some even with words spelled out with flowers. It was almost required to arrange flowers in the form of a soldier's regimental symbol when it was known. Each flower and plant had a symbolic meaning which everyone of the time was aware of — roses for youth, ivy for memory, laurel for honor, oak for immortality, goldenrod for loyalty, poppies for forgetfulness, etc.

An Anchor for "Hope"

When the ceremony moved from the cemetery to the town square, the emphasis on flowers necessarily declined. When flowers were present the varied and intricate arrangements were no longer in evidence, and the monument was sometimes decorated only with an evergreen wreath. Flowers, as a symbol of rebirth, lost their importance when the purpose of the ceremony was not to honor the dead but the cause they fought for. The intricate symbolic meaning of the plants, so well known in Victorian times, was also lost to future generations. In today's ceremonies the kind of flowers seem not to be as important as the color of the flowers, whether dyed or natural — red and white for Confederate; red, white and blue for Union.

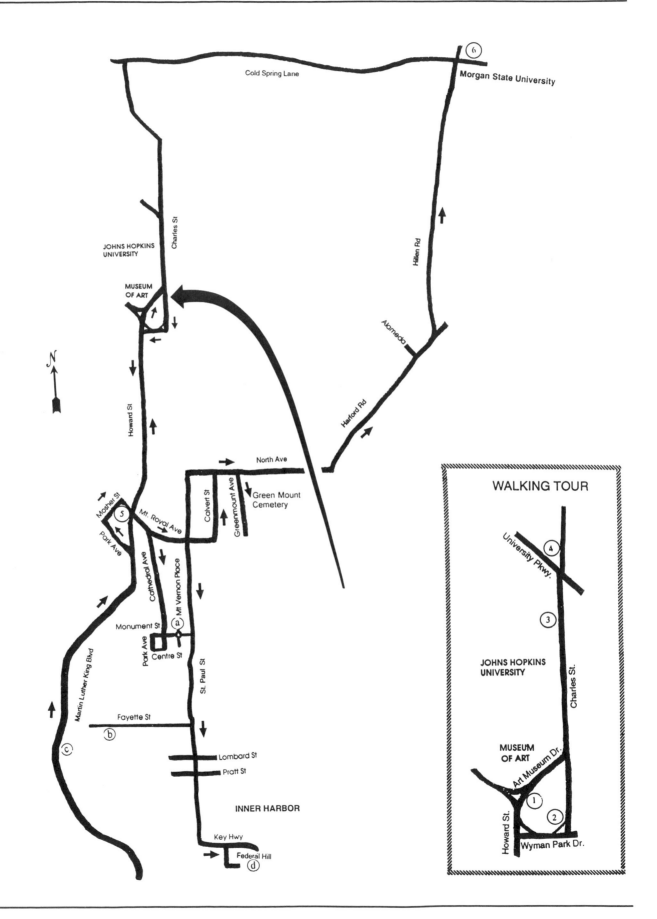

Cold Spring Lane

Morgan State University

Charles St

JOHNS HOPKINS UNIVERSITY

MUSEUM OF ART

N

Hillen Rd

Alameda

Harford Rd

Howard St

North Ave

Green Mount Cemetery

Mosher St

Mt. Royal Ave

Calvert St

Greenmount Ave

Park Ave

Cathedral Ave

Mt Vernon Place

Monument St

Park Ave

Centre St

St. Paul St

Martin Luther King Blvd

Fayette St

Lombard St

Pratt St

INNER HARBOR

Key Hwy

Federal Hill

WALKING TOUR

University Pkwy.

JOHNS HOPKINS UNIVERSITY

Charles St.

MUSEUM OF ART

Art Museum Dr.

Howard St.

Wyman Park Dr.

Chapter 1

BALTIMORE CENTRAL

fter the stifling military rule of the Civil War years, Baltimore sprang back to life with its discovery of the European sea trade and the advantages of diversified manufacture. Politics settled down to regular Democratic dominance and Machine rule. Benevolent associations took the place of the radical political gangs, and life took a more conservative turn. Veterans groups from both sides were powerful in the city and, for the most part, were congenial to each other.

The veterans actually took the first steps toward the reconciliation necessary for political and economic progress. Many had become politicians or businessmen and knew the benefits of reconciliation. Veterans of the war also tended to have a high degree of respect for the valor and loyalty of those who fought on the opposite side. That reconciliation process was reported in volume 28 of the *Confederate Veteran* magazine in 1909.

"In 1875 the 5th Regiment Maryland National Guard, Baltimore, paid a visit to Boston, Mass. The personnel of the regiment comprised veteran soldiers, the majority of whom had served in the Confederate army, and they took occasion to pay a tribute to their former foes by marching from their quarters on a Sunday afternoon without arms or music to the cemetery at Charlestown and placing on the soldiers' and sailors' monument therein a superb shield of flowers. There was no parade or ostentation connected with the simple ceremony, and it gave rise to the greatest surprise and enthusiasm throughout the entire North, coming, as it was deemed, from a representative Southern regiment."

The Baltimore Grand Army of the Republic (G.A.R.) posts returned the favor by decorating the Confederate monument at Loudon Park Cemetery, in spite of some reluctant members. In reply, William Pegram of the United Confederate Veterans, anonymously composed:

Cease firing! There are no foes to fight;
Grim war is o'er and smiling peace now reigns.
Cease useless strife! No matter who was right,
True magnanimity from hate abstains!
Cease firing!

This verse so inspired the Union veterans that they hung a plaque containing the words on the Confederate monument during their ceremonies there.

LEE/JACKSON

Dedication Date: May 1, 1948
Location: Museum Dr. & Howard St.
Medium: bronze
Donor: J. Henry Ferguson
Sculptor: Laura Gardin Fraser
Contractors:
      pedestal: Stony Creek Memorial Corp.,
          Guilford, Conn.
      statue: Gorham Company, Providence,
          R.I.

Inscriptions:

    pedestal:
*   So great is my confidence in
General Lee that I am willing to
Follow him blindfolded.
Straight as the needle to the pole
Jackson advanced to the execution
      of my purpose*

    front:
*   They were great generals and
Christian soldiers and waged
    war like gentlemen*
              — Ferguson

    right:
*   The parting of General Lee and
Stonewall Jackson on the eve
      of Chancellorsville*

    left:
Gift of J. Henry Ferguson of Maryland

Directions: From south of Baltimore take I-95 north to Rt. 395 into Baltimore. From Rt. 395 exit onto Martin Luther King Boulevard. Follow Martin Luther King Boulevard until it ends and turn left onto Howard Street. Continue north on Howard Street a little over a mile and bear right onto Art Museum Drive. The monument is on the right at the intersection of Howard Street and Art Museum Drive. The Baltimore Museum of Art is just beyond on the left. You should park on the street or in the Art Museum parking lot on the left (or in one of the Johns Hopkins University parking areas on weekends). This and the following three monuments are all within walking distance of each other.

This statue is a classical example of a commemorative memorial, bequested by a man who was just a boy at the time of the Civil War, but who had fond memories of his "boyish heroes." J. Henry Ferguson said in his will, "I feel that their example should be held up to the youth of Maryland." It is a monument relating a vision of history to posterity. Ferguson left his bequest of $100,000 to The Municipal Art Society of Baltimore to hold in trust for the memorial, and he named members of a committee to decide on the form of the memorial. A Baltimore banker, he is buried at Green Mount Cemetery.

The artist chosen in the resulting competition, Laura Garden Fraser of New York, had studied sculpture since she was a child, and already had many awards and public sculptures to her credit. She in turn hired the noted architect John Russell Pope to design the pedestal, and they worked together to complete a unified harmony in the monument. It is considered one of the finest statues in the world for its beauty of modeling and the symmetry of its unique double equestrian composition.

The *Baltimore Sun* (May 2, 1948) reported that more than 3,000 people gathered in Wyman Park for the Dedication Ceremony in 1948. Linking the past to the present, the grandchildren of the two revered generals were present. Also touching on the past, the old 5th Regiment appeared in full dress uniforms, not seen since 1938. Several companies from the modern Army were also present, along with the Army Band from Fort Meade. Dignitaries included the Governor of Maryland William Preston Lane, author Douglas Southall Freeman, representatives from the Virginia Military Institute (VMI), the United States Military Academy, the Army and the Navy. Virginia Military Institute cadets led the parade in their full dress uniform.

Governor Lane was the main speaker. He explained the appropriateness of a monument to these two Southern heroes being located in Maryland, a state which was split in loyalties during the Civil War, but was Southern before the war. He said "We honor here the character and the ability, the strength of conviction and the devotion to a cause" which made two men great. Douglas Southall Freeman then gave a stirring account of the events leading to the historic meeting depicted in the statue. R. E. Lee Marshall, Chairman of the Committee, presented the monument to the City of Baltimore, and mayor, Thomas D'Alesandro, Jr., gave a speech accepting the monument.

This monument has been the focus of many ceremonies since that time, its prominent location and its inspiring symbolism making it a perfect place for remembering the Civil War. The Sons of Confederate Veterans organization sponsors a wreath-laying ceremony there every January on a Saturday near the birthdays of the two generals.

CONFEDERATE FLAG

UNION SOLDIERS AND SAILORS

Dedication Date: November 6, 1909
Location: Charles St. & Wyman Park Dr.
Medium: bronze, 21'
Sculptor: Adolph A. Weinman
Donor: Maryland

Inscriptions:

> front:
>> *Erected by the State of*
>> *Maryland to commemorate*
>> *the patriotism and heroic*
>> *courage of her sons who*
>> *on land and sea fought*
>> *for the preservation*
>> *of the federal union in*
>> *the Civil War*
>> *1861-1865*

Directions: From the Lee/Jackson monument continue on the walkway around the park to the east along Art Museum Drive and south along Charles Street. The monument is on the opposite side of the park.

Maryland honored her native sons who "fought for the preservation of the Union" with one of the finest sculptures in Baltimore. The sculptor has masterfully arranged the three figures in a compact and balanced composition energized with a powerful forward momentum. The soldier, as he turns from his plow and anvil, buckling on his sword, seems almost to be stepping off the platform. The two angels behind him accentuate the forward movement with their hands, while their huge wings lend weight to the rear of the composition, keeping the forward movement in check. The angels represent Victory and Bellona (war).

The artist, Adolf Weinman from New York, studied under the famous August St. Gaudens for a time, and the statue here is reminiscent of St. Gaudens' Sherman and Shaw statues. Weinman immigrated to America from Germany at age 10 and studied art at the Cooper Institute in New York. He is well-known for his Lincoln sculptures in Madison, Wisconsin and Frankfort, Kentucky and for designing the 1916 dime and half-dollar.

"The erection of this monument was authorized by the General Assembly of Maryland, Act approved April 15th, 1906, Chapter 539," according to a tablet on the monument. The cost was $25,000. The dedication of the monument was a grand affair at the original site of the monument near the entrance to Druid Hill Park. There was a large reviewing stand for dignitaries opposite the monument, and the veterans of the war were seated in front of this stand, facing the audience.

The *Baltimore Sun* (Nov. 7, 1909) has a description of the ceremony. Gen. John King, president of the monument commission, was the master of ceremonies. He explained how the sculpture was the unanimous choice of the commission from a number of anonymous submissions. Governor Austin L.

Crothers then spoke. He praised the "fearless daring" of the soldiers from Maryland, that whatever the differences were of the past, "the people of Maryland stand today as a united people." After L. Barry Mahool, the mayor of Baltimore, accepted the monument, two little boys, sons of veterans, pulled the cords to reveal the statue while the band played "The Star-Spangled Banner" and a salute was fired.

The orator of the day, Major John I. Yellott, acknowledged the fact that many of Maryland's young men went to fight for the South, and that it was good that now the State "after a delay of nearly half a century, put its sign of approval" on the Union soldier of Maryland and commemorated his valor in doing his duty.

After the singing of "America" the parade of troops before the reviewing stand began. The 5th Regiment received an ovation from the crowd as it passed. There were about 800 Maryland members of the Grand Army of the Republic marching in the parade, as well as members from other states. A show of field artillery and cavalry brought up the rear.

SONS OF (UNION) VETERANS BADGE

SIDNEY LANIER

Dedication Date: February 4, 1942
Location: Johns Hopkins
         University, Charles Street
Medium: Bronze
Sculptor: Hans Schuler
Donor: The Municipal Art Society

Inscription:

> *Sidney Lanier*
> *Poet Musician*
> *1842-1881*

Directions: From the Union Soldiers and Sailors Monument walk back north along the park walkway to the intersection of Art Museum Drive with Charles Street. Cross Art Museum Drive and continue north. The monument is next to the sidewalk on the left about halfway to University Parkway.

The Lanier monument is not technically a Civil War monument, being erected as a tribute to Lanier as a poet and musician, but Sidney Lanier had been a Confederate soldier, serving with the 2nd Georgia. He was confined for many months in Point Lookout Prisoner-of-War Camp, where he contracted the tuberculosis which caused his death sixteen years later. His poetry was much loved in the South and the *Confederate Veteran* magazine (March 23, 1923), in an article against commercialism, said that "this poet, fighting disease, amassing little money, but singing many sweet songs, did more for the South than any captain of industry."

According to the *Baltimore Sun* (Feb. 4, 1942), more than 200 people gathered for the dedication of this statue, which many declare is the loveliest in the city. The Municipal Art Society's spokesperson, R. E. Lee Taylor, president M.A.S., at the ceremony said that the Society decided to pay tribute to Lanier "not only because he was distinguished in the field of letters, but also because he was a man of high ideals and lived up to them." On accepting the monument on behalf of the university Dr. Isiah Bowman, President of the University, pointed out that the monument faced east, which was appropriate for the poet who had written "Sunrise." The three-year old great-granddaughter of Lanier placed a basket of flowers in front of the monument, ending the ceremony.

There is a memorial "Sidney Lanier Room" at Johns Hopkins with some of the poet's original manuscripts, furniture from his house in Baltimore, and other memorabilia.

CONFEDERATE WOMEN

Dedication Date: November 2, 1918
Location: University Parkway and
       Charles St.
Medium: bronze, 12', on a red granite
       pedestal, 12'
Sculptor: J. Maxwell Miller
Donor: Maryland and United Daughters of
       the Confederacy

Inscriptions:

   front:

> To the
> Confederate Women
> of Maryland
> 1861-1865
> "The Brave At Home"

   rear:

> In difficulty and danger
> Regardless of self
> They fed the hungry
> Clothed the needy
> Nursed the Wounded
> and
> Comforted the dying

Directions: From the Sidney Lanier Monument continue walking north on Charles Street and cross University Parkway. The monument is at the intersection.

Dwindling in numbers, the United Confederate Veterans in 1902 appealed to its members to contribute to a fund to erect monuments to Southern women — "Your mother and my mother, who stood steadfast throughout those dreadful years, never wavering, never doubting the justness of our cause." Neither the Maryland Confederate veterans nor the Maryland United Daughters of the Confederacy were able to raise the necessary funds for such a tribute, so, in 1914, a delegation from the United Daughters went to the state legislature to request an appropriation from the state. They testi-fied before committees in both the House and the Senate, saying that "in all the Southern states monuments were being erected to Confederate women, and that the Confederate women [of Maryland] were worthy of being thus honored." The legislature replied with,

> "An act to erect a suitable monument in the city of Baltimore to commemorate the heroism, devotion, and self-sacrifice of the women of Maryland in their service to the wounded Confederate soldiers who came under their care in the War Between the States."

It appointed a commission of three men to oversee the project and appropriated $12,000.

J. Maxwell Miller won the competition for the commission. Miller was born in Baltimore in 1877, attended the Maryland Institute of Art and Design, and at that time was studying at the Rhinehart School of Sculpture. The winning of such a competition by a student was extraordinary, but was well-founded as Miller went on to create many beautiful public sculptures such as "Orpheus and Euridice" at the Peabody Institute, "Twilight" at the Walters Art Gallery, and "Cardinal Gibbons" at the Pennsylvania Academy of Fine Arts. The heroic size bronze grouping of three figures represents a mother holding a dying soldier while a younger woman stands behind.

The unveiling ceremony on a cold, blustery November day, as described in the *Baltimore Sun* (Nov. 3, 1918), was presided over by Rev. William Dame and the exercises began with the playing of the "Star Spangled Banner." The monument "was veiled by both the stars and stripes and the stars and bars, which were drawn aside by Miss Mary Ringgold Trippe, granddaughter of the late Gen. Andrew C. Trippe, chairman of the monument commission." The son of the General, Judge James Trippe, was the main speaker. He lauded the virtues of the women of the state who for four years suffered under hard circumstances for a cause doomed to failure. He praised the sculptor as having the artful talent to bring back to life "the most unique type of woman the world has produced," and portraying the "dignity, beauty, strength of character, loyalty, and passionate tenderness" in the features of the two women in the sculpture. Other musical selections during the ceremony were "Maryland, My Maryland," "Dixie," and "The Bonnie Blue Flag."

The inscription on the rear of this monument, paid for by the state, praises the very actions that women of Maryland would have been arrested and jailed by the Federal Government for doing during the war.

SEAL OF THE UNITED DAUGHTERS OF THE CONFEDERACY

CONFEDERATE SOLDIERS AND SAILORS

Dedication Date: May 2, 1903
Location: Mt. Royal Ave. and Mosher St.
Medium: bronze on red granite pedestal
Height: 18'
Sculptor: F. Wellington Ruckstuhl
Donor: Maryland United Daughters of the
Confederacy

Inscriptions:

front:
Gloria Victis

*To the
Soldiers and Sailors
of Maryland
in the Service of the
Confederate States of America
1861-1865*

right:
Deo Vindice

left:
*Fatti Maschi
Parole Femine*

rear:
*Glory
Stands Beside
Our Grief*

Directions: From Art Museum Drive turn left (south) on Howard Street. After you cross the bridge over the expressway and go under Mt. Royal Avenue, take the second right onto Park Avenue. Go three blocks and turn right on Mosher Street and take to the end (3 blocks). The monument is to the right on old Mount Royal Avenue. To exit after viewing the monument get onto new Mt. Royal Avenue and travel east a few blocks to a "Y" intersection. To go directly to Green Mount Cemetery take the left "Y" and turn left onto Calvert Street; to visit the downtown grave sites and monuments, take the right "Y" onto Cathedral Street.

In the early part of the century the United Daughters of the Confederacy (U.D.C.) of Baltimore decided to erect a monument that would "fitly commemorate the heroism of that martyr band who for us and for love of country gave fortune and life itself for the cause we love."

After raising sufficient funds, mainly through bazaars at the 5th Regiment Armory, the U.D.C. held a competition for a design for a monumental sculpture and chose the model submitted by New York sculptor, Frederick Wellington Ruckstuhl. It is a bronze sculpture, titled "Gloria Victis," of a standing winged female figure, an embodiment of "Glory," holding aloft a laurel wreath with her left hand while she supports a mortally wounded Confederate soldier with her right. The soldier tightly clasps a battered furled flag. The face of the soldier was modeled after an 1861 photograph of Lt. Henry Howe Cook of the 44th Tennessee, who was 17 at the time.

The sculptor, who was living in Paris at the time he entered the competition, said that he felt a deep sympathy for the South and was suddenly inspired with "a vision" of the design while attending an opera. The sculpture, however, closely resembles a sculpture by Antonin Mercie which at that time was located in the central courtyard of the Hotel de Ville in Paris. Mercie began his work, titled "Gloria Victis!" during the Prussian invasion of France in 1870, and it was originally a figure of Fame supporting a victorious soldier. When he found that France had surrendered, he changed the group, replacing the victorious soldier with a defeated one and changed the title to "Gloria Victis," which is a rejoinder to the ancient motto "Vae Victis" (woe to the vanquished).

Mrs. D. Girard Wright, President of the Maryland Division, U.D.C., described the monument in the *Confederate Veteran* (Oct. 1902) as an embodiment "of an idealization of the Confederacy in an allegorical representation of the glory of the South in her defeat,"

"Gloria Victis" by Mercie, 1874

The Cleveland Museum of Art,
Gift of Robert Hayes Gries 64.375.

and says that it is "the spirit of our motto - 'Glory stands beside our grief!'"

The unveiling ceremony for the Confederate Soldiers and Sailors Monument was attended by thousands. It began with a parade of veterans organizations and bands starting from Baltimore's Washington Monument. An observer later told her experiences: "As the line passed the house of Gen. Lawrason Riggs, an upstairs window was flung open and a woman waved the dear old flag. The sight of that was answered by a piercing Rebel yell, which was taken up in the ranks until the street was filled with it."

The ceremony began with the playing of "Dixie" and the singing of the long meter Doxology, after which Rev. William Dame, Chaplain of the U.D.C., gave the invocation which was filled with words like "righteous cause, call of truth, duty, sacrifice unto God, path of patriotism." Then the great-granddaughter of Major General Isaac Trimble, C.S.A., Margaret Lloyd Trimble and the great-granddaughter of Admiral Franklin Buchanan, C.S.A., Nannie Young Hardcastle, marched up to unveil the monument to the strains of "Tenting on the Old Campground."

After the unveiling, "Maryland, My Maryland" was played and flowers placed around the monument. Major General Andrew Trippe then gave a speech in which he gave a short history of the more famous Confederate leaders of Maryland, defended the legality of the war, and argued that the Southerners were not defeated, just worn down by overwhelming numbers.

Captain McHenry Howard delivered the featured oration. He denied that Marylanders were traitors, and said Maryland would have seceded if she could have. As he said: "The soldiers believed that they were not only taking up the sacred cause of liberty invaded, as their fathers had gone to Massachusetts after Lexington, but were in reality fighting the battle of their own state as truly as the sons of Virginia or Carolina." He ended praising the Southern women. The band struck up "We're the Boys So Gay and Happy" (Camp song of the Maryland Line), which was followed by the presentation of the monument to the mayor of Baltimore. The ceremony ended with the music "The Bonnie Blue Flag," the benediction, and finally, again "Dixie."

To show how far reconciliation had reached in 1903, the *Baltimore American* (May 3, 1900), a Republican newspaper which had not previously covered Confederate ceremonies, gave an account of the ceremony saying the monument was "a tribute to the heroism which animated the men representing the Confederacy when espousing a side they thought just," and that "the new loyalty is the stronger and purer because so steadfast to the memory of the old, and the symbolism of the memorial unites pathos, triumph, and hopefulness in such an inspiring degree that its spirit is as prophetic of a brighter future as it is tenderly remembering of the dead."

There is a second-casting of this statue in Salisbury, North Carolina. It is the only copy known to exist.

CONFEDERATE FLAGS

BALTIMORE CENTRAL'S OTHER STOPS

The 5th Regiment Armory is just a few blocks south of the Confederate Monument, on Howard Street, 29th Division (used to be Hoffman) Street, and Preston Street. This is not the original 5th Regiment Armory where bazaars were held to raise money for aid to Southern states and for monuments. That was located downtown and was destroyed by fire in the late 19th century. A new armory was completed at this site in 1903, burned down in 1933, and rebuilt in 1935. There is a Civil War Room in the museum in the building.

1.a   *Chief Justice Taney Statue Replica*
Mount Vernon Place Park

Directions: Go south on Cathedral Street five blocks from Mt. Royal Avenue to the park on the left. The Maryland Historical Society is on the right on Monument Street. There is an attended pay parking lot in the rear of the Historical Society buildings, with an entrance from Park Avenue. One block past the park turn right from Cathedral Street onto Centre Avenue and then right onto Park Avenue.

Many lovely statues surround the tall Washington Monument at Mount Vernon Place Park. To the north of the Washington Monument is a second-casting of the statue of Chief Justice Taney by Rinehart which sits in front of the State House in Annapolis (6.1). This replica was cast in 1887 and was a gift to the city from Mr. W. T. Walters.

Just one block west of Mount Vernon Place Park is the Maryland Historical Society Museum (Monument St. and Park Ave.) which has many Civil War Relics on display and informative interpretive exhibits about the war in Maryland. Temporary exhibits often feature the Civil War in Baltimore.

1.b   *Commodore George Nichols Hollins,*
CSA, 1799-1878
Westminster Burying Ground
Fayette and Greene Streets
(south of church in family crypt)

Directions: From Mount Vernon Place go south on Cathedral Street seven blocks. Turn right on Fayette Street and go four blocks to the cemetery on the left.

George Hollins was on a ship captured by the British in 1814, just after becoming a midshipman at age fifteen. He later served in the Mediterranean and in the Mexican War. He became a lieutenant in 1825, a commander in 1845 and a captain in 1855. In the Confederate Navy he commanded the New Orleans Naval Station then spent most of his time patrolling the James River in Virginia, where he was wounded in the arm, and serving on numerous boards and courts. After the war he was a court officer in Baltimore.

Hollins' most famous escapade was the capture of the Chesapeake Bay steamer St. Nicholas at the beginning of the war. His compatriot was dressed as a woman called Madame Zarvona who took passage on the steamer. Together they smuggled other Confederates aboard and at the right moment, threw off their disguises and captured the ship. They then used it to capture other vessels on their way up the Rappahannock River.

1.c   *Brig. Gen. Lewis A. Armistead, CSA,*
1817-1863 (Gettysburg)
Old St. Paul's Cemetery
Redwood St., Martin Luther King
Blvd., & Lombard St.
(SW corner of center)

Directions: From Westminster Burying Grounds walk two blocks south to Lombard Street and then two blocks west.

Armistead was a North Carolinian who attended West Point from 1834 to 1836. He served in the Mexican War and joined the Confederacy in May, 1861 as colonel of the 57th Virginia Infantry. In April, 1862 he was commissioned a brigadier general and given a brigade of Pickett's division. During the Battle of Gettysburg he led a company to capture a Union artillery battery and was mortally wounded. A monument to Gen. Armistead is on the battlefield.

1.d *Daughters' Sundial Federal Hill*

Directions: From Mount Vernon Place go south on Cathedral Street three blocks and turn left on Mulberry Street and then take the second right onto St. Paul Street. Follow St. Paul Street south until it becomes Light Street and continue past the waterfront. Turn left on Key Highway at the Science Museum and take the first right onto Battery Avenue which will take you to Federal Hill.

Not much is known about this little sundial except what is on the inscription — that it was erected by the Mother Sperling Tent [of the Women's Relief Corps] on April 23, 1935 "In memory of the Grand Army of the Republic." It is possible that it was originally at Smith Park on Pratt Street. That park was destroyed during the urban renewal of the waterfront, and the statue of Smith which had been in the park was moved to Federal Hill.

GREEN MOUNT CEMETERY

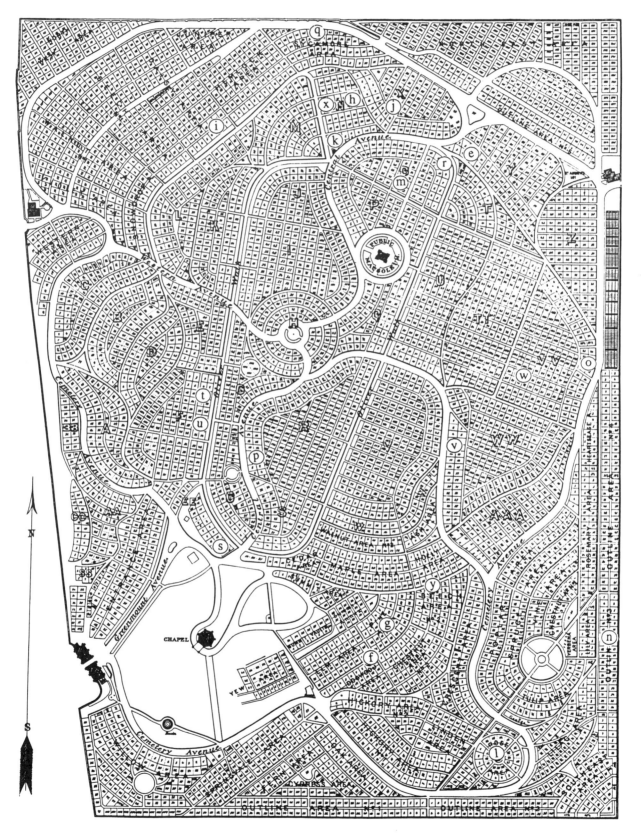

GREEN MOUNT CEMETERY

Greenmount Avenue & Oliver Street, Baltimore

Directions: From the downtown area take Calvert Street north about 2 miles to North Avenue. Turn right on North Avenue and go 3 blocks to turn right on Greenmount Avenue. The entrance to the cemetery is on the left five blocks down.

Although there are no major Civil War monuments in Green Mount Cemetery, there are seven Union generals, one Union admiral, eight Confederate generals, and five other important Civil War personages buried here, as well as many beautiful sculptures by William Henry Rhinehart and other masterful sculptors. The cemetery is included in the National Register of Historic Places.

The Green Mount Cemetery Corporation was founded in 1837 and bought the estate, called Green Mount, of Robert Oliver. The cemetery opened in 1839 as the fourth garden-park cemetery in America. Those cemeteries of the Victorian era were conceived as peaceful and secluded parks. Their shady avenues were laid out in a pattern conforming to the natural landscape and they were often visited just for strolling or picnicking as well as for paying tribute to those gone before. After the Civil War the cemetery expanded its boundaries and was the most popular and prestigious burial ground in Baltimore.*

1.e   *Brig. Gen. (brevet) Henry Bankhead, USA, 1828-1894 (section: Y, lot #7)*

Bankhead was born in Baltimore, October 5, 1828. He joined the army as a young man and began his service during the Civil War as a captain in the 5th U.S. Infantry. He became a lieutenant colonel in the 1st Corps, Army of the Potomac, then the 5th Corps, Army of the

Potomac. He was breveted a brigadier general April 1, 1865, for "gallant and meritorious service in the Battle of Five Forks, Virginia." He died in Bayonne, New Jersey Jan. 9, 1894.

1.f   *John Wilkes Booth (1838-1865) (section: Dogwood, lot #9-11, unmarked)*

The assassin of President Lincoln was born in Bel Air, Maryland, the son of the famous British-born actor Junius Brutus Booth. With his brother, Edwin Thomas Booth, John followed in the footsteps of his father and became a renowned actor, especially acclaimed for his tragic roles. After murdering the President he was hunted down and shot in a barn in Port Royal, Virginia. His grave is unmarked, but is probably south of the shaft that marks the grave of his parents.

1.g   *Brig. Gen. (brevet) Richard Neville Bowerman, USA, 1831-1920 (section: Pine, lot #11)*

Born in Baltimore May 31, 1831, Bowerman was employed by the U.S. Customs Service before the war. He entered the army as a corporal, then became a captain with the 11th New York Infantry. He ended his military career as a lieutenant colonel with the 4th Maryland Infantry. He was breveted a brigadier general March 13, 1865

---

* For more on this and the other cemeteries in Baltimore see Jane B. Wilson, *The Very Quiet Baltimoreans, A Guide to the Historic Cemeteries and Burial Sites of Baltimore.*

for "gallantry and good conduct at the Battle of Five Forks, Virginia." After the war he worked for the Consolidated Gas Company in Baltimore and died in that city August 9, 1920.

1.h Governor Augustus W. Bradford, 1806-1881 (section: N, lot #34)

Unfortunately the inscription on this gravestone was completely obliterated at the time of this writing by time and the elements. The identity of the occupant of the grave, however, is obvious by the close abutment on either side by the stones for the governor's wife and son. Elected governor of Maryland in 1862 as a Unionist, Bradford had a son who was an officer in the Confederate army. As governor of an occupied state, he did not have much power. He protested in vain to Lincoln about the escape of Maryland slaves to the District of Columbia after the District passed an emancipation resolution early in 1862. With Montgomery Blair and former mayor of Baltimore, Thomas Swann, he helped form the Conservative Unionist party in May, 1863, in opposition to Henry Winter Davis' Radical Unionist party. The new state constitution, passed in 1864 under his leadership, removed religious prohibitions on public office and established a state-supported public school system. He served as governor until 1866.

1.i Brig. Gen. Joseph Lancaster Brent, (promoted) CSA, 1826-1905 (section: Daisy, lot #3)

Before the war Brent was an attorney in California after graduating from Georgetown University. During the war he was a major of artillery under Gen. Magruder, then major and chief of artillery under Taylor in Louisiana. Appointed (though never actually com-

missioned) brigadier general of cavalry in October, 1864, he led "Brent's Cavalry Brigade" which fought in the western arena. After the war he travelled much in Europe, eventually settling in Baltimore where he practiced law until his death.

1.j Brig. Gen. (brevet) James Monroe Deems, USA, 1818-1901 (section: X, lot #76)

James Deems was a music teacher and composer born in Baltimore January 5, 1818. He served as lieutenant colonel in the 1st Maryland Cavalry during the war, becoming assistant inspector of cavalry on the staff of General Sigel. He was breveted brigadier general March 13, 1865 for "gallant and meritorious services during the war."

1.k Gen. (brevet) Andrew Woods Denison, USA, 1831-1877 (section N, lot #13)

Col. Denison lost an arm while leading the 8th Maryland in battle at Laurel Hill. He was wounded again near Petersburg and was breveted a brigadier general March 13, 1865 for valor at Wilderness and Spotsylvania, and major general for distinction at White Oak Road. He was postmaster of Baltimore after the war.

1.l Brig. Gen. (brevet) Levi Axrell Dodd, USA, 1833-1901 (section: Rose, lot #37½)

A native of Pennsylvania (born in Franklin, Aug. 13, 1833), Dodd was a merchant before the war. He was a captain with the 169th Pennsylvania Infantry, then a colonel with the 21st Pennsylvania Infantry. He was breveted a brigadier general April 2, 1865 for "gallant and meritorious services in the assault upon the enemy's works in front of Fort Sedgewick, Virginia. He was a court clerk and purchasing agent in Baltimore after the war and died August 5, 1901.

1.m *Maj. Gen. Arnold Elzy, CSA, 1816-1871*
(section: O, lot #33)

Born Arnold Elzey Jones at "Elmwood" in Somerset County December 18, 1816, he graduated from West Point and served in the Indian and Mexican wars as a captain. He entered the Confederate army in April, 1861 and was made colonel of the 1st Maryland Infantry. He was promoted to brigadier general after the battle of First Manassas, was wounded in the fighting around Richmond, and was made a major general in December, 1862. After the war he lived on a farm in Anne Arundel County until his death February 21, 1871.

1.n *Maj. Gen. Benjamin Huger, CSA, 1805-1877*
(section: Outline, lot #15)

Carrying out his family military tradition Huger (pronounced Eu-zhay) graduated from West Point in 1825 becoming an expert on modern artillery. He was chief of ordinance under Gen. Winfield Scott in the Mexican War, winning many brevets including that of colonel. He became a general in the Confederate army in April, 1861. His failures at Norfolk, Roanoke Island, and the battles of Seven Pines led to his reassignment to ordinance inspection duties in the western arena. After the war he retired to a life of farming in his home state of South Carolina.

1.o *Gen. Joseph E. Johnston, CSA, 1807- 1877*
(section: VV, lot #28-30)

Johnston was born at "Cherry Grove" near Farmville, Virginia February 3, 1807. He was a classmate of Robert E. Lee at West Point. During the Mexican War he rose to the staff rank of brigadier general. As a Confederate general he commanded the Army of Northern Virginia after the battle of First Manassas. He was severely wounded at Seven Pines and his command passed to Robert E. Lee. In 1863 he was in command of the Army of Tennessee. After the war he was elected to the U.S. House of Representatives from Virginia, and was a commissioner of railroads under President Cleveland. He died in Washington, D.C. March 21, 1891, supposedly after contracting a cold while marching in the funeral procession of his old adversary, General Sherman.

1.p *Maj. Gen. (brevet) John Reese Kenly, USA, 1818-1891*
(section: R, lot #11)

A lawyer before the war, Baltimorean John Kenly had seen battle before as a major of volunteers during the Mexican War. He began his Civil War career as a colonel of the 1st Maryland Infantry, serving garrison duty along the Potomac. His regiment fought the 1st Maryland, CSA at Front Royal, Virginia on May 23, 1862, and he was severely wounded and captured. Back in service after being exchanged, he was promoted to brigadier general and went on to command the Maryland brigade in western Maryland, and then the District of Eastern Shore. After the war he was breveted a major general and presented with a sword by the city of Baltimore.

1.q *Sidney Lanier, poet, 1843-1874*
(section: Sycamore, lot #32)

This simple boulder with a bronze plaque marks the grave of the poet Sidney Lanier who fought in the Confederate army. He is buried in the lot of his patron, Lawrence Turnbull. The inscription reads "I am lit with the sun." See also the Sidney Lanier Monument entry (1.3).

1.r *Brig. Gen. Lewis H. Little, CSA, 1817-1862*
(section: O, lot #11)

Born in Baltimore March 19, 1817, Little was the son of a noted Congressman. He had fought in the Mexican War and so was commissioned a major of artillery when he joined the Confederate cause in May, 1861. Soon he was promoted to colonel under General Price and distinguished himself at the Battle of Elkhorn, then being promoted to brigadier general. During the Battle of Iuka, September 19, 1862, he was conversing on horseback with three other generals when a ball from the federal lines passed under the arm of one of the others and hit Little in the forehead, killing him instantly.

1.s Rear Admiral Cadwallader Ringgold, USA, 1801-1867 (section: EE, lot #14-16)

Ringgold was a career navy officer, achieving the rank of lieutenant by age 27. He was a captain at the beginning of the Civil War, becoming a commodore in 1862, and a rear admiral by the end of the war. He died April 29, 1867.

1.t Brig. Gen. George Steuart, CSA, 1828-1903 (section: F, lot #80)

Born in Baltimore, Steuart served on the western frontier after graduating from West Point. He joined the Confederate army as a captain of cavalry and then became a lieutenant with the 1st Maryland, CSA. In March, 1862, he was commissioned a brigadier general under the command of Lieutenant General Richard S. Ewell. He was wounded at Cross Keys and captured at Spotsylvania. After the war he became a farmer in Maryland and for many years was the head of the Maryland Division, United Confederate Veterans.

1.u Governor Thomas Swann, 1809-1883 (section: F, lot #33)

Swann was the Know-Nothing mayor of Baltimore just before the war, and became

governor of Maryland in 1866 as a Conservative Unionist who quickly changed to Conservative Democrat following the lead of Montgomery Blair. He was instrumental in regaining the vote for the Southern sympathizers and Maryland Confederates after the war. For more information on this controversial governor see the "Hicks Monument" (5.4).

1.v Maj. Gen. Isaac Ridgeway Trimble, CSA, 1802-1888 (section: WW, lot #8)

Trimble was a native of Culpepper County, Virginia who had graduated from West Point in 1822 and served as a lieutenant of artillery until 1832 when he resigned to become an engineer for the Eastern and Southern Railway construction, living in Maryland. He was commissioned a colonel of engineering in the Confederate forces and constructed the defenses of Norfolk. He served as a brigadier general in the Valley campaign under Ewell. He was wounded at Second Manassas and returned just in time to participate in the Battle of Gettysburg where he lost a leg and was captured. He made his home in Baltimore after the war where he was involved in veterans activities.

1.w Maj. Gen. Erastus Barnard Tyler, USA, (Brevet) 1822-1891 (section: VV, lot #74)

Tyler was born in New York, but raised in Ohio where he went into the fur trapping and selling business after completing college. When war broke out he helped raise the Ohio volunteers and was elected their captain over James A. Garfield. He was made a brigadier general in May, 1861 and given command of several Pennsylvania regiments in the V Corps. He was then assigned to the defenses of Baltimore. After the war he married into a Baltimore family and remained in that city becoming active in the Grand Army of the Republic and the Masons. He was appointed

Postmaster of Baltimore by President Hayes in 1877.

1.x Severn Teackle Wallis, 1816-1894 (section: N, lot #36)

Not directly involved in the war, Wallis was a respected lawyer and writer in Baltimore who was involved in the political reform movement of 1858 and was influential in the Democratic party. He was a delegate to the special assembly on secession in Frederick in 1861 and was one of those arrested there.

1.y Brig. Gen. John H. Winder, CSA, 1800-1865 (section: Beech, lot #13)

Born in Somerset County, Maryland, Winder graduated from West Point in 1820. He then served in the Mexican War and rose to the rank of major. When he joined the Confederate army in April, 1861, he was made provost marshal of Richmond, a command which made him unpopular among the citizens. In 1864 he was assigned the duties of commissary general of prisoners east of the Mississippi. The federal government's refusal to effect an exchange of prisoners at that point, compounded by the lack of provisions, made his task almost impossible and brought him much criticism from the north. He died of anxiety and exhaustion in Florence, S.C., February 2, 1865.

OTHER STOP

1.z Brig. Gen. (Brevet) Leopold Blumenberg, USA, 1827-1876 Har Sinai Cemetery, Erdman Avenue at Edson Hwy.

Directions: (not on tour map) From Green Mount Cemetery, turn right on North Ave., then left on Belair Rd. After 9 blocks, turn right on Erdman Ave., right on Edison Highway and an immediate right into the cemetery.

The only Jewish Maryland general in the Civil War, Leopold Blumenberg was born in Prussia and moved to Baltimore with his family in 1854. He helped raise the 5th Regiment, USA, made up of Maryland volunteers. He was commissioned a major in 1861 and was wounded at Antietam, were he was serving with the 5th Regiment, in the fall in 1862. After the war Blumenberg served as Baltimore's postmaster and also as a representative of the Internal Revenue Service. He is supposed to have been breveted a brigadier general by President Andrew Johnson, but it is questionable whether he ever received his commission.

FREDERICK DOUGLASS

Dedication Date: October 20, 1956
Location: Morgan State University
Medium: bronze, 8'4", 4' pedestal
Sculptor: James E. Lewis
Donor: Maryland Education Association

Inscriptions:

> *Frederick Douglass*
> *1818 - 1895*
> *Humanitarian*
> *Statesman*

Photo Courtesy of Morgan State University

Directions: Morgan State University is in the northern part of Baltimore. From Green Mount Cemetery return to North Avenue and turn right. After ten blocks turn left on Harford Road and after fifteen blocks turn left on Hillen Road. After passing the reservoir park turn right on Cold Spring Lane into the university campus. Park in the first lot on the left in a visitor space and walk up the stairs behind the parking lot. The statue is in front of the building across the lawn from the top of the stairs.

It took a long time for a monument to a black hero of the Civil War to be erected in Maryland, but it is a lovely tribute to a most worthy man.

The Maryland Educational Association, the state teachers organization for Blacks, first conceived of a monument to Frederick Douglass in 1943. The association started a fund-raising effort and slowly the contributions from school children, parent-teachers associations, and service clubs accumulated until they finally amounted to the needed $10,000.

A competition was held and the sketch submitted by James E. Lewis, head of the Art Department at the then Morgan State College, impressed the association officers.

The statue completed by Lewis shows a larger-than-life Douglass striding forward in his forceful manner, hatless and holding a cane, with a serious, purposeful look on his face.

The dedication ceremony on October 20, 1956, featured Governor Theodore McKeldin who said Douglass was one "who chose hardship, labor and peril to serve a cause infinitely greater than self." Douglass was praised as a statesman, orator, and leader of emancipation.

Frederick Douglass was born and grew up a slave on a plantation on the eastern shore of Maryland, spending some time in a house-hold in Baltimore. Intelligent and defiant, he could not endure a life of slavery and escaped to the North as a young man. He became a brilliant orator and writer against slavery. His autobiography, *Narrative of the Life of Frederick Douglass, an American Slave*, excited abolitionists and inspired hope for the Blacks as no other book had done. Later in life he became secretary of the Santo Domingo Commission, Recorder of Deeds in the District of Columbia, and minister to Haiti.

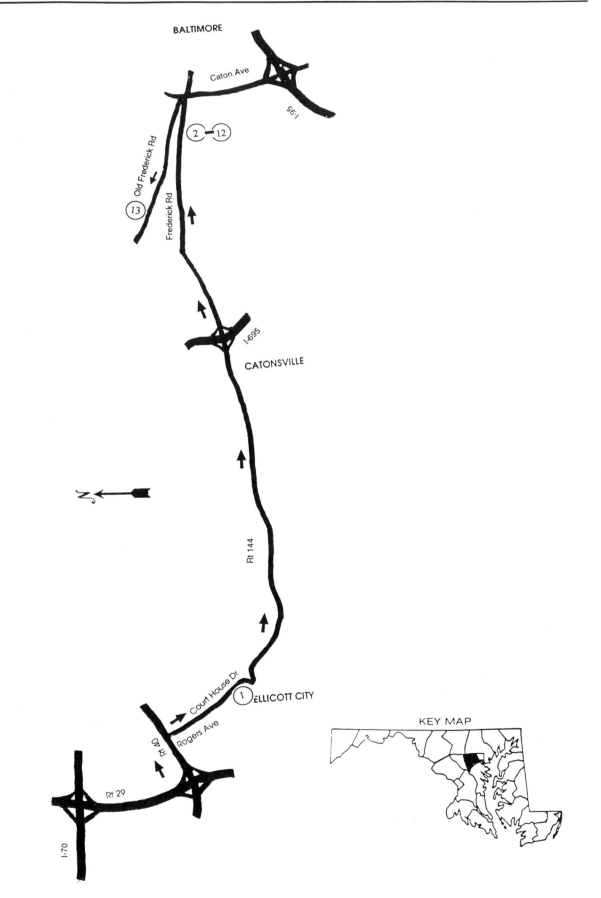

BALTIMORE

Caton Ave

I-95

Old Frederick Rd

Frederick Rd

② — ⑫

⑬

I-695

CATONSVILLE

Rt 144

N

Court House Dr

① ELLICOTT CITY

Rogers Ave

Rt 40

Rt 29

I-70

KEY MAP

Chapter 2

BALTIMORE AREA – WEST

Although some areas are now included within the boundaries of the City of Baltimore all of the towns discussed in this chapter were rural during and for many years after the Civil War. The towns were mainly agricultural in nature, supporting the farms surrounding them. Many of those farms were large plantations which used slave labor and were owned by old Maryland families which derived their heritage from England – similar to, and sometimes even having family ties with, Virginia. The area was dense with secessionists during the war, and many native sons went across the river to join the Confederate forces. Maryland Confederate officers, such as Frank Bond, Turner Ashby, William Murray, William Norris, and Harry Gilmor came from this area.

Industrialization had already begun before the war with the railroads that extended north, crossing the Gunpowder River north of Cockeysville, and west, going through Ellicott City, as well as south to Washington. These trains became important supply routes for Washington, D.C. during the war, and were thus targets for Confederate raiders during the war.

The most famous raid was that of Gen. Bradley Johnson's cavalry brigade in July, 1864, with Harry Gilmor leading his company through the countryside to the cheers of admirers. As a part of Gen. Jubal Early's offense against Washington Gen. Johnson's men were to cut telegraph wires and destroy railroad bridges around Baltimore, then proceed to Camp Lookout prisoner-of-war camp to release Confederate prisoners. They traveled from Frederick to Westminster, Randallstown, Reisterstown and finally Cockeysville, where they blew up the railroad bridge over the Gunpowder River. When they received the news that the offensive was called off the cavalry headed south, coming within 12 miles of Baltimore, and then west through Green Spring Valley to Owings Mills where they regrouped and proceeded to Poolesville to cross the Potomac River back into Virginia. A party of ten men lead by Harry Gilmor rode as far east as Pikesville, three miles from the city, then galloped west, cross-country and along local roads, to join the rest of the group at the Potomac River.

After the war, towns lying on the railroad lines such as Ellicott City and Owings Mills, became heavily industrialized along with the City of Baltimore. As agriculture declined and the population of Baltimore increased, the boundaries of the city were pushed further westward and farmland was turned into housing and factories. In the late 19th century streetcar lines ran out from the city like fingers to these new suburban developments.

The town of Catonsville, lying just outside the city limits, became the site of several cemeteries serving the city, demonstrating the custom that began in the early 19th century of burying the dead outside the city in park-like rural cemeteries. Of the three cemeteries discussed in this chapter, Loudon Park Cemetery was the only one established before the war. Loudon Park National Cemetery was separated from Loudon Park Cemetery after the war. New Cathedral Cemetery was established in the early 20th century when urban development forced the removal of Cathedral Cemetery in the city to this location.

ELLICOTT CITY

Dedication Date: September 23, 1948
Location: in front of courthouse, Ellicott City
Medium: bronze plaque on granite slab
Donor: Howard County Confederate
       Memorial Assoc.
Contractor: W. J. Dahle & Son

Inscriptions:

> *By the*
> *Howard County Confederate Monument*
> *Association*
> *in honor of the brave men*
> *who fought so courageously in the*
> *Confederate Army*
> (names of 5 officers & 87 enlisted men)*

Directions: From I-70 take Rt. 29 south to the Rt. 40 east exit, north of Columbia. At the second traffic light on Rt. 40 east turn right on Rogers Avenue. Instead of turning right to go to the Ellicott City Historic District continue straight onto Court House Drive. After ¹/₂ mile on Court House Drive turn right into a large parking area and park. The Court House is the large stone building on the right. The monument is on the other side, in front of the Court House.

To continue the tour after this monument stay on Court House Drive for one block and turn right onto Church Street and then left onto the main street and across the bridge. Note: Church Street is very steep. Large vehicles should return to the entrance into the Historic District off Rogers Avenue.

The Ellicott City monument has the dubious distinction of being the monument that took the longest time to erect. The Howard County Confederate Memorial Association was formed by 40 veterans of Company A, 1st Maryland Cavalry, CSA, at a reunion in 1898 at "Cherry Grove," the home of Edwin Warfield, a future governor of Maryland (1904-1908). They immediately began to work toward erecting a monument, but the Spanish-American War disrupted their fund raising efforts. After that war they continued their campaign and were able to raise a fair sum, but there was a controversy about who to list on the memorial — just officers, or enlisted men too; just Company A, or other Howard County Confederate soldiers. They finally decided to list Company A members only. When the First World War came the organization decided to invest the money they had collected in war bonds to help the country and erect the monument after the war.

---

* See Appendix G.

By the time the war was over there were few veterans of the Civil War alive. Although not a veteran, Judge William Henry Forsythe was in charge of erecting the monument. In a letter to Eleanor Thompson of the local United Daughters of the Confederacy (U.D.C.) in October, 1928, Judge Forsythe admitted that he had neglected the monument project because of a lack of free time. He said that he had gotten an estimate for a bronze tablet from Hans Schuler, Baltimore sculptor (see Lanier monument), but it was too expensive, and he would be more than happy if the U.D.C. would take over the project. Since, with the accumulation of interest over the years, there was about $1,000 available, the U.D.C. was able to erect a substantial monument. Why it took yet another twenty years is a mystery, but the further delay might have been caused in part by the national depression and the Second World War.

The bronze plaque mounted on a granite stele has a relief of a drum, bugle, rifle, saber, flag and laurel wreath and a border of oak leaves, ivy and forget-me-nots. There are five officers and 87 enlisted men named on the plaque. Most of those listed were from Company A, 1st Maryland Cavalry, organized by Ridgely Brown; but there are also names of Howard County men who were in Company M (later changed to K), 1st Maryland Cavalry, known as the Howard Dragoons, which was organized by George Gaither. Gaither had organized the original group from Howard County as Company K of the 1st Virginia Cavalry in the spring of 1861 since there was no Maryland cavalry at that time. In the spring of 1862 most of those men formed Company B of the 2nd Virginia Cavalry with Ridgely Brown as Captain. The 1st Maryland Cavalry was formed in the fall of 1862 with Ridgely Brown as its major, and Frank Bond took over the captaincy of the Howard County men who were now Company A of the 1st Maryland Cavalry.

Anita Cushing (Mrs. H. Stanley Cushing) attended the dedication ceremony for the monument, and the reception afterwards at the home of Mrs. Richard Talbott, member of the U.D.C. She recalled that there were many people in attendance, but no bands or singing. Judge William Henry Forsythe presided and the principal speaker was Edwin Warfield, son of the late Governor Edwin Warfield, who had been on the committee. According to the local newspaper account, Warfield did not dwell on the rights or wrongs of the two opposing sides in the conflict, but called the Union victory "providential...otherwise we might not have had the strong united nation to fight the more recent world wars and to face the world conditions which exist today."

LOUDON PARK CEMETERY
Confederate Hill – Section V

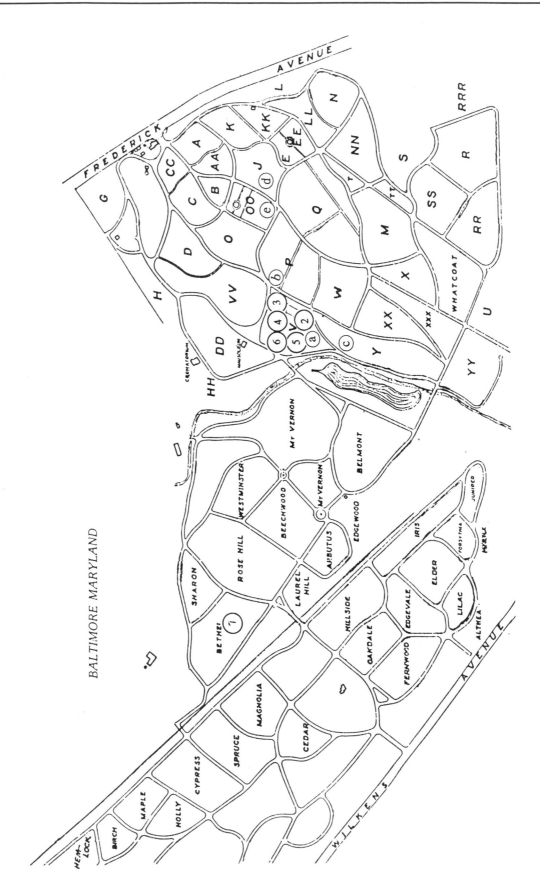

LOUDON PARK CEMETERY

3801 Frederick Avenue, Baltimore (Catonsville)

Directions: From Ellicott City follow Rt. 144, Frederick Avenue, 6.7 miles east to the entrance of the cemetery on the right. OR - From Rt. 95 inside the Beltway, take the first exit (Exit 50) onto Caton Avenue, north, about 1 mile, keep left and take the left "Y" toward Hilton Avenue, then turn left on Frederick Avenue and go three blocks to the cemetery entrance on the left.

Loudon Park Cemetery, a ten year old, park-style corporate cemetery on the outskirts of Baltimore, became a central resting place for many Confederate soldiers from the time that the first, John Scott, was buried there in May, 1862. Plots near that first burial were acquired privately by purchase or trade so that eventually a number of Confederate soldiers were buried near each other in an area of the cemetery which became known as Confederate Hill (section V). After the war, Confederate veterans formed the Loudon Park Memorial Association which held a Decoration Day ceremony on Confederate Hill every June 6. This date was the anniversary of the Battle of Harrisburg where the 1st Maryland Regiment, CSA, under Bradley Johnson, defeated the Pennsylvania "Bucktail" Regiment. The Decoration Days were well attended but subdued in character, with clergymen or judges as speakers. The speakers repeatedly said: "This is not the time or place for speeches," but almost always went on to praise the valor and honor of the men beneath the sod.

The Memorial Association was replaced in 1871 by the Society of the Army and Navy of the Confederate States in Maryland (S.A.N.C.) (See Chapter 1.) In 1874, with the aid of an appropriation from the state, the Association gathered the remains of Maryland Confederates who fell in battle in other states and brought them for reburial in Loudon Park Cemetery. If the remains were already buried in a cemetery, as at Winchester, Virginia, and Gettysburg, Pennsylvania, the Society raised funds to erect a monument over the graves where they were.

There was a horse-trolley, and later a street-car, running to this Loudon Park Cemetery, so it was a popular place for burials, ceremonies, and weekend excursions. There are a number of important former Confederate personages buried in the cemetery, and one Union general. More than 250 Confederates are buried on Confederate Hill.

CONFEDERATE CEREMONY BADGE

LOUDON PARK CONFEDERATE STATUE

Dedication Date: 1870
Location: Confederate Hill
Medium: marble
Donor: by public subscription
Sculptor: Frederick Volck

Inscription:

Erected
To the memory of the
Confederate dead
by the
Loudon Park Confederate
Memorial Association
1870

The Confederate Memorial Association raised contributions for a monument to be placed on Confederate Hill in 1870. The monument is a life-sized marble statue of Lt. Gen. Thomas Jefferson "Stonewall" Jackson. There was originally a sculpture on the front of the pedestal of two angels holding a wreath and a torch, which represented "Peace."

The statue was sculpted by a Baltimore artist, Frederick Volck, who completed the work in Munich, Germany. Some references have reported that the sculpture was by Frederick's brother Adalbert Volck, the famous Baltimore cartoonist, because the signature on the base of the statue is "F. Volck" and the "F" has been allegedly mistaken for an "A" due to deterioration of the inscription. Frederick Volck also sculpted a statue of Stonewall Jackson which stands in front of the State House in Richmond, Virginia. The statue in Richmond is similar to this one.

Frederick Volck was at the Decoration Day ceremony at Confederate Hill in June, 1870 according to the *Baltimore Gazette* (June 9, 1870) and the *Baltimore Sun* (June 9, 1870) to help raise funds for the completion of the monument. On that occasion he said the statue was to be of Jackson and could be in place by next September if the necessary funds were forthcoming. Unfortunately, the death of Gen. Robert E. Lee the following fall and the heavy involvement of the Baltimore Confederate veterans in the ceremonies surrounding his funeral most likely precluded any dedication ceremony for the Loudon Park monument, but it was in place for following Decoration Days.

MURRAY ASSOCIATION

Dedication Date: unknown
Location: Confederate Hill
Material: marble, 7'
Donor: Murray Association
Contractor: D. Kern, York, Pa.

Inscriptions

front:
[Maryland Seal]
Captain Wm. H. Murray
Born at West River Md April 30, 1839
Killed at Gettysburg Pa July 3, 1863

left side:
Erected by the surviving members
of Co. H, 1st Md & Co. A, 2nd Md Infantry, CSA
as a just tribute to the worth and gallant lives
of their fallen comrades
(Names of 46 privates and
7 non-commissioned officers)*

It was not uncommon for the veterans of an individual unit of the army to form a group after the war and raise money for a monument to their former unit as well as for the purchase of a number of cemetery plots so they could all be buried together when they died. Although some groups were formed as a part of a larger established association, some, like the Murray Association, were independent groups.

The inscriptions on the monument list all of the members of Companies H and A who were killed during the war. Some of the members of the Murray Association, as well as some of those listed whose bodies were moved here, are buried around the monument.

They were formed mainly from the pre-war 1st Rifle Company, Baltimore Home Militia under Col. George Peters, and went on to participate in Stonewall Jackson's Valley Campaign.

Captain Murray is buried at Owensville, Maryland, in Christ Episcopal Church Cemetery (Rt. 255, east of Rt. 2 – 12 miles south of Annapolis).

* See Appendix G.

LT. COL. GILMOR

Unveiling Date: 1883
Location: Confederate Hill
Material: marble
Donor: veterans
Sculptor: G. W. Staylor, Baltimore

Inscriptions:

front:

> [crossed sabres]
> *In*
> *memory of*
> *Harry Gilmor*
> *Lt. Col 2nd Md Cavalry*
> *Army of Northern Virginia*
> *C.S.A.*

right:

> *Harry Gilmor*
> *b. Jan. 24, 1838*
> *d. Mar. 4, 1883*
> *Distinguished in 1877 as a*
> *Police Commissioner*
> *in the service of his native*
> *state and city*

left:

> *Mentoria N. Strong*
> *Beloved Wife of*
> *Harry Gilmor*
> *b. Feb. 6, 1845*
> *d. Dec. 13, 1879*
> *Death is swallowed in Victory*

back:

> *OUR GALLANT HARRY*
> *Dauntless in Battle,*
> *Splendid in Success,*
> *Constant in Defeat.*
>
> *This dashing Cavalry Chief*
> *Outrode the Storm of War.*
> *And in the downside of Life*
> *Entered the Valley of Death*
> *Where he was a Conqueror.*
>
> *Life's Battle ended, he sleeps well*
> *Beside the Wife*
> *Who, on Earth as in Heaven,*
> *Heralding the better life*
> *Was a helpmate worthy of a hero.*

Harry Gilmor enlisted as a private in the Confederate Army in Virginia at the beginning of the war. He helped organize the 2nd Maryland Cavalry and became their commander leading them on daring raids throughout Virginia, Maryland and Pennsylvania. One of his most famous raids was the capture of a train filled with Union supplies at Harpers Ferry in February, 1862.

In July, 1864, as a part of Lt. Gen. Jubal Early's planned offensive against Washington, Gilmor led his cavalry from Frederick into his home area, threatening Baltimore and planning to then attack the federal prison at Point Lookout to free the Confederate prisoners there. Gilmor's cavalry burned the bridges over the Gunpowder River and the home of Governor Augustus W. Bradford, and then, receiving notice of Early's retreat, raced back through Howard and Montgomery counties to cross the Potomac River into Virginia at Edward's Ferry.

By the end of the war Gilmor had attained the rank of lieutenant colonel. After the war he became police commissioner of the City of Baltimore and was active in veterans affairs until his death. He was a hero to the veterans of Maryland and the epitome of the dashing gentleman warrior to the women. Even today, there is both a Sons of Confederate Veterans camp and a United Daughters of the Confederacy chapter named after him. He was the author of *Four Years in the Saddle*.

GREAT SEAL OF THE CONFEDERACY

JANE CLAUDIA JOHNSON AND
BRIG. GEN. BRADLEY T. JOHNSON

Dedication Date: June 6, 1901
Location: Loudon Park Cemetery,
          Catonsville (Baltimore)
Medium: granite
Donor: Confederate veterans

Inscriptions:

front:
*Jane Claudia
March 8, 1832 - December 31, 1899
Daughter of
Hon. Romulus M. & Anna H. Saunders,
of North Carolina,
and honored wife of
Genl. Bradley Tyler Johnson
of Maryland*

rear:
*In memory of
Bradley Tyler Johnson
Brigadier General C.S.A.
Born September 29, 1829
Died October 5, 1903*

right:
*April 1861 Captain
June 16, 1861 Major
July 21, 1862 Lieut. Colonel
March 18, 1863 Colonel
June 28, 1864 Brigadier General*

left:
*"He is bold & intelligent,
Ardent and true."
R. E. Lee to President Davis
June 26, 1864.*

This is the first Civil War monument to an individual woman in Maryland, and it was erected not by a woman's organization but by the Confederate veterans who loved and respected her. The dedication of the monument merited a long column in the *Baltimore Sun* (June 7, 1901) and five pages in the *Confederate Veteran* (July, 1901) magazine.

Jane Claudia Johnson was born in North Carolina, the daughter of Romulus M. Saunders, a distinguished congressman and ambassador to Spain. She entered society in Spain and was a confidante of Empress Eugenie of France when they were young girls. When she was 16 she married Bradley T. Johnson, a young Maryland lawyer at the time, and they went to live in Frederick, Maryland.

At the outbreak of the Civil War Bradley Johnson gathered a group of local young men and led them across the Potomac to join the Confederate army. Mrs. Johnson actually left first, taking their five-year-old son, and leaving their home in Frederick in the charge of friends, as she went to Chestnut Hill in Virginia, the home of friends. Soon there were more than 500 Maryland men in Harpers Ferry and Point-of-Rocks who needed uniforms, arms and supplies. Mrs. Johnson volunteered to go to her native state of North Carolina and ask for assistance, which was readily given in the form of rifles and money. On the way back from Raleigh she stopped in Richmond and procured camp supplies from the Confederate government. In the short space of ten days she returned to the camp of the newly forming Maryland Line with a good supply of uniforms, arms, camp equipment and food.

She didn't stop there, but followed her husband's army throughout much of the war caring for the sick and wounded, setting up hospitals, arranging for church services, organizing a traveling library, and generally boosting the morale of the men. She even did courier work for the Confederate army.

On being mustered out after the war, the soldiers of the Maryland Line unanimously voted to give her their flag, the famous banner decorated with the bucktail of the Pennsylvania troop which they had defeated at Harrisburg.

The Johnsons lived in Richmond until 1879 when they moved to Baltimore. Jane Claudia was very active in volunteer work in the city, becoming president of the Hospital for Women and president of the Board of Visitors of the Maryland Line Confederate Home when it was founded. She was known for her tremendous organizational talents.

The dedication of the monument took place on Decoration Day a year after her death. All of the Confederate veterans of the state who could come were there, including many distinguished members of the state government.

Brig. Gen. Bradley T. Johnson, CSA (1829-1903)

The other three sides of this monument are dedicated to Jane Claudia's husband, Brig. Gen. Bradley T. Johnson, a native of Frederick who had graduated from Princeton and was admitted to the Maryland bar in 1851. Before the war he was a lawyer, State's Attorney, chairman of the state Democratic Committee, and delegate to the 1860 convention where, as a staunch supporter of Breckenridge, he was one of the leaders in the split in the party.

As major and then colonel of the 1st Maryland Infantry, CSA, he participated in First Manassas, the Valley Campaign, and the Seven Days battles. He was promoted to brigadier general June 28, 1864. While serving under Brig. Gen. John McCausland he executed Early's orders to McCausland to burn the city of Chambersburg.

After the war, he served for four years in the Virginia Senate before moving to Baltimore where he was the head of the Society of the Army and Navy of the Confederacy in Maryland and was prominent in founding the Maryland Old Line Home for Confederate veterans.

CONFEDERATE MOTHERS & WIDOWS

Dedication Date: November 16, 1906
Location: Confederate Hill
Medium: dark granite, 6'
Donor: Confederate Memorial and Aid
     Society
Contractor: unknown

Inscriptions:

To the memory of
Confederate Mothers
and Widows
Erected by the Ladies
Confederate Memorial
and Aid Society of
Maryland in Baltimore
City
November 16, 1906

    This lovely black granite monument was erected to honor the mothers and widows of the Confederate soldiers, who suffered patiently through the war and often helped the war effort by raising money for the South and by making clothing, bandages, and flags. There is a recorded instance of the Southern sympathizing ladies donating their silk dresses to the Confederacy for the construction of a hot-air balloon.

    This monument pre-dates the Confederate Women's Monument in Baltimore (1.4). It is placed near the graves of several mothers and widows of Confederate soldiers.

LOUDON PARK CONFEDERATE WOMEN

Dedication Date: October 15, 1913
Location: Bethel Section, #342
Medium: granite, 5'
Donor: Confederate Women's Home Board
Contractor: unknown

Inscriptions:

> front:
>> *Confederate Women*
>
> rear:
>> *Erected*
>> *by the*
>> *Board of Managers*
>> *of the*
>> *Confederate*
>> *Women's Home*
>> *Incorporated*
>> *Dedicated October 15, 1913*

In the lot around the monument are the marked graves of nine women who died between 1908 and 1922, and the unmarked grave of a tenth, Annie Anderson, who died in 1932, many years after the Confederate Widow's Home was closed and she was moved to other facilities.

The Confederate Widow's Home was founded by Baltimore businessman and former Confederate soldier, James Russell Wheeler, who was also chairman of the board of the Old Line Confederate Soldiers' Home in Pikesville for 24 years.

The dedication of the monument was a small but impressive ceremony with a band, speakers, poetry, and, as always, Rev. Dame, who had participated in almost every Confederate ceremony since 1870. Six of the women from the Home were already buried in the lot. Ten others attended the ceremony, four of whom would eventually also be buried there.

OTHER MEMORIALS IN LOUDON PARK CEMETERY

**2.a   Capt. Frank Bond, CSA, 1838-1923
(Confederate Hill)**

Frank Bond served with Stonewall Jackson in Co. A, 1st Maryland Cavalry, and saw much action during the war, but he earned his fame after the war by being appointed Adjutant General of Maryland by the governor in 1874. He was very active in veterans groups and much admired by his comrades. In 1907 he was chairman of the Maryland Democratic Party.

**2.b   Brig. Gen. James Herbert
(Major in Civil War), CSA, 1833-1884
(across the street from
Confederate Hill, next to the road)**

James Herbert was a native Marylander from Howard County. He became a merchant of grain, tobacco and produce in Baltimore. During the war he was lieutenant colonel of the Independent Grays (Company D, 2nd Maryland Cavalry). After the war he was elected colonel of the 5th Regiment, Maryland Guard, and was made brigadier general by the governor in 1871. Like Harry Gilmor, Herbert became a police commissioner in Baltimore after the War.

The 8' granite stone is decorated with Confederate flags and colonettes and a cross. The inscription on the front reads: "James R. Herbert, Born August 18th 1833, Died August 5th 1884." [biographical details] "As a Memorial of a brave soldier and good citizen, his friends have erected this monument."

**2.c   Maj. Gen. Charles W. Field, CSA,
1828-1892
(section: Y, #168)**

Born in Kentucky, Field graduated from West Point in 1849. Joining the Confederacy in 1861 he was made colonel of the 6th

Virginia Cavalry. In 1862 he made brigadier general of infantry and was wounded at Second Manassas. After recovering, in February, 1864, he was commissioned a major general in command of Hood's old division of the First Corps. He travelled much after the war and died in Washington, D.C.

**2.d   Brig. Gen. (brevet) James Watt Horn,
USA, 1834-1897
(section: J, #115)**

Born in Scotland, Horn became a carpenter and a military instructor after immigrating to America. During the Civil War he was captain of the 5th Maryland Infantry (USA) and then colonel of the 6th Maryland Infantry. After the war he was warden of the Maryland State Penitentiary and superintendent of the Cheltham Home for Colored Children. He died in Mitchelville, Maryland.

**2.e   Pvt. Joseph R. Stonebraker, CSA
(section: OO, #16)**

Among the spectators at the unveiling of the monument to Jane Claudia Johnson was Joseph R. Stonebraker. Stonebraker served in Company C, 1st Maryland Cavalry. His stone carries the unusual inscription — "Having done his duty faithfully to the present time, is permitted to go where he pleases until called for, signed by 1st Md. Cavalry, CSA."

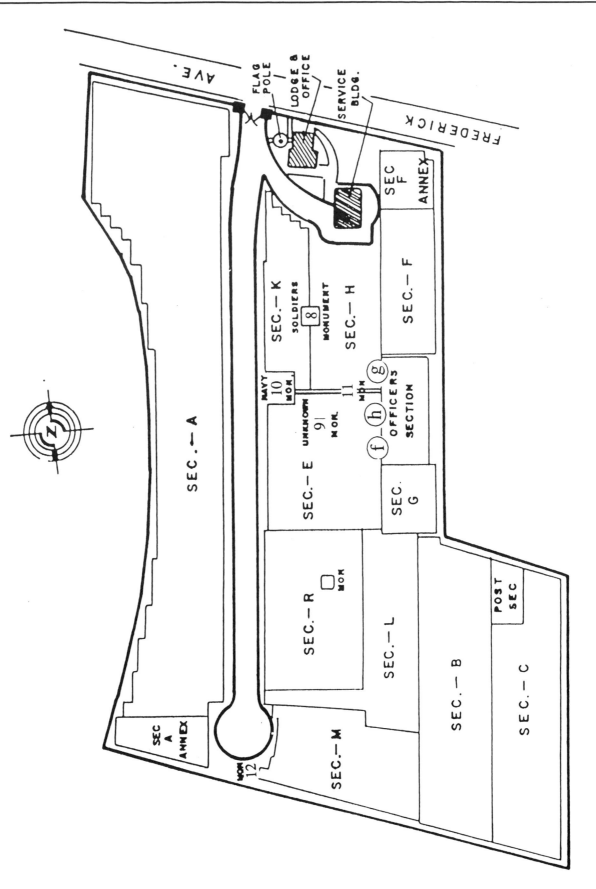

LOUDON PARK NATIONAL CEMETERY

Courtesy of Loudon Park National Cemetery

LOUDON PARK NATIONAL CEMETERY

3400 Frederick Avenue, Baltimore (Catonsville)

Directions: The entrance to this cemetery is on Frederick Avenue, just east of the entrance to Loudon Park Cemetery. (Not to be confused with the more recent National Cemetery, 3 miles west on Frederick Avenue.)

The *Baltimore Sun* reported on December 24, 1861 that a sanitary commission had selected a portion of Loudon Park Cemetery for the burial of deceased soldiers. A subscription for a monument was begun at that time. The federal government purchased the 3.7 acre lot in 1874, adding additional property over several years until it reached 5.45 acres (present size) in 1883.

The cemetery currently holds the bodies of 7,118 veterans and their wives. 2,300 of these are Union dead from the Civil War, and there are 700 Confederate dead. The largest section is of the U. S. Colored Troops. About 1,000 of them were removed from Laurel Hill Cemetery in Baltimore in 1911 because of the building of a road through that cemetery. The remaining Civil war dead were removed from Laurel Hill to Loudon Park National Cemetery in 1957 when that cemetery was condemned.

The superintendent of this cemetery for the first twenty years or so, was apparently rather incompetent, according to letters and reports of the inspectors to be found at the National Archives. There are no records for the monuments erected here before 1900.

UNION OBELISK

Dedication Date: October, 1884
Location: left of entrance
Medium: granite obelisk, 35', with a 3' terra
cotta frieze
Donor: Daughters of Union veterans
Sculptor: (frieze) Casper Buberyl
Contractor: unknown

Inscriptions:

front:
Crescite et multiplicamini
[Md. seal w/ laurel]

right:
How sleep the brave who sink to rest
By all their country's wishes blest
By fairy hands their knell is rung
There honor comes a pilgrim gray
To bless the turf that wraps their clay,
And freedom shall a while repair
To dwell a weeping hermit there.

rear:
E. Pluribus Unum
[U.S. seal w/ laurel]

left:
To the sons of Maryland
Who perished in preserving
to us and posterity
the government of the people
secured by our fathers
through the Union
this memorial
is erected
By her loyal and grateful daughters

A letter from the Army's inspector of that site to the Quartermaster General, dated Sept. 27, 1884 says that work will begin on the foundation on Monday and the Monument will be erected next month by the "loyal ladies of Maryland."

The terra cotta frieze around the base of the monument is cast from the same molds as the frieze on the Pension Building in Washington, D.C. (now the National Building Museum) which was made about the same time. Casper Buberyl (1834-1899), a Bohemian-born sculptor who was very popular at the time, was hired to create the 1,200 foot long frieze for the new Pension Building designed by Montgomery C. Meigs. Meigs directed the sculptor to model the horses after the famous 5th Century Parthenon frieze, and to use the recent scientific studies of motion by Edward Muybridge to help him model the marching men and prancing horses. Buberyl created 28 panels in clay, each from two to four feet in length, which could be repeated in varying order and changed by removing or adding figures. The panels were cast into terra cotta at the Boston Terra Cotta Company.

The verse on the monument is from an ode by the English poet William Collins who was writing about those who lost their lives defending England against the Scottish Jacobites led by Bonnie Prince Charlie in 1745 (Appendix E). It was a popular poem in America after the Civil War and can be found on several monuments. Not all the lines were quoted.

FRIEZE ON THE U.S. PENSION BUILDING

UNION UNKNOWN SOLDIER

Dedication Date: 1895
Location: South of the Union Obelisk
Medium: marble, 5'8" ht., 4'3" × 7'11" base
Donor: Women's Relief Corps, GAR, of Md.
Contractor: Wilkins & Neville, Builders,
    Baltimore
Sculptor: J. M. Dibuscher

Inscriptions:

> front:
>> To the memory of the
>> Unknown dead
>> Erected by the Women's Relief Corps
>> Auxiliary to the Grand Army of the Republic
>> [bronze plaque]
>> Department of Md WRC
>> (list names of committee)

> rear:
>> But there upon the sodden earth
>> he bides his last long sleep,
>> to sleep un-named, unknown
>> Until God's angel on the whirlwind rides
>> to claim his own

All that is known about this poignant memorial is that the Women's Relief Corps (W.R.C.) of the Grand Army of the Republic paid $1,550 for this monument. The names of the committee were Ruth A. Graham, Florence Fink, Sallie A. Moore, Mary E. Wright, Clara A. Alford, and Mary J. Kirby.

This was the time of the peak of the Women's Relief Corps. In a time of popularity for associations, this organization had managed to attract a large number of women from all walks of life. The Corps was instrumental in having American flags placed on public buildings, and the "Pledge of Allegiance" recited in schools, as well as the erection of such monuments as this.

The sculptor was also a local dealer in marble gravestones and monuments.

U.S. NAVY

Dedication Date: November 26, 1896
Location: next to road
Medium: granite, 23'6" ht., 6'8" × 6'8" base
Donor: Naval Veterans Association of Md.
Contractor: unknown

Inscriptions:

front:

[anchor]
Maryland's tribute
To her loyal sons
Who served in the
United States Navy
During the War for
The preservation
of the Union
Don't Give Up The Ship
(list of committee members)

right:

[ship's wheel]
(lists sea battles fought by Md. men in U.S. Navy)

rear:

Erected by the Naval
Veteran Association
of Maryland
September 12, 1896

left:

[compass and crossed cannons]
Maryland furnished
The United States Navy
4152 men who participated
in the important Naval
Battles of the Civil War

The figure in this monument is a ship's quartermaster on watch with a spyglass in his hand. The Naval Veterans Association raised $2,000 for the monument, and arranged an impressive ceremony which was attended by the mayor of Baltimore, members of the City Council, and representatives of the Army and Navy.

The *Baltimore Sun* (Nov. 27, 1896) describes the parade preceding the unveiling of the monument as unique because it began in the center of the city, at Water and Gay Streets, and proceeded west to Lombard and Freemont Streets where the entire parade of over 500 men boarded street cars which took them to Frederick Avenue, west of the railroad tracks where they all alit and resumed the parade to the Loudon Park National Cemetery.

The parade was led by the 4th Regiment with their band and included representative companies from the Army and Navy, the Association of Naval Veterans, and Grand Army of the Republic Veterans. About 5,000 spectators greeted the parade as it arrived at the cemetery.

The ceremony was opened with the singing of the hymn "Nearer My God to Thee," followed by a prayer, and an introduction by H. F. Dorton, executive of the Naval Veterans Association. The monument was unveiled by two little boys, sons of veterans, while the band played "Columbia, the Gem of the Ocean," and "Maryland." The monument was accepted by Alcaeus Hooker, the mayor of Baltimore, and passed on to the superintendent of the cemetery, Maj. Walter A. Donaldson.

Lieutenant Colonel J. Frank Supplee, the orator of the day, gave a long and impressive speech, praising the United States Navy, lamenting the fact that Britain was still "Mistress of the Seas," and making the prophecy,

> "But the day is not far distant when our population shall be so dense that we will be compelled to reach out for new worlds to conquer and the American sailor will, upon the ocean, wrest from England the prestige she has so long enjoyed, for the ultimate glory of the Anglo-Saxon race will only be attained when it has proclaimed that America is greater than Britain."

The exercises closed with Mrs. Theodore Wilcox reading her original poem, "Heroes", a benediction and the playing of "Taps" by a single bugler.

The most significant aspects of this ceremony are the playing of "Maryland" [Maryland, My Maryland] and the speech of the orator. The playing of "Maryland" showed that the animosities of war had faded enough for the song of the pro-southern Marylanders to be a part of a Union celebration, foreshadowing the song's later acceptance by all Marylanders as their special song. Supplee's speech, dwelling as it did upon the might of the American Navy and its competition with its British counterpart, reveals the general sentiment of the people on the eve of the Spanish-American War. His reference to the "glory of the Anglo-Saxon race" reflects the newly forming social and political concept of eugenics, the spread of which would ultimately lead to America's restrictive immigration laws of the early twentieth century.

DODGE POST, G.A.R.

Dedication Date: November 24, 1898
Location: east of Navy monument
Medium: marble, 5'6½" statue,
      11' pedestal
      bronze plaque, 3½ × 1½'
Donor: Dodge Post, G.A.R.
Sculptor/contractor: A. C. May, Baltimore
Plaque: William Gisrell & Son

Inscriptions:

front:

In memory of
Our comrades
A. W. Dodge Post 44
erected Nov. 24, 1898
(names of the committee)

left:

LOYALTY
On fame's eternal camping ground
Their silent tents are spread
But glory guards with solemn round
The bivouac of the dead

right:

FRATERNITY
(list of officers)

rear:

CHARITY
(list of names of members on a bronze plaque)*

Snow covered the military graves at the Loudon Park National Cemetery when the American flag was pulled off to reveal this handsome statue. Members of the Women's Relief Corps sang a hymn as two volleys were fired by the 4th Regiment. The principal orators at the event were Major General Robert St. George Dyrenforth, and S. R. Stratton, commanders of the Union Veterans' Union. Musical selections included "Our Soldier Heroes are Sleeping," and "Nearer My God to Thee." The ceremony concluded according to the *Baltimore Sun* (Nov. 25, 1898), with the singing of the "Star-Spangled Banner."

The statue, costing $1,200, was crafted locally, which makes it one of the "itinerant" sculptures rather than a commercially made sculpture and also makes it one of a kind. The names of 198 members of the Grand Army of the Republic Post #44 are listed on the monument. That list included the names of both the dead members, and those still living when the monument was erected.

---

* See Appendix G.

CONFEDERATE PRISONERS OF WAR

Dedication Date: 1912
Location: far south end of the cemetery
Medium: bronze plaque on 5' granite slab
Donor: U.S.A.
Contractor: unknown

Inscriptions:

*Erected by the United States
To mark the burial place of
twenty-nine Confederate soldiers
Who died at Fort McHenry, Maryland
While prisoners of war,
And whose remains were there buried/
But subsequently removed to this section
Where the individual graves
Cannot be now identified*
(list of names)*

The bodies of Confederate prisoners of war who died at Fort McHenry were reinterred here in 1884. The monument was erected in 1912 by the Federal Government in compliance with the 1906 Law (see Point Lookout Monument, 6.5). This law did not appropriate money for dedication ceremonies, so those federal monuments to Confederate prisoners did not have dedication ceremonies unless they were sponsored by a local group. The names of 29 Confederate soldiers and three camp followers are listed on the monument, but there are actually 136 Confeder- ates buried there according to the records. The individual graves are not marked.

Because this is a National Cemetery, Confederate flags are not allowed to be placed on the site.

---

* See Appendix G.

OTHER MEMORIALS IN LOUDON PARK NATIONAL CEMETERY

2.f *Brig. Gen. (brevet) Adam Eckfeldt King, USA, 1837-1910 (officers' section, #4)*

Born in Chester County, Pennsylvania, King was a lieutenant with the 31st New York Infantry during the Civil War. He was breveted brigadier general March 31, 1865 for "gallantry during the campaign of 1864 and distinguished good conduct throughout the war." After the war he was a U.S. Customs official and diplomat, becoming Consul at Paris, France in 1890.

2.g *Brig. Gen. (brevet) David Leroy Stanton, USA, 1840-1919 (officers' section, #29)*

Stanton was a merchant in Baltimore who became a colonel in the 1st Maryland Infantry during the war. He was breveted brigadier general for "gallant conduct in the Battle of Five Forks, Virginia." He returned to Baltimore after the war where he was a U.S. pension attorney.

2.h *2nd Lt. William Taylor, Co. H & Co. M 1st Md. Infantry, USA (officers' section, #16)*

2nd Lt. Taylor is a Medal of Honor recipient. While fighting at Front Royal he burned a bridge preventing its use by the enemy, after being wounded. At Weldon Railroad, while a lieutenant, he volunteered to take the place of a disabled officer and undertook a hazardous reconnaissance beyond enemy lines and was taken prisoner.

NEW CATHEDRAL CEMETERY

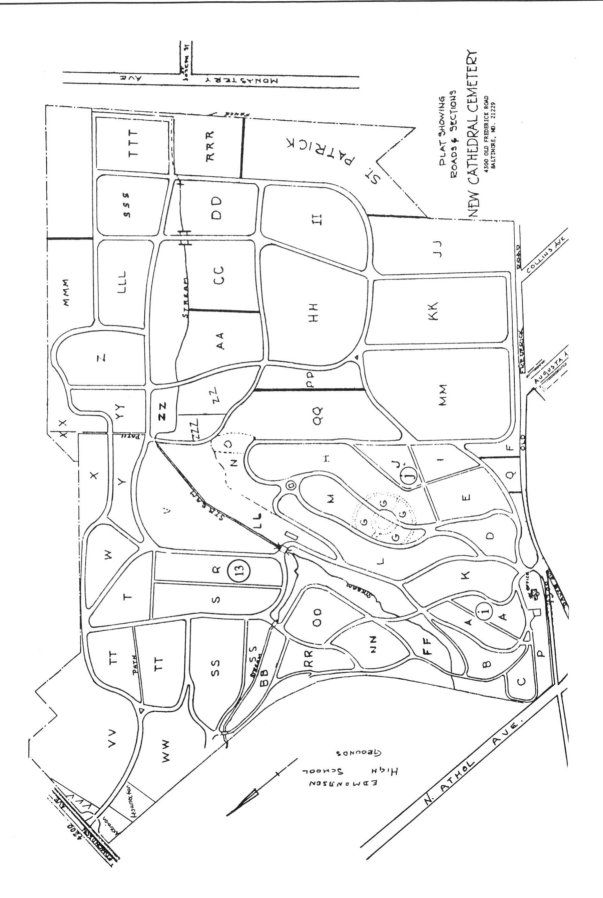

PLAT SHOWING
ROADS & SECTIONS
NEW CATHEDRAL CEMETERY
4300 OLD FREDERICK ROAD
BALTIMORE, MD. 21229

Courtesy of New Cathedral Cemetery

GLEESON

New Cathedral Cemetery
4300 Old Frederick Road, Baltimore (Catonsville)

Dedication Date: 1866
Location: Section R, #123
Medium: granite
Designer: E. G. Lind, architect
Contractor: Hugh Sisson
Donor: Monument Association

Inscription:

front:

> *Erected*
> *To the memory of*
> *Capt. John P. Gleeson*
> *5th Regiment U.S.V.*
> *By the loyal citizens of*
> *Baltimore in*
> *commemoration of his*
> *gallantry as a soldier*
> *and his devotion*
> *to his native country*

right:

> *Captured with his command in the Valley of*
> *the Shenandoah and taken to Richmond,*
> *Virginia where he died a prisoner of war*
> *October 2nd, 1863, aged 30 years,*
> *a martyr to the cause of human liberty.*
> *Here repose his remains, which were forwarded*
> *to this city by permission of the insurgents,*
> *November 17th, 1863.*

Directions: From Loudon Park National Cemetery turn left out of the entrance. Go six blocks, and turn right on Augusta. Go four blocks and turn left onto Old Frederick Avenue and then right into the cemetery entrance.

This was the first Civil War monument erected in Maryland, and the only one for which money was raised during the war.

John Gleeson was born in Baltimore in 1835 and became a lawyer there. He joined the United States Army at the outbreak of the Civil War and was promoted to captain for meritorious conduct on the field at Antietam. Captured at the Battle of Winchester, he died in Libby Prison in Richmond. His body was exchanged for the body of Captain Stamp of Mississippi, nephew of Jefferson Davis. He was buried with military honors at Cathedral Cemetery in Baltimore in November, 1863, and the funeral cortege was one of the largest ever witnessed in Baltimore. The graves in Cathedral Cemetery were later moved to New Cathedral Cemetery, sometimes called "Bonnie Brae."

The importance of this monument lies not just in the fact that it was the first Civil War monument erected in Maryland, but also in the reasons why it was erected, which can be learned from the members of the monument association and the wording on the monument.

The Gleeson Monument Association was formed on January 2, 1864 and was spearheaded by the Hon. Montgomery Blair, who was president, and William Prescott Smith, who was chair of the building committee. The governor of Maryland, Thomas Swann, and Mayor John Lee Chapman of Baltimore were vice presidents. Dr. E. I. Chaisty, William Nichols, and Capt. J. M. Stevens, made up the rest of the board.

The monument was of classical design of the simple Doric order which can demonstrate both purity and discipline, with ample space for inscriptions. The committee did not want to draw attention to the art of the structure, but to what it stood for.

The members of the association's board were all political figures who vigorously supported the Union. They wanted to continue their political careers and let everyone know how well they supported the Union. They called themselves the "loyal citizens of Baltimore." Gleeson was not only gallant, but also "devoted to his *native* country." Some of the members of the association had been of the know-Nothing or Nativist party before the war. Gleeson was a "martyr to the cause of liberty," and his remains were released by "*insurgents*." This kind of language would not have been acceptable in the later, reconciliation stage of these monuments, but while the war was still going on (when the inscription was devised by the committee) the words reflected the feelings of many of Baltimore's citizens.

2.i   *Brig. Gen. Lucius B. Northrop,*
(promoted) CSA, 1811-1894
New Cathedral Cemetery
(section: A, #136)

"An honest man is the noblest work of God" is the inscription on this stone. Northrop was born in Charleston, South Carolina, and graduated from West Point in 1831. He was severely wounded in the course of Cherokee Indian encounters in Oklahoma Territory and returning to Charleston, he practiced as a physician. He was a life-long friend of Jefferson Davis who appointed him Commissary General of the Confederacy. His obstinate and cantankerous personality won him few friends, and the inefficiency and poverty of the Confederate government made his job next to impossible. He was arrested and imprisoned at the end of the war on suspicion of having willfully starved prisoners, but quickly gained his freedom. After the war he turned to farming.

2.j   *John Surratt (died 1916)*
New Cathedral Cemetery
(section: J, #264)

John Surratt, son of Mary Surratt who was hanged for the Lincoln Assassination, had fled the country after the assassination. He was found and extradited in 1867, tried and found "not guilty" by a Civil Court. After the war he taught at St. Joseph's school in Emmitsburg. After marrying Victoria Hunt he settled in Baltimore and worked as an auditor for the Old Bay Line, a steamship company, until his retirement.

BALTIMORE – WEST'S OTHER STOPS

2.k *Brig. Gen. (brevet) Charles Edward Phelps, USA, 1833-1908 Woodlawn Cemetery, Gwynn Rd., Woodlawn (N. Howard Sec., #130)*

Directions: From I-695 (Baltimore Beltway) take Rt. 26 (Liberty Road) and exit east. Proceed a little less than a mile to the cemetery on the right.

Phelps was a native of Vermont who graduated from Princeton in 1852 and went on to attend Harvard Law School. During the Civil War he was a colonel of the 7th Maryland Infantry. He was breveted a brigadier general for "gallant and meritorious services." He practiced law in Baltimore after the war and became a judge.

2.l *The Pikesville Soldiers' Home (now the State Police Headquarters) Reisterstown Rd., Pikesville*

Directions: From The Baltimore Beltway (I-695) take the Pikesville exit and follow Reisterstown Road south 3/4 mile to the State Police Headquarters building on the left.

In 1880 the Society of the Army and Navy of the Confederacy in Maryland formed an associate organization, The Association of the Maryland Line, which raised money for the care and housing of Maryland Confederate veterans who otherwise had no pensions or alternatives for care in their aging years. Although it could not legally give pensions to Confederate veterans, the state could support a non-profit organization which aided them. In 1888 the state gave the old Pikesville Arsenal, along with a maintenance stipend of $5,000 a year, to this association for use as a Confederate veterans home. The Women's Auxiliary of this organization, headed in the beginning by Jane Claudia Johnson, was active in the renovation of the arsenal building and later in the care of the aging veterans. It was formally opened and dedicated in April, 1888. From the opening until 1893 there were 139 admissions to the home. It remained open until 1932, when there were only three residents left. Most of those who died at the Home were buried at Loudon Park Cemetery.

There is a museum at the facility which is open Wednesdays and Saturdays.

2.m *Col. William Norris, CSA, 1820-1896 All Saints Episcopal Church Cemetery (east side) Reisterstown*

Directions: From the Baltimore Beltway (I-695) take I-795 west to Reisterstown. Exit onto Franklin Boulevard, east, then turn left at the light onto Reisterstown Road. Travel a little over a mile and turn right on Bond Street. The cemetery is in the second block on the right.

After graduating from Yale Law School in 1840 Norris went to New Orleans to practice law. He returned to his home in Reisterstown in 1851 and became president of the Baltimore Mechanical Bakery. He offered his services to the Confederacy when war broke out and became head of the Signal Corps when it was formed in April, 1862. He was also head of the Confederate Secret Service and set up a "Secret Line" from New York to Baltimore to Washington to the South. There is a Sons of Confederate Veterans Camp named for him.

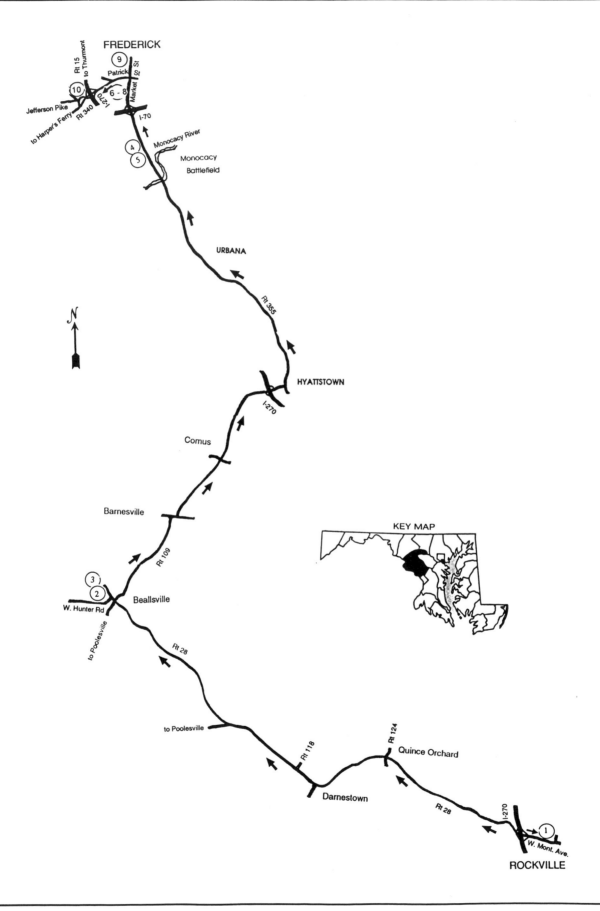

Chapter 3

MONTGOMERY COUNTY, MONOCACY BATTLEFIELD AND FREDERICK

The area of Maryland just north of the capital city was like a revolving door for Union and Confederate troops during the Civil War. Armies from both sides crossed the area many times on their way to and from major battles, and Confederate raiders attacked whenever they could to wreak havoc on the Union forces camped in the area and disable the Chesapeake & Ohio Canal.*

The political atmosphere of the area reflected that of the rest of the state. Those people living close to the Potomac River, many having family ties with people across the river in Virginia, were mainly secessionists. The enclave of Quakers in the Sandy Spring area in the eastern part of Montgomery County was pro-Union and anti-slavery. They were about the only people in the county who voted for Lincoln in the 1860 election. The rest of the area was intermixed with both pro-unionists and secessionists, sometimes living right next door to each other, sometimes even within the same family. As one moved north of the city of

Frederick there were more and more landowners of German descent — many of whom had moved there from Pennsylvania — whose political leanings were more and more pro-Union.

When Lincoln suspended *habeas corpus*, essentially putting Maryland under martial law, to protect Washington in the summer of 1861, the tension between citizens supporting opposite causes heightened. Many of the pro-South men from this area "went south" early in the war to join the Confederate Army, most of them joining either the 35th Virginia Cavalry under Col. Elijah White or later the 1st Maryland Cavalry of the Confederate States under Col. Ridgely Brown.

After the war many of the former Confederate soldiers became powerful political figures and were elected to major offices in the local and state government. Those included Spencer Jones, Edward Chiswell, John Sellman, John Clark, and Henry and Edward Wootton.

---

* For more information on war activities in the area see Charles Jacobs, *Civil War Guide to Montgomery County.*

ROCKVILLE

Dedication Date: June 3, 1913
Location: Maryland Avenue and Courthouse
     Square
Sculptor: M. J. Falvey of Washington, D.C.
Medium: bronze, 6', granite pedestal, 8'
Donor: United Confederate Veterans and
     United Daughters of the Confederacy

Inscription:

To
our heroes
of Montgomery Co.
Maryland
That we through life
may not forget to love
the thin gray line
erected A.D. 1913
1861 CSA 1865

Directions: From I-270 take the Rockville, West Montgomery Avenue (Rt. 28), exit. Follow West Montgomery Avenue about one mile east to Jefferson Street and then turn left on Monroe Street. Take the first left into the parking garage under the Executive Office Building. Proceed to the lower parking area, park in a visitor space and take the rear elevator to the first floor of the Judicial Building. Exit the front entrance of the Judicial Building and walk straight ahead toward the Old Red-Brick Courthouse. The monument is in the middle of the trees on the Judicial Building side of the Old Red-Brick Courthouse.

Confederate veteran Richard Poole Hayes (Co. B., 35th Virginia Cavalry) made the first suggestion that such a monument be built – at a memorial service at Monocacy Cemetery in 1906. But no action was taken until the E. V. White Chapter of the United Daughters of the Confederacy (U.D.C.) was formed in 1911 (see Monocacy Chapel, monument 3.2). This group spearheaded the movement which was joined by the Ridgely Brown Chapter, U.D.C., and the Ridgely Brown Camp United Confederate Veterans (U.C.V.).* Members of the committee included Hayes, George Rice (1st Maryland Cavalry), Spencer C. Jones (Co. A, 1st Maryland Cavalry), Edgar Tschiffely (Co. A., 1st Maryland Cavalry) and Frank Kilgore (Co. D, 35th Virginia Cavalry).

After $3,600 was raised through charity events and public subscription, Michael J. Falvey of Washington was hired to construct the monument which was, according to the E. V. White Chapter, "to honor our soldiers in this county who left home and firesides to cast their lot with the Southland, and to be an inspiration to the youth of our land to hold principle, honor, and a firm trust in God above all else."

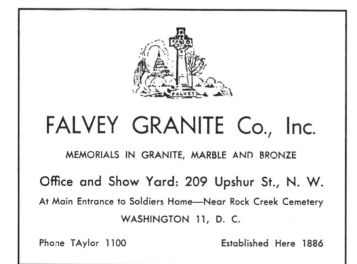

FALVEY GRANITE Co., Inc.

MEMORIALS IN GRANITE, MARBLE AND BRONZE

Office and Show Yard: 209 Upshur St., N. W.

At Main Entrance to Soldiers Home—Near Rock Creek Cemetery

WASHINGTON 11, D. C.

Phone TAylor 1100   Established Here 1886

The Falvey Granite Company was founded by Michael J. Falvey (1859-1921) in 1886 after he had been working as a stonemason on the Washington Monument. The company, located near Rock Creek Cemetery in Washington, D.C., specialized in cemetery monuments and usually the artist would make a small model in plaster which would then be transferred to stone by a stonemason. In the case of a bronze statue such as this, however, the artist would have made the model full size in order to have it cast at a foundry. Although the Falvey Company is still in operation, records before 1927 no longer exist. The 1993 owner, Merle L. Cox, Jr., thought that the artist for this statue may have been Fred E. York, a well-known monument artist who is known to have worked for the company in the 1920s and 1930s.

The monument is a life-size bronze of a cavalry private, arms folded and looking into the distance, standing on an eight-foot granite pedestal. The model for the statue was reportedly Spencer C. Jones who had been a private in Company A, 1st Maryland Cavalry, and had gone on to become a prominent politician in Montgomery County. Jones' daughter married a Thomas Falvey of New Orleans, but the relationship between Thomas and Michael Falvey is not known. The monument was placed in front of the county courthouse, facing south, and was unveiled on June 3, 1913.

The dedication ceremony for this monument was a dramatic demonstration of the reconciliation stage of monument building. It climaxed with the unveiling of the monument that had been draped with the Confederate and Maryland flags. When those flags were pulled down, an American flag was unfurled to fly above the statue in the breeze to the accompaniment of the band playing "Dixie," and then the "Star Spangled Banner."

---

* Because this guide book is organized for the convenience of those who will follow its driving tours and not chronologically, the discussion of an earlier monument, the Ridgely Brown Camp erected in Silver Spring, is on page 129, monument 6.1.

The *Montgomery Sentinel* (June 6, 1913) reported that the location was

> ...almost within a stone's throw of the place where our Revolutionary fathers gathered to express their repudiation of the assumed right of Great Britain to levy taxation on our people without representation....More than three thousand souls assembled to do homage to those who, dominated by a like courage and patriotic spirit, voluntarily enlisted in the cause of the South.

The speakers stood on the courthouse porch while 50 to 75 veterans lined the sidewalk in front, facing the audience. The band played "Maryland, My Maryland," and then Judge Edward C. Peter gave the welcoming address in place of Spencer C. Jones who was ill. He named the Confederate officers from the county and spoke of the courage and importance of their service, and of the men who served under them. There was an invocation by Reverend James Taylor of the Presbyterian church of Washington, D. C., and then a choir sang, "Nearer, My God, To Thee." The Honorable J. Thomas Heflin from Alabama was the featured speaker. He spoke of the gallantry of the Confederate soldiers and the hardships they endured and their devotion to a cause which was never lost, only overpowered. He pointedly defended the soldiers as not being traitors, and ended with a tribute to the "fortitude and majestic loyalty" of the women of the South. As the newspaper recorded, "one of the most pathetic scenes of the day occurred when the veterans present responded in tears to the sentiments of the speaker."

In 1971 the monument was moved to the side of the old courthouse to make way for an urban renewal project. It is surrounded by tall bushes.

3.a   *Plaque to Col. Ridgely Brown*

Dedication Date: November 13, 1924
Location: St. John's Episcopal Church interior, Olney
Donor: Ridgely Brown Chapter, U.D.C.
Inscription:

> *In memory of*
> *Lieut. Col. Ridgely Brown*
> *Co. A, 1st Md. Cavalry, CSA*
> *Army of Northern Virginia*
> *Born Nov. 13, 1833*
> *Died June 1, 1864*
> *after being mortally wounded that*
> *day in a victorious charge near*
> *Ashland, Virginia*

Directions: Travel east on Rt. 28 from Rockville about 5 miles to Georgia Avenue (Rt. 97). Turn left and take Georgia Avenue north 3 miles to Olney. Turn left onto Rt. 108, go one block and turn right into the parking lot for St. John's Church. The plaque is on the wall inside the church next to the entrance leading to the church annex. The church is not always open, so it is best to call before going to view this memorial.

Brown was born November 11, 1833 on his family's estate, Elton, near Unity. He enlisted as a private in the Confederate service June 1, 1861, and soon became a lieutenant in Company K, 1st Virginia Cavalry, which fought at 1st Manassass. In 1862, with Frank Bond, James Griffith, and J. A. Pue, he helped to organize the nucleus of what was to become the First Maryland Cavalry, CSA. Brown was elected captain of Company A and eventually became a lieutenant colonel. His battalion was in the Valley and Peninsula Campaigns and he was wounded at Greenland Gap in April, 1863, but was still able to fight at Gettysburg. He was killed in action at South Anna River on June 1, 1864.

The *Confederate Veteran* magazine in 1913, page 575, referred to him as "a brave and modest Christian soldier, the memory of whose chivalrous and heroic deeds is a bright page in Maryland's history and a cherished ideal in the hearts of his comrades." There was both a Confederate veterans group and a Daughters group named in his honor. It was that U.D.C. Chapter that erected this plaque to the young hero of Montgomery County on November 13, 1924.

Col. Brown's body was brought home to be buried in the family cemetery at Elton.

3.b Grave of Private William Scott
St. Rose of Lima Catholic Church
Clopper Road, Gaithersburg

Inscription:

*Private William Scott, Co. D,
14th Virginia Cavalry, CSA*

Directions: From Rockville travel north on I-270 and take the Clopper Road exit. The church is about three miles north on Clopper Road on the right at the top of the second hill. The grave is in front of the old white church building, next to the road.

This grave is of interest not because it is that of a general or famous person, but because it demonstrates the terribly difficult time it was for Marylanders – both Northern and Southern sympathizers – living under military rule. This small lonely gravestone standing in front of a historic church is a stark reminder of those dark and treacherous days.

Scott was a member of a scouting unit for Jubal Early's troops when they invaded Maryland en route to attack the capital in July, 1864. He was wounded by a Union sharpshooter and rode to Woodlands, the home of the Francis Clopper family, Union supporters. Members of the family carried him inside the house and found a passing Confederate surgeon to tend to him. The doctor removed the bullet but could not save the young man's life. Before he died Scott asked to be baptized and Francis Clopper's son-in-law, William Hutton, performed the ceremony. When the soldier died the family, wanting to assure that he rest in hallowed ground, had a coffin made and buried him in the front of their church. This was done in secret and at night because the family did not want to be arrested for harboring an enemy soldier, as some of their friends and neighbors had been. Many years later the U.D.C. had a stone erected over his lone grave. Scott was from Greenbrier County, Virginia (West Virginia today).

MONOCACY CHAPEL

Dedication Date: Cornerstone Laying –
    June 17, 1915
Location: Beallsville, Rt. 28 and Rt. 109
Medium: cement block, pine-paneled interior
Donor: U.D.C., E. V. White Chapter

Directions: From Rockville go west on Rt. 28 about 18 miles to Beallsville where there is a traffic light. Immediately past the traffic light turn left onto West Hunter Road. The cemetery and chapel are on the right.

The E. V. White Chapter, U.D.C., continued their zealous efforts to honor the Confederate Veterans of Montgomery County by raising funds for another monument after the Rockville statue, but this monument is unlike any other one in this book because it is in the form of a chapel. The motives for constructing this monument were also different than for earlier monuments because they were centered on the living rather than the dead. On June 17, 1915 (postponed from June 3 because of inclement weather) the Daughters laid the cornerstone for a memorial chapel dedicated to the Confederate veterans of the county. The site chosen for the chapel was the site of an original Anglican Chapel-of-Ease in Beallsville, one of the first in the county, dating from before 1748. That earlier chapel had been destroyed by Union troops camped in the vicinity during the Civil War, who used the pews and siding for firewood and stabled their horses under the roof.

There was a large cemetery at the site and the people from nearby Episcopal churches had been gathering informally for many years at the Monocacy Cemetery every spring to clean and decorate the graves. When the E. V. White Chapter, U.D.C., formed, it began a special annual ceremony at the cemetery to honor the Confederate veterans buried there. "Every June 3rd we'd meet there, rain or shine," according to Charles Elgin, Board member of the Monocacy Cemetery Association. "There would always be a speaker, a congressman from the South, and the ladies would always bake a cake for him." There would be prayers, singing of hymns and the decorating of the graves with flowers. Afterwards there would usually be a "box social" picnic in the cemetery.

Because Decoration Day was always held on June 3, no matter what the weather, the Daughters decided that a chapel to house the annual ceremony would be a useful monument. The chapel could also be used for funeral services for those being buried at the cemetery. This utilitarian type of monument was very unusual for the time, but has since become more popular.

The laying of the cornerstone for this chapel was an elaborate ceremony conducted in part by the local order of the Ancient Free and Accepted Masons, Pentalpha Lodge of Gaithersburg. There were about 700 people in attendance. The program opened with a prayer, a musical rendition, and then a recitation of "The Conquered Banner." The Masons then performed their detailed prescribed ceremony after which there was an address by Col. Robert E. Lee, grandson of the General, who paid a great tribute to Col. Elijah "Lige" White, for whom the U.D.C. Chapter was named. The program closed with a benediction and the singing of "Maryland, My Maryland" by a chorus. Then the children marched off to decorate the graves with flowers and miniature Confederate flags. Col. Lee's speech was not only a special tribute to White, but also included an appeal to the audience for loyalty to a united nation. The ceremony was covered in detail in the *Sentinel* (June 23, 1915).

When the chapel was completed, it served as both a meeting place and a monument to the Confederacy with a stained glass window depicting "Faith," and a picture of Robert E. Lee hanging on the wall on one side of the window and a picture of Thomas "Stonewall" Jackson on the other, flanked by Confederate American flags. On the wall next to this configuration is a framed map of the Confederate States, overlaid by pictures of famous Confederate generals, produced in 1910 as a "Half-Century Confederate Memorial." Over the archway to the chancery is the inscription "Lest We Forget." This is a quote from Rudyard Kipling's "Recessional," a poem proclaiming God's Will in war, and is found on numerous Civil War monuments.*

OLD SEAL OF THE UNITED DAUGHTERS OF THE CONFEDERACY

---

* See Appendix E.

MONOCACY CEMETERY CONFEDERATE NAMES TABLET

Dedication Date: 1975
         (replacing 1913 tablet)
Location: Beallsville, Monocacy Cemetery
Medium: marble, 4' × 6'
Donor: E. V. White Chapter, U.D.C.

Inscriptions:

"In loving memory of the valor and self-sacrifice of the Maryland soldiers in the Confederate Army whose names are inscribed hereon"
(32 names)*
[Confederate flag in a laurel wreath]

Outside the door of the Monocacy Chapel is the memorial tablet listing 32 names of Confederate soldiers from the community. It was erected in November, 1911 and replaced in 1975 after a falling tree damaged it.

In 1911, primarily through the efforts of Mrs. Ann Virginia Jones, the "Ladies of Old Medley's District" (an organization pre-dating the E. V. White Chapter of the U.D.C. and named for that historic voting district) persuaded John Collinson White of Bucklodge to donate a marble slab, and they raised money to have that slab engraved with the names of all the Confederate soldiers from that area. White had inherited the marble slab with his father's farm. It reportedly had been brought over from England by his great-grandfather for use in a tanning yard. That block of stone became the centerpiece for an increasingly popular Decoration Day celebration.

Two of the people named on the slab were local heroes Lt. Edward Chiswell (1836-1906) (Lot 9, Area F), and his brother, Capt. George Chiswell (1819-1882) (Lot 7, Area C).

---

* See Appendix G.

MONOCACY BATTLEFIELD

Directions: From Beallsville take Rt. 109 (at the traffic light) northeast 9 miles through Barnesville and Comus to Rt. 355. Turn left on Rt. 355 and travel about 8 miles to the Monocacy Battlefield Visitor Center which is on the right, just before the Monocacy River.

The Battle of Monocacy was a comparatively minor battle in terms of casualties, but a major battle in terms of its effect on the outcome of the war. Under orders from Lee to menace Washington and Baltimore in order to draw Grant's forces away from Virginia, Early led his 14,000 strong Army of the Valley across the Potomac River at Shepherdstown to attack Washington from the north. On the morning of July 9, 1864 his army left Frederick traveling down the Georgetown Pike (Rt. 355) toward Washington. They were met at the bridge crossing the Monocacy River by a force of about 5,800 Union troops under the command of Major General Lewis Wallace. The day-long battle ended in a clear victory for the Confederates, over the numerically weaker Union forces. The Confederates lost about 900 killed and wounded, while the Union lost 1,968 men. But Wallace's troops saved the federal government from major disaster by delaying Early's army a day which allowed Grant to bring in troops to reinforce the defenses of the capital city.

The first monument to be erected on Monocacy Battlefield was the New Jersey monument, located just across the river from the Visitor Center, on the west side of Rt. 355. This statue of a soldier atop a tall pedestal was erected by the state of New Jersey to the 14th New Jersey Regiment of Volunteers on July 11, 1907. A little more than a year later, November 24, 1908, the state of Pennsylvania erected a monument on Araby Church Road to the 67th, 87th and 138th Pennsylvania Regiments of Volunteers. The monument is in the form of a 35-foot granite shaft surmounted by a ball with a Greek cross on its face, the symbol of the 6th Army Corps. The Vermont monument to the 10th Vermont Infantry was put up in 1915. It is a 6-foot rectangular monolith with a bronze plaque in the form of a Greek cross and is situated at the intersection of Araby Church Road and Baker Valley Road, across from the Pennsylvania monument.*

---

* For more information on the Battle of Monocacy and on those monuments see Glenn H. Worthington, *Fighting for Time: The Battle That Saved Washington* (originally published 1932, and reprinted by White Mane Publishing Company, Inc., 1988).

MONOCACY BATTLEFIELD CONFEDERATE

Unveiling Date: July 9, 1914
Location: Monocacy Battlefield, Rt. 355,
    2 m. south of Frederick,
    1 m. north of the Monocacy River
Medium: granite slab
Donor: Fitzhugh Lee Chapter, U.D.C.,
    Frederick, Md.

Inscriptions:

front:

> *This boulder overlooks*
> *the Monocacy Battlefield*
> *and is in memory of*
> *The Southern soldiers*
> *Who fell in the Battle*
> *Fought July 9, 1864*
> *Which resulted in*
> *a Confederate victory*

Nearly 1,000 people gathered for the unveiling of this monument on the 50th anniversary of the Battle of Monocacy. The monument, in the form of a rough-cut boulder, is situated not on the battlefield itself, but on the point from which the Confederates launched their attack. At this spot the entire scene of the engagement can be viewed. The message engraved on the monument attests to the defeat of the federal troops there. The message gives no indication that the battle also delayed Early's army by one day so that Union forces in Washington had more time to bring in reinforcements to protect the capital, and thus were able to fend off Early's attack. Gen. John Floyd King gave a moving recollection of the battle which, according to newspaper accounts, brought tears to the eyes of many of the veterans of the battle who were in attendance.

Col. Robert E. Lee, grandson of Gen. Robert E. Lee, was the principal speaker at the unveiling ceremony. Col. Lee, in his address, defended the South's right to secede, and referred to slavery as "the South's calamity, but, thank God, not her sin." It was being promoted by northern shippers and slave traders until prohibited, the South passing the first legislation on that prohibition, according to Col. Lee.

The ceremony, embellished with band music and singing, opened with "Maryland, My, Maryland" and closed with "The Star Spangled Banner," according to the *Frederick Post* (July 10, 1914).

MONOCACY BATTLEFIELD MARYLAND

Unveiling Date: July 9, 1964
Location: Next to the Monocacy Confederate
Monument
Medium: granite shaft w/bronze open book
on top
Donor: Maryland Civil War Centennial
Commission

Inscriptions:

The Battle of Monocacy
[state seal]
The battle that saved Washington

Here along the Monocacy River on
July 9, 1864, was fought the battle between
Union forces under General Lew Wallace
and Confederate forces under
General Jubal Early

The battle, although a temporary victory
for the Confederates, delayed the march
on Washington one day, thereby enabling
General Grant to send veteran reinforcements
from Petersburg, Virginia, to the defenses
of Washington in time to forestall the
attack by Confederates and thus save
the capital from capture.

dedicated on July 9, 1964
to honor the Maryland soldiers
who fought here
for the Union and Confederacy

J. Millard Tawes, Governor of Maryland
Maryland Civil War Centennial Commission
George L. Radcliffe, Chairman

The Maryland Civil War Centennial Commission, in order to compensate for the omission of information in the earlier U.D.C. monument, erected this monument next to it (See 3.4). The dedication of this monument was part of a two-day celebration following July 4 in 1964. On Sunday, July 5 there was a program in Frederick commemorating the ransom of Frederick, followed by a program at the Pennsylvania monument in celebration of the Civil War Centennial. The program on Thursday, July 9 began with a wreath-laying ceremony by the United Daughters of the Confederacy at the Mt. Olivet Cemetery Confederate monument and continued with a dedication ceremony for this monument with Governor J. Millard Tawes as the main speaker. Governor Tawes expounded on the importance of this battle and said: "We no longer think of a victorious North or a vanquished South, we think of a triumphant United States of America." This dedication ceremony began with the playing of "The Star Spangled Banner" and ended with "Maryland, My, Maryland."

MOUNT OLIVET CEMETERY

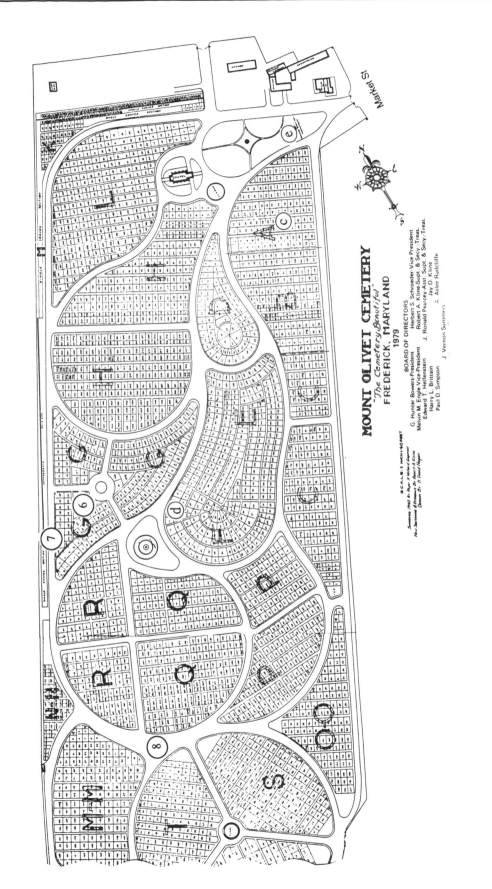

MOUNT OLIVET CEMETERY
"The Cemetery Beautiful"
FREDERICK, MARYLAND
1979

BOARD OF DIRECTORS
G. Hunter Bowers-President   Herbert S. Schroeder-Vice President
Melvin M. Engle-Vice-President   Robert A. Kline-Supt. & Secy.-Treas.
Edward T. Helfenstein   J. Ronald Pearcey-Asst. Supt. & Secy.-Treas.
Harry L. Brittain   Jay D. Kline
Paul D. Simpson   J. Vernon Summers   Atlee Rutcliffe

MOUNT OLIVET CEMETERY

515 South Market Street, Frederick

Directions: Continue on Rt. 355 north 2 miles from the Monocacy Battlefield. After crossing I-70 the cemetery can be seen at the top of the hill on the left. The entrance is off Rt. 355 (Market St.).

Mount Olivet Cemetery in Frederick, Maryland, a private corporate owned cemetery on the city's southern edge, had only been in existence for ten years when it began to receive the bodies of soldiers killed in the battles of South Mountain and Antietam in the fall of 1862. South Mountain was eight miles west of the town and Antietam 20 miles to the northwest. Hospitals had been set up in Frederick after the battles, and those who died in the hospitals were buried either at Mount Olivet or at church cemeteries in the town. The Battle of Monocacy in July, 1864, occurred about two miles south of the town, and once again hospitals in town received the wounded, although the dead of both sides were buried on the battlefield as at Antietam and South Mountain. The Union dead from the battlefields were later moved to Antietam National Cemetery.

After the war prominent citizens formed the Frederick County Confederate Memorial Association, the members of which were all men, and the purpose of which was

> to remove and reinter, when deemed necessary by the Association, the remains of any Confederate dead now lying in Frederick County, to renovate and keep in good order the remains of said dead, and especially those now buried at Mount Olivet Cemetery...and to assist the relatives and friends of said soldiers to identify and recover and remove the remains of said soldiers, whenever they desire so to do.

The association gathered as many of the remains as they could locate in the battlefields of Monocacy and South Mountain and other local cemeteries and reinterred them at Mount Olivet. There were 409 Confederates buried at Mount Olivet in 1881.

The association did not formally incorporate until 1869, and they did so to be able to request $2,000 of the $5,000 which had been appropriated by the state legislature in 1868 for the burial of Confederate soldiers in the state. They used the $2000 they received to erect headstones for the graves and to beautify the grounds. Most of the graves at Mount Olivet are from the nearest battle, that of Monocacy, as well as those who died in the Frederick hospitals.*

The first official Decoration Day Ceremony was arranged by the association on June 18, 1869, and the tradition was repeated every year. The exercises of the early ceremonies were religious in character with hymns and prayers, recitations of local poetry composed for the occasion, and long, flowery speeches filled with references to the valor of the fallen heroes. In 1869 the featured orator, John Ritchie, Esq., said: "We believe that enduring conciliation and harmony can be most surely promoted by securing a correct appreciation of the motives and a just understanding of the cause which animated the southern people in the late Civil war." He goes on to defend the ideas that the South fought to protect states'

---

* For a list of the names of those buried here see Steven Stotelmyer, *The Bivouacs of the Dead*.

rights, not to defend slavery; that secession was a legal alternative and the Confederates thus not traitors; and that the result of the war did not decide who was right, only who was strongest. He ends his oration by praising the women and turns the conclusion of the ceremony over to them with, "The perfume of your floral tributes may not woo the sleeping warrior back to life, but it will be wafted to many a stricken southern home, and there be redolent of the only solace now left to the bereaved, that of knowing that the remains of their precious dead are tenderly watched over and cared for by sympathizing friendship."

The ceremonies always ended with the formation of a procession, led by little girls dressed in white, to lay flowers on the graves. Many of these flowers were beautifully arranged in the forms of crosses, stars, and anchors, red and white being the predominant colors.

MOUNT OLIVET CEMETERY CONFEDERATE STATUE

Unveiling Date: June 2, 1881
Location: Mt. Olivet Cemetery, section G
Medium: Cararra marble, 6', granite base, 8'
Donor: Monument Association of Frederick
    County

Inscriptions:

front*:*
Erected A.D. 1880
by the Ladies' Monument Association
of Frederick county
in honor of the soldiers
of the Confederate Army who fell in the
Battles of Antietam, Monocacy and elsewhere
and are here buried
HONOR TO THE BRAVE

right:
Soldiers rest, thy warfare o'er
Sleep the sleep that knows not breaking
Dream of battlefields no more
Days of danger, nights of waking

left*:*
To the unknown soldiers
Whose bodies here rest
We cannot inscribe their names
Upon tablets of stone, but we may
Hope to read them on a purer and
Unchangeable record

rear:
Their praises will be sung
In some yet unmoulded tongue
Far on in summers that we
shall not see

In 1879 the Confederate Memorial Association formed the Confederate Monument Association to raise funds for the erection of a monument at the cemetery. This association consisted of ladies, who raised over $1,500 through a food booth at the local county fair, selling raffle tickets and holding concerts.

The resulting monument was the figure of a private soldier leaning on his rifle. This was a commercially produced statue, but being very early, is a particularly good example of the first "private soldier at parade rest" statues. This one is distinguished by the full beard and cocked hat on the soldier. Similar statues can be found in Macon, Georgia, and Mt. Olivet Cemetery in Nashville, Tennessee.

According to the *Frederick Daily Times* (June 3, 1881), the rain wouldn't stop for the unveiling ceremony on June 2, 1881, so, after the statue was unveiled and the graves decorated with flowers (including the Union graves), the crowd proceeded to the City Hall, accompanied by the Frederick Cornet Band playing "Dixie." Prominent in the ceremony and seated on the stage were Gen. Bradley T. Johnson and Capt. McHenry Howard representing the Society of the Army and Navy of the Confederacy in Maryland. The ceremony was similar to the previous Decoration Day ceremonies with hymns and local poetry. The move toward reconciliation can be seen in the emphasis on the then living heroes, and on the words of the orations. The orator was the Hon. James M. Buchanan of Baltimore, who, after praising the valor of the "sons of the old Maryland Line," and the worthiness of erecting a tribute to the private soldier, turned his talk toward the future and spoke of the prosperity of the land and how that prosperity and improvements in communication have helped to reunite the nation. "And now if there be any animosities surviving, let them be buried in the graves of our great and loved ones on either side...and their offspring, wherever they may live, rise up in the majesty of a united faith and a fast reconciliation and command the peace." At the end of Buchanan's speech there were calls for Johnson to speak. He rose and gave a brief talk on the valor of his men in the defense of his regimental flag, which had been presented to him by the ladies of Frederick at the beginning of the war.

MOUNT OLIVET CEMETERY CONFEDERATE NAMES TABLET

Dedication Date: June 4, 1933
Location: Mt. Olivet Cemetery, west border, section M
Medium: bronze plaque on brown marble slab, 6'
Donor: local committee, U.D.C. & S.C.V.

Inscriptions:

In memory of
The young men from Frederick County
Who fought for southern rights
1861-1865
(220 names)*
This tablet erected through the efforts of the
following committee
William J. Grove, Chairman
G. Mantz Besant   Lewis A. Rice
Albert S. Brown   Glenn H. Worthington
G. Raymond Shipley, Pres.
1933

This monument represents a movement to erect markers naming all of the men from an area who fought for one side or the other during the Civil War. That trend began after the First World War as part of the historical commemoration stage. This Frederick County names tablet, sponsored by a local committee of prominent men in the area, represents that movement. The local United Daughters of the Confederacy and Sons of Confederate Veterans chapter supplemented the committee's fund raising efforts for the memorial.

The monument was unveiled at the annual Decoration Day ceremonies at the cemetery. Members of the committee were the principal speakers, one of whom, Judge

Glenn H. Worthington, was a witness to the Battle of Monocacy. He and the others spoke of the "valor, chivalry, and devotion to duty" of the southern soldier, and also paid tribute to the Union soldiers, while still defending the southern cause. The music accompanying the ceremony included "Onward Christian Soldiers," "Tenting on the Old Campground," and "Taps."

Those early commemorative memorials had the effect of reinforcing the myths of the lost cause and of the victorious cause which were so prevalent in the first half of this century. The main speech in this ceremony was described in detail in the *Frederick Post* (May 30, 1933).

* See Appendix G.

BARBARA FRITCHIE

Dedication Date: September 9, 1914
Location: Mt. Olivet Cemetery, between sections T & Q
Medium: bronze plaque on granite boulder, 8'
Donor: Barbara Fritchie Memorial Association
Designer of medallion: J. E. Kelly
Contractor: U. A. Gough & Son, Md.

Inscriptions:

front:
circular bronze medallion with profile portrait of Barbara Fritchie
rectangular bronze plaque with entire text of poem by John Greenleaf Whittier*

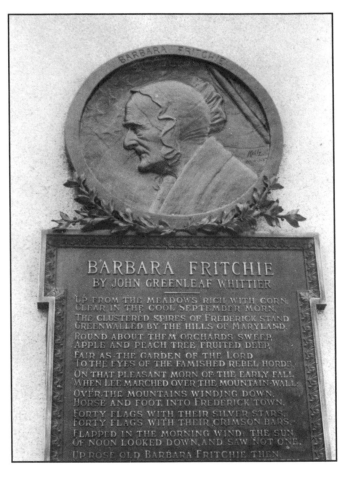

* See Appendix E.

The movement for a monument to Barbara Fritchie began about the same time as the movement to construct a monument to the Confederates at the Battle of Monocacy (see 3.4). It is not known which movement began first, both formed in 1912, but the two groups certainly vied with each other for local funds and contributions. Both fund raising committees were made up entirely of women, but the Barbara Fritchie Memorial Association had more prestige because it had as honorary members the Governor of Maryland, Phillips Lee Goldsborough, the wife of the president, Mrs. William Howard Taft, the Vice President and Mrs. Thomas Marshall, and Congressmen William Griest and David Lewis.

The legend of Barbara Fritchie was well-known in the town, having been tremendously boosted, if not created, by the poem by John Greenleaf Whittier. The poem had been published in the October, 1863 *Atlantic Monthly* and acquired vast fame, bringing renown to the town of Frederick. As legends go, it was quite romantic and had appeal to the respect for elderly people as well as for women in general. Women who fought for the cause they believed in with courage and loyalty, were especially revered at this time of the second generation after the war.

It had been proven, by the time this memorial was erected, that Jackson had definitely not taken the route through town that passed Barbara's house. Other Confederate soldiers may have taken that route, since they marched through town all day, and Mrs. Fritchie may have waved the stars and stripes out of her window at them. She also may not have been the only one.

In nearby Middletown there is a story of a 17 year old girl, Nancy Crouse, who, ordered by Confederate soldiers en route to Antietam, to remove a Union flag displayed from her house, wrapped the flag around her instead saying "You may shoot me, but never will I willingly give up my country's flag into the hands of traitors." She did, however, finally release the flag when a gun was placed to her head.

The monument, then, was more of a promotion for the town of Frederick and an honor to Whittier — and a tribute to the courage of women during the war — than a reflection of facts. The ceremony was attended by the national director of the federation of women's clubs, whose presence emphasized the monument's importance as a tribute to women. The main speaker at the dedication ceremony was the Hon. Alfred S. Roe of Worcester, Massachusetts, the home of the poet. Roe not only praised Whittier and Frederick, and read selections from the poem, but also emphasized the contributions of women during the war, referring to one of the effects of the poem as being "the ennobling of women." Details of his speech can be found in the *Frederick Semi-Weekly News* (Sept. 11, 1914).

A reconstruction of the house where Barbara Fritchie lived is open to the public and is located at 154 West Patrick Street in Frederick.

OTHER MEMORIALS IN MOUNT OLIVET CEMETERY

3.c *Brig. Gen. James Cooper, USA*
(1810-1863)
(section: A, #46)

General Cooper was born in Frederick on May 8, 1810. He was a lawyer by profession and settled in Gettysburg, Pa., where he was twice elected to the U.S. House of Representatives as a member of the Whig party. He served four terms in the Pennsylvania legislature, was a State's Attorney, and was elected a U.S. senator in 1849. He was appointed a brigadier general in May, 1861 and assigned by Lincoln to recruit troops in Maryland. He served briefly in the Shenandoah campaign and then was assigned as commander of Camp Chase prisoner of war camp in Columbus, Ohio, where he died March 28, 1863.

3.d *Capt. George Tyler, 2nd Cavalry,*
USA (1839-1881)
(section: E, #9)

Captain Tyler's gravestone is a beautiful example of Victorian sentiment as expressed in cemetery sculpture. It is in the form of a classical column from which is suspended a sword and belt above a helmet, gloves and spurs.

3.e *Francis Scott Key (1779-1843)*
(entrance)

At the entrance to Mount Olivet Cemetery is an extraordinary monument over the grave of Francis Scott Key, author of "The Star-Spangled Banner."

Although the "Star-Spangled Banner" was not often sung during the Civil War and was not officially adopted as the national anthem until 1931, it was a part of many of the early 20th century monument dedication ceremonies of both sides. Key was also the brother-in-law, law partner, and close friend of Roger Brook Taney.

The magnificent monument was paid for through nationwide subscription, supplemented by the State of Maryland. Designed by Alexander Doyle of New York City, it was dedicated August 9, 1898. The female figure at the base of the monument is a symbol of patriotism, the young man with a sword a symbol of war, and the child with a lyre is a symbol of music.

CHIEF JUSTICE TANEY BUST

Dedication Date: September 26, 1931
Location: Court and Church Streets,
    Frederick
Medium: bronze
Donor: Taney Memorial Association
Sculptor: Joseph Urner

Inscriptions:

(dates of the highlights of Taney's career)

Directions: Turn left out of Mount Olivet Cemetery and continue north on Market Street. After the intersection with Patrick Street the old courthouse is in the second block on the left.

In spite of his controversial decision on the Dred Scott case and his avid support of states' rights, the people of Frederick still considered native son Roger Brooke Taney a hero. Chief Justice Taney lived in Frederick for 22 years, from the time of his graduation from Dickinson College and post-graduate work in Annapolis, until 1823. During that time he practiced law in Frederick, became one of the incorporators of the Frederick County National Bank, served as a member of the Maryland Senate, and was Attorney General of Maryland. In 1806 he married Anne Key, sister of his life-long friend, Francis Scott Key, and they had six daughters. The Taneys resided at 121 South Bentz Street from 1815 to 1823. The house is now a museum.

The movement to erect a monument to Taney in Frederick was organized by Dorsey Etchison after a bust of Governor Thomas Johnson was placed in front of the courthouse in 1929. Etchison felt it would be fitting to honor Frederick's own Chief Justice in the same manner. The two busts stand in line with each other on either side of the entrance to the courthouse.

The elaborate ceremony for the dedication of the monument as described in the *Frederick Daily News* (Sept. 26, 1931) involved day long events culminating with the unveiling and a speech by the then Chief Justice, Charles Evans Hughes. Appropriately three associate justices, as well as judges from the Maryland Court of Appeals and Circuit Court attended the event.

Hughes' speech concentrated on the history and importance of the Supreme Court, not dwelling on any of the controversies surrounding Chief Justice Taney. The ceremony was accompanied by a local band playing patriotic music.

The sculptor, Joseph Urner, who also sculpted the bust of Governor Johnson, was the son of Chief Justice Hammond Urner of the 6th Judicial Circuit Court. Both were natives of Frederick.

For more information on Taney's association with the Civil War see the Taney Monument in Annapolis (5.1).

3.f ROGER BROOKE TANEY GRAVE
St. John's Catholic Cemetery,
E. 2nd Street, Frederick
(3 blocks east of the old courthouse)

Roger Brooke Taney was born March 17, 1777 in Calvert County and died in Washington, October 12, 1864. The monument over his grave was erected by the Knights of Columbus and dedicated October 24, 1954.

GENERAL MEADE

Dedication Date: June 28, 1930
Rededicated: June 28, 1963
Location: Jefferson Pike and exit road onto
Rt. 340
Medium: granite boulder, 10', with bronze
plaques
Donor: Pennsylvania

Inscriptions:

[Pennsylvania State seal]
Major General
George Gordon Meade
took command
of the Army of the Potomac
under orders from
President Lincoln
seven hundred feet
north of this marker
June 28, 1863
He pursued the Confederates
into Pennsylvania
and at Gettysburg July 1, 2, 3
Fought the decisive battle
of the Civil War

Marked by
The Pennsylvania Historical Commission
1930

Directions: From the old courthouse go around the block and turn right (west) on Patrick Street. After a few blocks bear left at the split onto Jefferson Street (Rt. 340) and drive west on Jefferson past the interchange with Rt. 15 and I-270. Get into the far right lane and take the next exit onto Jefferson Pike (Rt. 180). At the traffic light at the intersection of the exit ramp with Jefferson Pike continue straight across the Pike onto the road which leads to the entrance ramp to Rt. 340, and the monument is on the left next to an entrance into Prospect Hall Seminary.

This is actually a battlefield monument, even though it is not on a battlefield, but on the site of a military camp. It marks the place where Major General George G. Meade received the order from Lincoln transferring the command of the Army of the Potomac from Major General Joseph Hooker to himself. On June 28, 1863, just before the Battle of Gettysburg, that historic change of command led to the defeat of the Confederate Army at Gettysburg, the great turning point of the war from which the Confederacy could not extricate itself and which led to the final surrender of Lee at Appomattox.

The monument is a boulder taken from a point near Devil's Den on Gettysburg Battlefield. The 25' × 25' plot of ground was donated to the state of Pennsylvania by former Congressman Joseph Himes of Ohio. The principal speaker at the ceremony was Governor John S. Fisher of Pennsylvania. The two daughters of Congressman Himes unveiled the monument.

In 1963 the Civil War Centennial Commission rededicated the monument and added a plaque to the side of the boulder commemorating this rededication. George Meade III, grandson of the general, unveiled the new plaque. The main address at this ceremony was given by the Honorable George L. Radcliffe, representing Governor Tawes of Maryland. His remarks centered on the history of the area and the historic significance of the event. Bronze commemorative coins were made especially for the occasion, with a representation of Meade and Hooker on the face. One of those coins is on display at the C. Burr Artz Library in Frederick.

To continue from here on the South Mountain, Antietam and Hagerstown Tour return to Rt. 340 traveling west. To go to Rt. 340 west continue down the same road leading to the exit ramp which the Meade Monument is on.

BADGE, ARMY OF THE POTOMAC

WINFIELD

Dedication Date: unknown (est. 1880-1910)
Location: Ebenezer Methodist Church,
        Winfield
Medium: granite, 7', 3' concrete base
Donor: Women's Relief Corps (W.R.C.)

Inscription:

> *Erected by WRC No. 16*
> *to our*
> *Brave and loyal sons*
> *1861-1865*

Directions: From Frederick take Rt. 26 east about 26 miles east to Winfield. Turn right onto Woodbine Road at the traffic light. The church and cemetery are ¹/₂ mile on the left. The monument is one row back from the road, near the center of the cemetery.

This is one of the forgotten monuments. Erected with love and remembrance by the mothers of soldiers killed in the Civil War, it sits near the center of a church cemetery surrounded by the graves of the young men to whom it was dedicated. It was the focus of many Memorial Day ceremonies in the past. Ebenezer Methodist Church was built in 1888 and the monument was probably erected about that time, since that is the time of the height of the Women's Relief Corps' influence. The concrete base of the monument is of similar consistency to the concrete of the porch of the church.

It is a handsome monument of the best quality granite. The highly polished front and top are inscribed with unique and artistic decorations. It obviously cost much money, which was most likely raised in the community by the mourning mothers.

Today, no one is left who remembers the purpose of the monument or who the ladies were who erected it. It is just one of the many memorials in the cemetery – a token of the past.

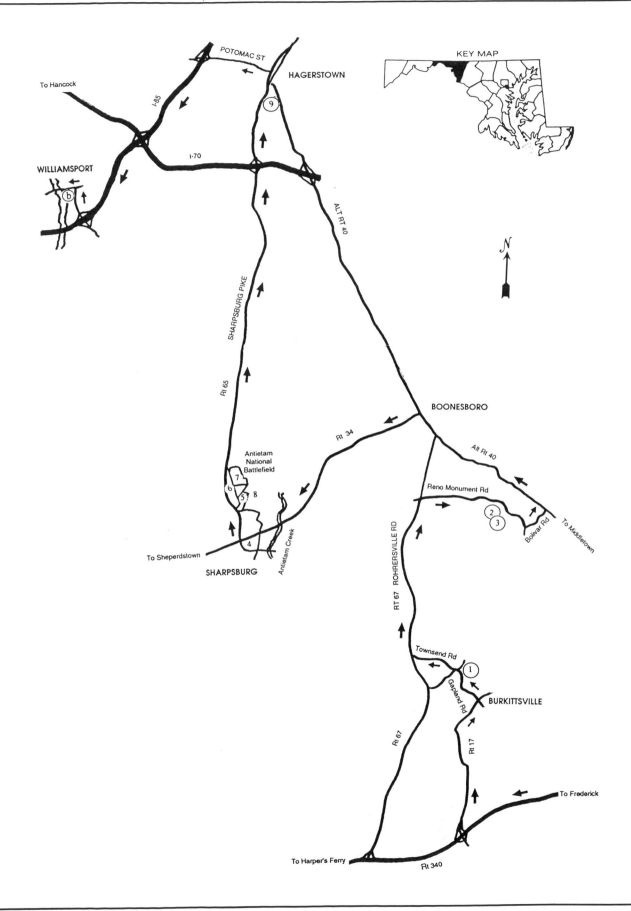

CHAPTER 4

ANTIETAM, SOUTH MOUNTAIN AND HAGERSTOWN

When Lee invaded the North in early September, 1862, he found Harpers Ferry heavily garrisoned with 14,000 Union troops impeding his supply and communication lines. Camped just south of Frederick, Lee decided to split his army and sent Stonewall Jackson with three columns, more than 20,000 men, to Harpers Ferry to drive out the federals and then meet with him again at Boonesboro. While Jackson was occupied at Harpers Ferry, the Union army under Maj. Gen. George B. McClellan advanced unexpectedly on Lee's rear, having discovered Lee's orders. The Union troops pushed back the Confederate units which had been established in a defensive line across South Mountain, running from Boonesboro to Harpers Ferry. Lee, even though Harpers Ferry had surrendered, was forced to stand and fight the threatening Union forces or give up his invasion of the North.

The Battle of Antietam, or Sharpsburg as it is referred to by Southerners, was fought at Sharpsburg, Washington County, Maryland, on September 17, 1862. It has often been called the "bloodiest day of the war" because 4,800 soldiers from both sides were killed between dawn and dusk on that fateful fall day. Almost another 20,000 lay wounded. Lee hurriedly retreated with his army across the Potomac River leaving his dead and wounded in the field. The wounded were transported to makeshift hospitals in Hagerstown and Frederick, but it was left to the Union army and the local townspeople to bury the thousands of dead. Most of the bodies were buried in makeshift shallow graves on the battlefield. First, attention was given to the Union dead, and the Confederate dead were left to lie in the field for days until they were deposited in shallow trenches, sometimes barely covered with soil, or in one case, dumped down a well.*

The story of the two cemeteries established by the State of Maryland for those killed in this battle — one for the Union dead and one for the Confederate dead — demonstrates the gradual progression from antagonism to reconciliation that took place after the war.

The first monument on this tour, the War Correspondents Arch, shows how far the people of Maryland had come by 1896 in respecting the contributions that were made by those working on either side of the conflict by paying tribute to both Southern and Northern journalists and artists on the same monument.

---

* For more information on the burial of the dead from the battle see *The Bivouacs of the Dead* by Steven Stotelmyer.

WAR CORRESPONDENTS ARCH

Dedication Date: October 16, 1896
Location: Gathland State Park, Crampton's
    Gap
Medium: Fieldstone arch, 40' wide x 50' tall
Donor: George Alfred Townsend and others
Contractors: Hummelstone Brownstone Co.
    Daniel Martin, mason

Inscriptions:

south end:
> *Out of Zebulun they that handle*
> *the pen of the writer*
> > *Judges*

> *It is with labor that they were*
> *ascertained because those who were*
> *present in the several affairs did not*
> *give the same account of the same things.*
> > *Thucydides, 425 B.C.*

> *Xenophon assured him with an oath*
> *that he should not have enough for*
> *his expenses in traveling home unless*
> *he sold his horse and what he had*
> *about him.*
> > *Anabasis, 399 B.C.*

> *On quitting school I boldly under-*
> *took to write and relate the wars*
> > *Froissart, 1357*

> *I and my son staid with General*
> *Braddock several days at Frederick-*
> *town dined with him daily and had*
> *full opportunities.*
> > *Franklin, 1755*

> *Know Mr. Trumbull as a man and an*
> *artist.*
> > *Washington to Lafayette, 1791*

> *The enemy's fire emptied several sad-*
> *dles, among others Theodore Wilson's,*
> *the correspondent*
> > *General Sheridan, 1865*

> *"Dr. Livingston, I presume?"*
> > *Henry M. Stanley, 1871*

> *"Viu kto?" "Americanetz."*
> > *MacGahan at Kiva, 1873*

west:
(names of 151 correspondents, writers & artists
of North & South)

north end:
> *"To the army correspondents and artists,*
> *1861-65, whose toils cheered the camps,*
> *thrilled the fireside, educated the provinces of*
> *rustics into a bright nation of readers and*
> *gave incentive to narrate distant wars*
> *and explore dark lands.*
> *Erected by subscription, 1896."*

Directions: From Frederick take Rt. 340 west toward Harpers Ferry. Exit at Rt. 17 and travel 4 miles north to Burkittsville. Turn left and go 1 mile to Gathland State Park. The monument is on the right.

The most intricate in symbolism of all the Civil War monuments in Maryland is this arch dedicated to the correspondents and artists who brought the war to the public in words and pictures.

George Alfred Townsend was a Civil War correspondent, author, poet, and playwright, born in Georgetown, Delaware, in 1841. He began his journalism career as a youth in Philadelphia and in 1862 began working for the *New York Herald*. In 1868 he adopted the pen name "Gath" and began one of the first syndicated columns in the U.S. The first three letters of the pseudonym are Townsend's initials, and addition of the "h" is linked with the first recorded account of news censorship in the Book of Samuel in the Bible (Chapter 1, verse 20): "Tell it not in Gath, publish it not in the streets of Askelon." What was not supposed to be told was that David's army of Israelites had been defeated by the Philistines at Mt. Gilboa, and Saul and Jonathan had been killed.

Townsend was a prolific writer, producing novels, poetry, and plays as well as his newspaper columns, sometimes writing as much as 18,000 words a day. While researching one of his novels, *Katy of Catoctin*, about John Brown's raid and the Civil War, he visited the lovely area around South Mountain and decided to build his estate there. He purchased the land atop Crampton's Gap in 1885 and built several houses of stone for himself, his wife, and his children. The house he built for his daughter was called Askelon. He always summered at this estate, and entertained many guests.

His inspiration for the War Correspondents Memorial came when he was on a train passing through Hagerstown and saw the Antietam Fire Company building under construction. The configuration of the stonework reminded him of Henry Stanley's words, "Experience is an arch wherethro gleams that untraveled world." Having seen the monuments going up at Gettysburg Battlefield, he then conceived of the idea of a monument to the war correspondents and decided to make it in the form of an arch, sketching preliminary plans on the spot. He formed a committee of friends and began raising money for the project, but most of the funding came from his own pocket.

The finished monument is a 50-foot crenelated tower flanked by a horseshoe-shaped Moorish arch (standing for the horse, on which the correspondent depended for speed), topped by three Roman arches which were intended to contain busts. It is made of fieldstone, much of which came from nearby Civil War battlefields. The faces of "Electricity" and "Poetry" appear above the words "Speed" and "Heed."

The new muse "Electricity" symbolizing the telegraph

The statue in the niche of the tower is probably a personification of the war correspondent idealized in the form of a Greek youth. He is shown sheathing the sword of Ares (Mars), the god of war; wearing the helmet of Hermes (Mercury), the swift messenger of the gods; and taking up the pipes of Pan, the satyr-god who was known as a beguiler with music and words. He may have been meant by Townsend to represent Philippides (Greek: Pheidippides), the

Personification of the war correspondent as a Greek youth with the symbols of Pan, Hermes and Aries

correspondent who died after running from Marathon to Athens to announce the Greek victory on the Plains of Marathon. Philippides is mentioned by Herodotus as being favored by Pan. The statue is hollow and made of zinc (manufactured by J. W. Fisk, Park Place, New York), which made it difficult to repair when it was broken into pieces by vandals in the summer of 1987. It was more than five years before it was finally repaired by experts in Colonial Williamsburg and replaced in its niche.

Texts from war correspondents of the past deck the walls, and even the weathervane is symbolic, being a sword wrapped with a pen. On the rear, or west face, of the monument are listed the names of 157 war correspon-

dents and artists of the Civil War, both northern and southern. In every aspect the monument embodies the author's ideas of a free press in symbolism and word.

The monument was dedicated October 16, 1896 amid a large crowd and much publicity. Governor Lloyd Lowndes of Maryland was the main speaker.

In 1905, Townsend's wife, Bessie, died, and he left Gathland, the place where they had spent so many happy years together, never to return. He died in Philadelphia in 1914.

A period of deterioration began at the once busy estate. The heirs, finding the upkeep too expensive, sold the entire property in 1922. The once grand buildings went to ruin, reclaimed by nature and marred by vandals. A church bought the property in 1943 for use as a retreat, but found it impossible to restore. In 1947 nine Frederick County citizens raised the money to purchase 100 acres of the former estate in 1959 and turned the property over to the state. The one restored building now houses a museum.

On October 16, 1946, the monument was rededicated in a ceremony which honored modern correspondents and journalists. The guest speaker was Maj. Gen. Milton A. Reckord, who had been Provost Marshal of the U.S. during World War II. There were plans by the state to construct a Newspaper Hall of Fame and Museum next to the monument in the 1960s, but the plan was abandoned due to lack of funds.

The most recent rededication of the monument was on Sept. 13, 1962 with Maryland Governor Tawes as the speaker.

GENERAL RENO

Dedication Date: September 14, 1889
Location: Fox's Gap, South Mountain
Medium: granite, 8' ht., 4' sq. base,
     40' sq. plot
Donor: survivors of the 9th Army Corps

Inscriptions:

> front:
> > *IX Army Corps*
> > *RENO*
> right:
> > *This mon. marks the spot where*
> > *Maj. Gen. Jesse L. Reno*
> > *Commanding the Ninth Army Corps*
> > *of the Union Army*
> > *was killed in battle*
>
> left:
> > *Erected by the survivors of the*
> > *Ninth Army Corps*
> > *to their commander and comrade*
> > *Sept. 14, 1889*
>
> rear:
> > *Battles*
> > *Vera Cruz, Cerro Corod,*
> > *Contreras, Churubusco,*
> > *Chapultepec, Roanoke Island*
> > *New Berne, Camden, Bull Run,*
> > *Chantilly and South Mountain*

Directions: From Gathland State Park proceed west across the pass on Townsend Road to Rt. 67. Turn right on Rt. 67 and travel about 5 miles to Reno Monument Road and turn right. Follow this road about 2 miles to the monument on the right.

About twenty years after the end of the Civil War, there was a great movement by veterans groups in both the North and the South to erect monuments to their leaders, regiments, and companies in the battlefields where they had fought. It is not known how this custom started, but it spread widely and today the battlefields are decorated with numerous monuments of all kinds. This was one of the first.

At the annual meeting of the Society of the Burnside Expedition and of the Ninth Army Corps in 1888 it was decided to solicit subscriptions for a monument to honor Maj. Gen. Jesse L. Reno, Ninth Corps commander at the Battle of South Mountain.

The monument is a 6-foot polished granite shaft on a one foot base, situated on a 40-foot square plot of ground near where Reno was killed, and surrounded by a 4-foot concrete wall with an iron gate. The anchor on the front of the monument is the badge of the Ninth Corps.

Although the monument states it is on the spot where Reno fell, Jonas Gross, the owner of the property in the 1880s would not sell the property where Reno died, which contained a large oak tree, but was willing to part with the nearby property next to the road. This is where the monument stands today. The monument was originally at the intersection of Old Sharpsburg Road (Reno Monument Road) and Ridge Road, but Ridge Road has been moved and the original road made a part of the Appalachian Trail.

Maj. Gen. John F. Hartranft, former governor of Pennsylvania, was chairman of the monument committee and spoke at the dedication ceremony. The main speaker at the ceremony, which drew about 1,000 spectators, was Maj. Gen. Orlando B. Willcox, commander of the first division of the Ninth Corps at South Mountain. He spoke of the life of the Virginian Jesse Lee Reno and how his was a brilliant career cut short.

A rededication of the monument on September 14, 1989 is described in the *Frederick News* (Sept. 19, 1989).

INSIGNIA OF THE UNION IX CORPS

GENERAL GARLAND

Dedication Date: September 11, 1993
Location: Fox's Gap, South Mountain
Medium: concrete, 4' x 24"
Donor: Garland/Rodes Camp, SCV,
     Lynchburg, Va.
Contractor: Baer & Sons Memorials, Inc.,
     Lynchburg, Va.

Inscription:

> [2 crossed Confederate flags]
> *Near here in*
> *Wise's field on the*
> *Morning of Sept. 14, 1862*
> *Brigadier General*
> *Samuel Garland, Jr. C.S.A.*
> *of Lynchburg, Virginia*
> *Fell mortally wounded*
> *While leading his men*
>
> *Erected by*
> *Garland-Rodes Camp 409*
> *S.C.V.*

Directions: Next to and west of the General Reno Union Monument.

This most recent monument was erected by the Garland-Rodes Camp, SCV from Lynchburg, Virginia. It is dedicated to Brigadier General Samuel Garland, Jr. (1830-1862), of Lynchburg, Virginia, who was leading the Confederate forces defending the hill Reno was attacking. Garland fell just yards from Reno.

Garland had attended the Virginia Military Institute (VMI) and was a lawyer in Lynchburg when the war began. He had helped form the Lynchburg Home Guard in 1859. He began service during the Civil War as captain of Company G, Eleventh Virginia Cavalry. After leading North Carolina troops

he was wounded at Williamsburg and, upon his recovery, was made a brigadier general and assigned command of the brigade of the wounded Jubal Early. This was the brigade that was posted at Fox's Gap on September 14, 1862.

The erection of the monument was delayed for a few years because the landowner wouldn't give permission for the monument to be placed. In 1993, the Central Maryland, Heritage League (CMHL) was able to purchase the 9^1/$_2$ acres of land surrounding the Reno monument. They could not purchase the land inside the wall of the Reno Monument because that is owned by the National

Park Service. The CMHL is only responsible for the upkeep of the land outside the wall and the Garland Monument. The federal government takes care of the space and the monument inside the wall.

The dedication ceremony on September 11, 1993 is an excellent example of how a modern commemorative type of ceremony is carried out. It was attended by more than 100 people. A contingent of Union and Confederate Civil War re-enactors opened the ceremony with a presentation of colors (including the Confederate flag) and the reverend/historian John Scheildt gave the invocation. The ceremony was presided over by CMHL President George Brigham who introduced the first and most prominent speaker, Governor of Maryland, William Donald Shaefer.

Shaefer was followed by the representative from the Sons of Confederate Veterans (SCV), Elliott Cummings, the representative from the Garland/Rodes Camp, SCV, Robert Doss, and local historian Steven Stotelmyer. The microphone was then turned over to Maryland Secretary of Transportation, James Lighthizer; Maryland Secretary of Planning, Ron Crichton; former Congresswoman, Beverly Byron; and the Burgess of Middletown, Louise Snodgrass.

After presenting the story of the battle and the life of Samuel Garland, the speakers mainly dwelled on the importance of Wise's field to history, the historical significance of the battle which took place there, and the importance of preserving this space and honoring the brave men who fought there.

The monument was unveiled by Robert Doss and a wreath was laid. Following the benediction there was a rifle salute, and a single bugle played by Dennis Fraley rang out Taps.

THE SONS OF CONFEDERATE VETERANS

ANTIETAM NATIONAL BATTLEFIELD

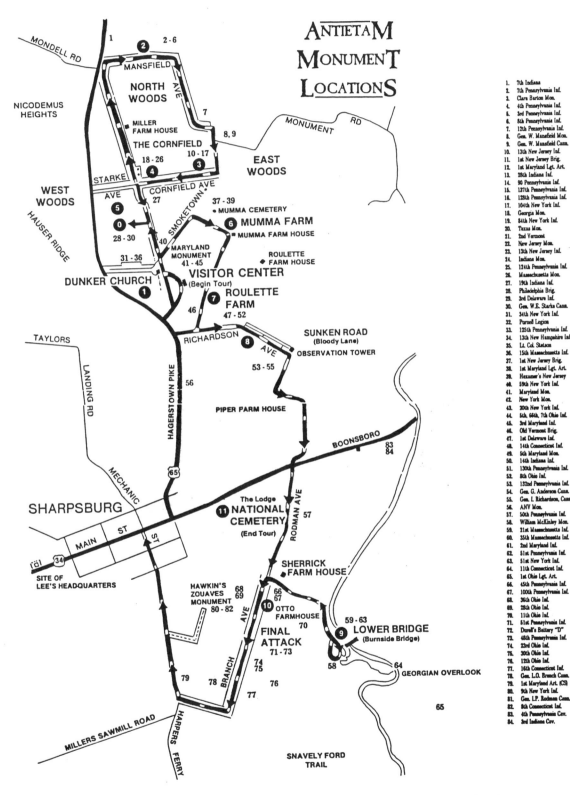

ANTIETAM
MONUMENT
LOCATIONS

1. 7th Indiana
2. 7th Pennsylvania Inf.
3. Clara Barton Mon.
4. 4th Pennsylvania Inf.
5. 3rd Pennsylvania Inf.
6. 8th Pennsylvania Inf.
7. 12th Pennsylvania Inf.
8. Gen. W. Mansfield Mon.
9. Gen. W. Mansfield Cann.
10. 13th New Jersey Inf.
11. 1st New Jersey Brig.
12. 1st Maryland Lgt. Art.
13. 28th Indiana Inf.
14. 90 Pennsylvania Inf.
15. 137th Pennsylvania Inf.
16. 128th Pennsylvania Inf.
17. 104th New York Inf.
18. Georgia Mon.
19. 84th New York Inf.
20. Texas Mon.
21. 2nd Vermont
22. New Jersey Mon.
23. 13th New Jersey Inf.
24. Indiana Mon.
25. 124th Pennsylvania Inf.
26. Massachusetts Mon.
27. 19th Indiana Inf.
28. Philadelphia Brig.
29. 3rd Delaware Inf.
30. Gen. W.E. Starke Cann.
31. 34th New York Inf.
32. Purnel Legion
33. 125th Pennsylvania Inf.
34. 13th New Hampshire Inf.
35. Lt. Col. Stetson
36. 15th Massachusetts Inf.
37. 1st New Jersey Brig.
38. 1st Maryland Lgt. Art.
39. Hexamer's New Jersey
40. 59th New York Inf.
41. Maryland Mon.
42. New York Mon.
43. 20th New York Inf.
44. 5th, 66th, 7th Ohio Inf.
45. 3rd Maryland Inf.
46. Old Vermont Brig.
47. 1st Delaware Inf.
48. 14th Connecticut Inf.
49. 5th Maryland Mon.
50. 14th Indiana Inf.
51. 130th Pennsylvania Inf.
52. 8th Ohio Inf.
53. 132nd Pennsylvania Inf.
54. Gen. G. Anderson Cann.
55. Gen. I. Richardson, Cann.
56. ANV Mon.
57. 50th Pennsylvania Inf.
58. William McKinley Mon.
59. 21st Massachusetts Inf.
60. 35th Massachusetts Inf.
61. 2nd Maryland Inf.
62. 51st Pennsylvania Inf.
63. 51st New York Inf.
64. 11th Connecticut Inf.
65. 1st Ohio Lgt. Art.
66. 45th Pennsylvania Inf.
67. 100th Pennsylvania Inf.
68. 36th Ohio Inf.
69. 23th Ohio Inf.
70. 11th Ohio Inf.
71. 51st Pennsylvania Inf.
72. Durell's Battery "D"
73. 48th Pennsylvania Inf.
74. 23rd Ohio Inf.
75. 30th Ohio Inf.
76. 12th Ohio Inf.
77. 16th Connecticut Inf.
78. Gen. L.O. Branch Cann.
79. 1st Maryland Art. (CS)
80. 9th New York Inf.
81. Gen. I.P. Rodman Cann.
82. 8th Connecticut Inf.
83. 4th Pennsylvania Cav.
84. 3rd Indiana Cav.

Courtesy of Antietam National Battlefield Park

ANTIETAM NATIONAL CEMETERY

Directions: From the Reno Monument continue east on Reno Monument Road 1.2 miles to Bolivar Road. Turn left and travel .7 mile to Alternate Rt. 40 and turn left. Take Alt. Rt. 40 4.8 miles to Boonesboro. Turn left in the center of Boonesboro onto Rt. 34. Go 6 miles to Sharpsburg. The cemetery is at the top of the hill to the left. For the battlefield turn right at the next intersection onto Rt. 65 and proceed 2 miles to the Visitor Center.

In March, 1864, the Maryland legislature approved a bill introduced by Lewis Fierey to establish a cemetery near Antietam Battlefield to properly bury the dead from that bloody battle. In March, 1865, the bill was refined incorporating a Board of Trustees with representatives from each state that contributed money for the cemetery and reburial of the dead. This second bill also stated that "the remains of the soldiers of the Confederate army to be buried in a part of the grounds separate from those of the Union army." But the Board refused to bury the Confederate dead in the cemetery, in spite of the objections of the General Assembly and many private citizens.

Although all the Northern states did not contribute money, they all had representation on the board. Those that did contribute were: Maryland, New Jersey, Minnesota, Maine, Rhode Island, Pennsylvania, West Virginia and Massachusetts. The total amount collected was $62,229.77 ($15,000 from Maryland).

The cemetery was dedicated September 17, 1867, without the remains of the Confederate soldiers. The trustees set up a committee in June, 1868, to look into the purchase of property adjoining the cemetery for the interment of the Confederate dead, but, since this proposition rested on the destitute southern states contributing money for the purchase, it was never carried out. The remaining money in the coffer was used instead to construct a large Keeper's House – which ended up costing more than was budgeted.

In 1870, the Maryland legislature established a new commission for the reburial of the Confederate dead (see Washington Cemetery 4.9). The U.S. took over the Antietam National Cemetery in 1877, paying off the remaining debt.

ANTIETAM NATIONAL BATTLEFIELD PARK

August 30, 1890, Congress passed an act authorizing the preservation and marking of the lines of battle of the Army of the Potomac and the Army of Northern Virginia at Antietam, Maryland. This was the beginning of the Antietam National Battlefield Park. By 1898 the Park had 35.5 acres, numerous historical markers, an observation tower, and thirteen monuments. By 1990 this had grown to more than 2,000 acres and more than ninety monuments. The first monument of record was the 5th Regiment Maryland Infantry, 1890 (4.8). In 1933 the Battlefield Park was transferred from the War Department to the Department of the Interior.

CONFEDERATE BODY NEXT TO A UNION GRAVE

THIS RARE PHOTOGRAPH CLEARLY SHOWS THE PRACTICE OF BURYING ONE'S OWN BATTLE DEAD BEFORE TAKING CARE OF THOSE OF THE OTHER SIDE AS A DEAD CONFEDERATE LIES NEXT TO A TEMPORARY UNION GRAVE ON THE ANTIETAM BATTLEFIELD.

Courtesy of the Library of Congress, Gardner Collection

ANTIETAM NATIONAL CEMETERY STATUE

Dedication Date: September 17, 1880
Location: center, rear of cemetery in
    Sharpsburg
Medium: granite, 44'7" ht. (soldier, 21')
Donor: National Cemetery Board of Trustees
Designer: George Keller
Sculptor: Carl H. Conrads
Artisan: James Pollette, Westerly, R.I.
Contractor: James Batterson, Hartford,
    Conn.

Inscriptions:

Not for themselves but for their country
Sept. 17, 1862

Not only is this a huge monument, it is also an example of the commercial production of monuments at its best. Its designer, George Keller, was a well known architect who was employed at that time by the Batterson firm in Hartford, Connecticut, and Carl Conrads was the firm's house artist. James Pollette was the stonemason who carved the statue. Keller also designed the Soldiers Monument at Gettysburg.

The colossal statue of a private soldier at parade rest was completed in 1874, but was detoured to stand at the gate of the National Centennial Exposition in Philadelphia in 1876. It was then transported by ship to Washington, D.C. where, while being transferred to a C&O Canal barge in several sections, the top section fell into the Potomac River. It was many months before the section was finally retrieved and brought up the C&O Canal to Sharpsburg where the entire 86-ton statue was reconstructed. The statue has been nick-named "Old Simon." The cost of the statue was $35,000.

A number of prominent persons and veterans groups attended the unveiling ceremony on September 17, 1880. In the place of honor at the procession as well as the ceremony was the 5th Regiment band of Baltimore. A special permanent stand was built for this occasion and those to follow. Henry Kyd Douglas, who was later to play a prominent part in the Washington Cemetery and the Maryland Monument at Antietam, was listed as being on the stand at the time of the unveiling. The orator of the day was Col. William Lambert of Philadelphia, who paid eloquent tribute to the dead interred in the cemetery.

Antietam National Cemetery Statue – Unveiling Ceremony September 17, 1880
Courtesy of the Washington County Historical Society

MARYLAND MONUMENT AT ANTIETAM BATTLEFIELD

Dedication Date: May 30, 1900
Location: Antietam Battlefield, #41
Medium: granite and bronze , 35' high
Donor: State of Maryland

Inscriptions:

On one of the plaques —
*"Erected by the State of Maryland to her sons,
who on this field offered their lives in maintenance of their principles."*

In 1898, the Maryland Legislature en-
acted a bill to "form a commission of nine
persons, six of whom shall have served in the
Union Army, and three of whom shall have
served in the Confederate Army, and all of
whom shall have participated in the battle of
Antietam...for the erection of a State Monument to the Maryland soldiers of both sides
engaged in said battle." The legislature appropriated $12,500 for the project.

There are no documents stating whether
this bill had any connection with the previous separate cemeteries for Union and Confederate dead of Antietam, but one member
of the appointed Commission, H. Kyd Douglas, had previously been president of the
Washington Cemetery Board of Trustees.
According to *The Washington Star*, "the movement to erect the monument grew out of a
desire of the Maryland members of the Grand
Army of the Republic to honor the dead of
Maryland who fell in the battle." Norman C.
Scott, state senator from Washington County
in 1898 was influential in having the monument include the Confederate regiments from
Maryland.

The Commission wanted the monument to
be distinct from other monuments already in
place on the battlefield and to be a special
symbol of Maryland. They wanted to demonstrate to the public how the men of Maryland
fought for both sides, but were now united in
brotherhood. Major Henry G. Graham of
Maryland's 5th Regiment created the original
design which was modified by the Harrison
Granite Company of Barre, Vermont, who
erected it. In form it is a small octagonal
Greek temple topped by a bronze statue of
"Peace" in the form of a classical female
figure with sword sheathed and holding a

laurel wreath over the sword. The eight columns represent the eight Maryland commands at the battle, two Confederate and six Union, which together support the dome on which stands Peace. On four faces of

"Peace"

the monument are four bronze bas-reliefs depicting scenes from the battle; inside are eight plaques listing the battles fought by each of the eight commands. According to the

One of the four bronze bas-reliefs

Baltimore Morning Herald, the unique design of the monument was chosen because it "typified a mighty nation strengthened, rejuvenated and glorying in a reunited people, in 'a union of hearts and a union of hands' cemented and made indissoluble at the campfires of the Army of the Spanish war."

Possibly as many as 25,000 people attended the unveiling ceremony for the monument. President William McKinley attended with most of his cabinet and many members of Congress. Also in attendance were the Governor of Maryland, John Walker Smith, and many nationally known men such as Generals Joseph Wheeler and James Longstreet, Senator John W. Daniel of Virginia, Maj. Gen. John R. Brooke, and Representative George B. McClellan (son of the general). There were "hundreds of southern veterans and thousands of northern veterans present." Each veteran who had participated in the battle at Antietam wore a special "survival badge." President McKinley and many others on the reviewing stand sported this badge on their lapels. Many of the newspapers *(Hagerstown Morning Herald, Washington Evening Star, Hagerstown Morning Globe)* began their coverage with the statement: "Another link in the chain which binds together the once warring factions of the north and the south was forged Wednesday by the dedication of a monument erected to the memory of men who wore the gray as well as those who wore the blue."

The ceremony began, without a procession, with Col. Benjamin Taylor, president of the Monument Commission, calling everyone to order and introducing the master of the ceremonies, Gen. H. Kyd Douglas, who then called on Reverend B. F. Clarkson to offer a prayer. Col. Taylor, after a brief speech, then officially presented the monument to the State of Maryland through Governor Smith. Governor Smith's long speech was interrupted by the appearance of the 5th Regiment Veterans Band that was supposed to play at the end of Smith's speech, but marched up to the reviewing stand playing "Maryland, My Maryland" in the middle of the speech. After he finished his speech, the monument was then presented to Elihu Root, Secretary of War, who accepted it on behalf of the United States government. Root's speech, which was interrupted frequently by applause, spoke of the valor of the soldiers of both sides and how that valor had been transferred to a national patriotism.

The band played "Hail Columbia" and then Douglas introduced Generals Longstreet, Brooke, and Wilcox and some other prominent people who each gave a brief address, mainly of reminiscences of the battle and the war. One of the most memorable statements came from Senator John B. Daniel, a former officer in the Confederate army, who said: "I have one advantage over Generals Brooke and Hawley. They have never seen the United States except from one standpoint, from one side. I have seen it from both sides, outside and inside. After observation it is my honest and deliberate judgement that the United States looks much better from the inside."

Then President McKinley was introduced and the band played "Dixie" and "Yankee Doodle." Also interrupted frequently by applause and cries of "yes!" he spoke of his personal experiences in the battle and then said: "We meet after all these intervening years, with but one sentiment – that of loyalty to the government of the United States, love of our flag and our free institutions, and determined, men of the North and men of the South, to make any sacrifice for the honor and perpetuity of the American Nation." McKinley ended with a commendation of the men who fought in the Spanish War saying: "The men of the South and the men of the North vied with each other to show their devotion to the United States...together in those far-off islands are fighting and dying for the flag they love, the flag that represents more than any other banner in the world, the best hopes and aspirations of mankind."

The exercises concluded with "The Star Spangled Banner," and a benediction by Reverend William Dame, chaplain of Maryland's 5th Regiment.

The monument was restored by an appropriation of $12,000 from the Maryland General Assembly in 1988.

MARYLAND BATTLEFIELD MARKERS

Dedication Date: May 30, 1900
Location: Antietam Battlefield
Medium: 4-to 5-foot granite shafts
Donor: Maryland

Inscriptions:

Battle action of each unit

All eight of these markers are the same design: four- or five-foot shafts with a slanted top bearing a bronze relief of the Maryland seal. The inscription on the front of the shaft relates the action in the battle by that unit.

They were placed and unveiled in conjunction with the Maryland Monument in 1900 and were restored in 1988 with the Maryland monument. In the order in which they appear on the Antietam Battlefield tour, with the map number in parentheses, these monuments are:

1st Maryland Light Artillery, Snow's Batt. B, USA (#12)
　　north side of Cornfield Ave.

1st Maryland Light Artillery, CSA (not on Park's map)
　　rear of Philadelphia Park

Purnell Legion Infantry, USA (#32)
　　Confederate Ave., near Dunkard Church

1st Maryland Light Artillery, Wolcott's Batt. A, USA (#38)
　　Smoketown Road at Mumma Lane

3rd Maryland Regiment Infantry, USA (#45)
　　Hagerstown Pike in front of Visitor Center

2nd Maryland Regiment Infantry, USA (#61)
　　northeast corner of Burnside Bridge, east of Creek

1st Maryland Artillery, Dement's Battery, CSA (#79)
　　Old Harpers Ferry Rd., just north of Branch Ave.

5th Maryland Infantry, USA (#49)
　　Sunken Road, north end

CLARA BARTON

Dedication Date: September 9, 1962
Location: Antietam Battlefield, (#3)
Mansfield Ave.
Medium: bronze plaque on rough marble slab
Donor: Maryland Civil War Centennial Commission
Contractor: bronze plaque designed by Medallic Art Co.
Base of mon. fr. Hagerstown Lumber Co.
Marble block donated by Washington Co. Quarry, cut and placed by C. E. Darner & Son, Hagerstown
Bricks from chimney of Clara Barton's birthplace

Inscription:

Clara Barton
During the Battle of Antietam
September 17, 1862
Clara Barton brought supplies
and nursing aid to the wounded
on this battlefield
This act of love and mercy
led to the birth of the present
American Red Cross

This symbolic red cross
has been made from a brick
from the chimney of the house
where Clara Barton was born
at North Oxford, Massachusetts
on Christmas Day, 1821

"Members of the Maryland Civil War Centennial Commission were largely involved in the design, erection, and dedication of the Clara Barton Memorial," according to the 1963 report of that Commission.

The American Red Cross wanted to erect a memorial to their founder on Antietam Battlefield, but they wanted to avoid using Red Cross funds for such a purpose. They assigned the project to the local Red Cross chapter, who in turn contacted the Maryland Civil War Centennial Commission (CWCC) who were only too willing to help. The Red Cross wanted a large rock for the memorial which would symbolize Clara Barton's rugged individualism and resolute dedication to her principles and beliefs. Park Loy, executive director of the CWCC, found a rough marble slab which had been quarried nearby and which the owner donated.

The only cost incurred for this monument was the plaque, paid for by the CWCC. Other materials and labor were donated.

The monument was erected within sight of the old Middlekauf place, where Barton had nursed the wounded. Gen. Alfred M. Gruenther, chairman of the American Red Cross, gave the address at the dedication of this, the first, monument erected to the memory of Barton. Gruenther tied the purpose of the Red Cross organization with world problems, pointing to the individual responsibility to administer to the suffering, and to the danger that the United States was in when it was thought of as too materialistic by other nations. The ceremony concluded with the playing of "America."*

Clara Barton nursed the wounded and dying at 28 battlefields at home and abroad, before retiring, with ill health, to Europe. She soon came back to America, however, and founded the American Red Cross, as president of which she traveled to Cuba during the Spanish-American War. After that the organization assisted in national disasters such as floods, famine, epidemics, earthquakes, tornadoes, and forest fires, earning a reputation for organization, speed of assistance, and reliability.

---

* The Hon. Charles McMathias, representative from Maryland, placed a description of the ceremony in the Congressional Record, September 10, 1962.

5TH REGIMENT

Dedication Date: September 17, 1890
Location: Antietam Battlefield, north side of
  Bloody Lane, on hill (no number on
  map)
Medium: granite, 8' ht., w/ 4 bronze
  medallions
Donor: 5th Maryland veterans
Contractor: medallions by J. Page & Son,
  Philadelphia

Inscriptions:

front:
  [badge of the Union II Corps]

Erected by the survivors of Company A & I
to the memory of our fallen comrades
who fell on this spot Sept. 17, 1862.
This stone marks the extreme advance of
Weber's Brigade, French's Div.,
2nd Army Corps
Can their glory ever fade?
5th Md. Vet. Vol. Inf'y

4 10' bronze circular medallions:
  1. 1854 Maryland seal w/motto
     "crescite et multiplicamini"
  2. Infantryman firing a rifle at
     charging bayonets
  3. 3 crossed rifles
  4. [medallion missing]

This is the only Maryland monument on Antietam Battlefield not erected by the state of Maryland. It is also the first monument to Maryland men placed on the battlefield. The Union veterans of Cecil County wanted to honor their comrades who fell in that bloody battle. Company A lost half its men that day, and Company I also had heavy losses. Those fallen heroes had been well honored at home and at Antietam National Cemetery, but the survivors wanted to place a memorial at the site where they fell, having experienced the horror of the battle themselves at that site and watched their comrades die.

They raised the money and had this impressive monument with artfully made bronze medallions erected. They hired an excursion train from Cecil County to Sharpsburg especially for the unveiling of the monument.

A Hagerstown newspaper, *The Herald and Torch Light* (Sept. 25, 1890), described the monument as being "of highly polished Quincy granite, five-feet high and two and a half feet square, resting on a base of Cecil County granite four-feet square. On each face is a bronze medallion. The one on the front bears the 1854 Maryland Coat-of-Arms; the others represent respectively, a soldier carrying arms, a soldier at charging bayo-

nets; and a soldier firing at full length extended and over an embankment, as was done at Bloody Lane."

The newspaper account goes on to say that there were 18 members of those two companies present, but the addition of other veterans from around the state increased the number to about 65. The ceremony consisted of a march, prayer and oration, followed by the laying of wreaths.

Charles A. Foster, a native of North East, Maryland, who had been a member of Co. A, was the leader of the movement to erect the monument. He also designed the monument, the stone engraving of which was done by a Wilmington, Delaware, firm, and arranged the dedication ceremony.

On March 30, 1892, the Maryland legislature appropriated $530 to the survivors of the Fifth Regiment Maryland Volunteers as partial compensation for the debt of $940 incurred in the erection of this monument.

The monument was rededicated on September 14, 1962, with descendants of the members of the original companies in attendance. Lt. Gen. Julian Smith gave the memorial address with special tribute to those who died in the Civil War. Both Union and Confederate re-enactors took part in that ceremony.

II CORPS INSIGNIA

WASHINGTON CONFEDERATE CEMETERY

Directions: From Antietam Battlefield drive 10 miles north on Rt. 65 to Hagerstown. Rt. 65 becomes Potomac Street and Rose Hill Cemetery is on the right just after crossing over the railroad tracks. The entrance is at Potomac Street and Memorial Boulevard. Inside the entrance turn to the right to Washington Cemetery.

After the Antietam National Cemetery Trustees refused to bury the Confederate dead, Governor Oden Bowie of Maryland, successor to Swann, took it upon himself to request Thomas A. Boult of Hagerstown, one of the Maryland Trustees, to "employ agents to go over the battlefield and mound up the graves and also make careful notes of their location and as far as possible identify the dead." The resulting pamphlet, describing in detail the terrible conditions and various locations of the Confederate remains, incensed the Maryland General Assembly. In April, 1870, it reappropriated the $5,000 last given to the Antietam Board to a new Board of Trustees which would purchase ground within one mile of Hagerstown for a cemetery for the Confederate dead, to be called Washington Cemetery. According to the Act this was necessary "by reason of the persistent refusal of the trustees of said Antietam National Cemetery to allow the remains of said Confederate soldiers to be interred therein." An additional $5,000 was later appropriated by Maryland and $500 each by Virginia and West Virginia.

The governor appointed Henry Kyd Douglas, George Freaner, and James T. Gambrill as trustees from Maryland. Douglas had been a colonel under the command of Stonewall Jackson, and George Freaner had been a major on the staff of Fitzhugh Lee, both of the Confederate army. It was almost two years before the Trustees were able to purchase 2 1/2 acres adjacent to the Rose Hill Cemetery in Hagerstown. This delay was due to their "inability to procure suitable grounds with the limited means at our disposal." They were afraid that if they established the cemetery, without providing a fund for its upkeep, the grounds would soon be neglected and eventually disappear in the overgrowth. The site of Rose Hill Cemetery was chosen, according to Trustee George Freaner in his speech at the dedication ceremony, because it was run by "a corporation composed of our own citizens, having their dead buried within its enclosures, and our whole community interested in its preservation and ornamentation."

The locating, exhuming and reburial of the bodies took five years. The identified remains were placed in a single coffin and the unknown deposited two to a coffin. A total of 2,447 were buried in Washington Cemetery at the time of its dedication, of which 380 were identified by name. A few more were added over the years as they were discovered, the last being in 1987. The Trustees were proud of the fact that the cost per body of $1.50 was about one-tenth of the cost per body for the Antietam National Cemetery, as was even more true of their monument ($1,440 to $35,000).

The Washington Cemetery Board of Trustees is still in operation and sponsors annual Decoration Day ceremonies at the cemetery. It is the only Civil War cemetery administered by the state of Maryland.

WASHINGTON CEMETERY STATUE

Dedication Date: June 12, 1877
Location: Washington Cemetery section of
　　　Rose Hill Cemetery, Hagerstown
Material: marble on granite pedestal
　　　height: 19'
Donor: States of Maryland, West Virginia and
　　　Virginia
Sculptor: A. Steinmetz

Inscription:

*"The State of Maryland has provided this
cemetery and erected this monument to
perpetuate the memory of the
Confederate dead who fell in the battles of
Antietam and South Mountain."*

The monument is a statue of "Hope" in the form of a classical semi-clad female figure leaning on an anchor. The statue by A. Steinmetz of Philadelphia is of Italian marble, and the pedestal is of Richmond and Scotch granite. It cost $1,440.

More than 6,000 people attended the dedication ceremony for Washington Cemetery and the unveiling of the monument on June 12, 1877. Details of the dedication ceremony can be found in the *Hagerstown Mail* (June 15, 1877). The procession assembled at the town square at 2 p.m. and proceeded to the cemetery where the marchers were met by the Trustees. Confederate veterans groups, many with bands, came from all over the state. The ceremony opened with a prayer by Reverend Levi Keller of Funkstown. "He thanked Almighty God for the restoration of love and unity between the late contending armies and offered an earnest supplication for the President and officers of the United States."

After music by the Baltimore band, Trustee George Freaner gave an historical account of the Washington Cemetery. This was followed by the singing of a dirge* by a sixty-member choir accompanied by an organ. The words of the dirge were composed by Kyd Douglas and it ends:

———————
* See Appendix E.

"And on each tomb his foe shall write
God only knows which one was right."

The featured orator, Gen. Fitzhugh Lee, nephew of Robert E. Lee, spoke next. He quoted from Father Ryan's poem, "The Conquered Banner,"* gave vignettes of famous southern generals and ended with, "We now have a common country and it behooves us to love and cherish it and to let strife and discord not be known among us. Eternal harmony must prevail." Following this was more band music and then the reading of an original poem, followed by more music and the strewing of flowers over the graves. At the end of the decoration rites, a drum roll called the people together again. The drum was played by five year old Harry Greenwood, who was accompanied by his grandfather on the fife. The choir then sang "Farewell" followed by the long-meter doxology accompa-

nied by the Hagerstown band. The ceremony ended with a benediction by the minister of the Episcopal church, and the firing of three volleys over the graves by the Berkley Light Infantry.

The Civil War Centennial Commission had a bronze replica of the map of the cemetery, including the names of the known dead, erected next to the statue.** The stone slab on which the plaque rests was donated by D. M. Erskine of Roanoke, Virginia, who had wanted to donate the slab for the Clara Barton memorial but whose gift was rejected in favor of a marble slab. The plaque was dedicated June 9, 1963 with the local National Guard, reenactment Civil War units, the Washington Jr. High school band, and the U.S. Army Band participating. The address was given by Paul Sedgewick, a descendant of Gen. Charles Sedgewick.

MARKER FOR THE CEMETERY WITH THE MARYLAND STATE SEAL

---

* See Appendix E.
** For a list of these names see: *Bivouacs of the Dead* by Steven R. Stotelmyer.

OTHER MEMORIALS OF INTEREST

4.a *Maj. George Freaner, CSA*
(1831-1878)
Rose Hill Cemetery, Hagerstown

Maj. Freaner was aide-de-camp on the staff of Gen. J.E.B. Stuart until Stuart's death, at which time he became a member of the staff of Fitzhugh Lee. A native of Hagerstown, he was practicing law there when he was elected to the Maryland House of Delegates in 1859. He enlisted in the Confederate army in the fall of 1861. After the war he returned to his law practice and was a member of the board of commissioners appointed by the governor to establish the Washington Cemetery for Confederates.

4.b *Doubleday Hill Union*

Dedication Date: July 4, 1897
Location: Riverside Cemetery, Williamsport
Medium: 3 cannons and a flagpole
Donor: U.S.

Directions: From Hagerstown or I-70 take I-81 South to Rt. 11 west into Williamsport. After passing the traffic light marking the intersection with Rt. 68, turn left onto Vermont Street and then the second right into the cemetery entrance.

This is a secondary monument because it is not a construction, but a compilation of objects, a park, and also because it has little historical significance.

Maj. Abner Doubleday, commanding a Union artillery unit, constructed a battery consisting of three cannons overlooking the ford across the Potomac River. After having occupied the spot for several months he realized that the river could be crossed above and below that spot, out of view of his battery because of a bend in the river. He reported this to his superiors and then evacuated the position.

In 1897, the site was made a monument consisting of the breastworks, three cannons supplied by the federal government, and a flagpole. The dedication ceremony took place on July 4th, 1897, culminating in a parade and demonstration in the town. The speakers were Senator L. E. McComas, the Hon. John Findlay, and Thomas McCardell, editor of the *Cumberland Times*, all of whom had been born in Williamsport. Although a flag still flies above the cannons, the battery has been sadly neglected and can only be reached through the cemetery.

4.c *Maj. James Breathed, CSA*
(1838-1870)
St. Thomas Episcopal Church
Cemetery, High St., Hancock

Directions: From I-70 west take left exit #3, Rt. 144. Turn right at the traffic light and travel 1¼ mile to turn right on Church Street. Go 1 block to High Street. The church and cemetery are in front of you. The grave is just to the left of the church entrance.

Fitzhugh Lee spoke of the "proverbial intrepidity of the reckless Breathed upon every battlefield of the Army of Northern Virginia." James Breathed was born in Morgan County, Virginia, and graduated in medicine from the University of Maryland. During the Civil War he was a captain with the 1st Stuart Horse Artillery and joined with the famous Pelham to form the first horse artillery battery to serve with Stuart. He was promoted to major, in command of a battalion, in February, 1864. Wounded at Yellow Tavern, he recovered to fight in the Shenandoah Valley Campaign of 1864. After the war he returned to the practice of medicine in Hancock, Maryland.

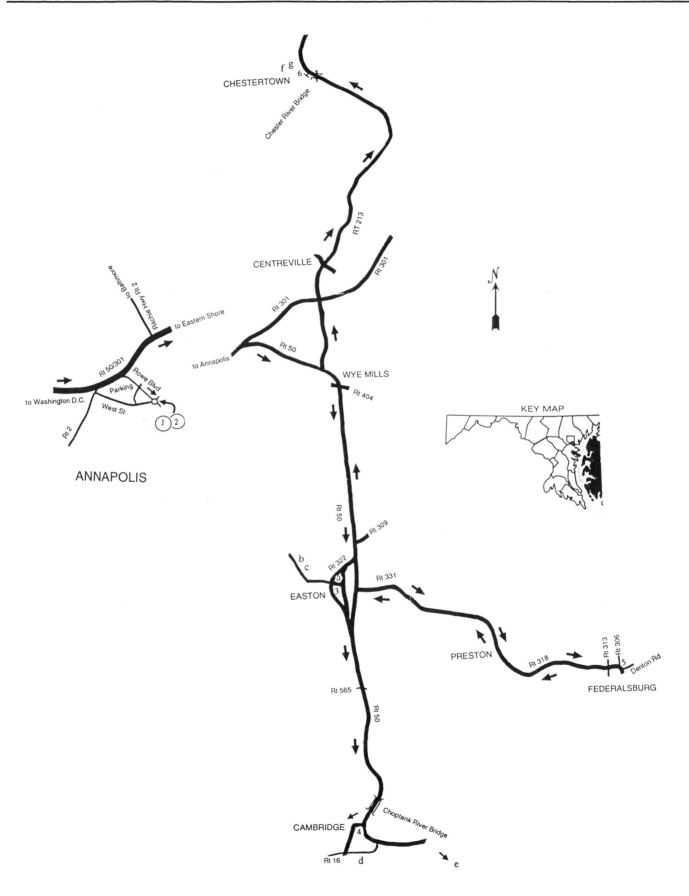

CHESTERTOWN

Chester River Bridge

RT 213

CENTREVILLE

Rt 301

Rt 301

to Baltimore
Rt 2

Ritchie Hwy
to Baltimore

to Eastern Shore

Rt 50/301

Rowe Blvd

Parking

to Washington D.C.

West St

Rt 2

① ②

to Annapolis

Rt 50

WYE MILLS

Rt 404

ANNAPOLIS

Rt 50

Rt 309

b
c
Rt 322

Rt 331

EASTON

③

Rt 318

PRESTON

Rt 313
Rt 306

⑤
Denton Rd

FEDERALSBURG

Rt 565

Rt 50

KEY MAP

N

Choptank River Bridge

CAMBRIDGE

④

Rt 16
d

e

CHAPTER 5

ANNAPOLIS AND EASTERN SHORE

During the war Annapolis had become the site of the first occupation of the state by federal troops as Brig. Gen. Benjamin Butler and the 8th Massachusetts volunteers arrived by ferry on April 21, 1861. They were joined by the 7th New York on April 22. The troops were able to secure a locomotive and repair tracks to Washington so that new troops approaching the capital city from the north would not have to travel through Baltimore, but could take a ship to Annapolis, then board a train to Washington. The U.S. Naval Academy in Annapolis – under the command of Capt. George S. Blake since the former superintendent, Capt. Franklin Buchanan, left for the South on April 22, 1861 – was transferred to Newport, Rhode Island, on April 24 for the duration of the war.

After the war the Maryland State House, having been occupied by staunch Union supporters during the war, became a haven for southern sympathizers and even some former Confederate soldiers after the new 1867 Maryland Constitution was put in place, according to an article by William Russ in the *Maryland Historical Magazine* (June, 1958). Pro-southern decisions in the State House – legislation, appropriations of money, honoring of citizens – can be seen as an indication of the sentiments and apprehensions of a majority of the people of the state as they struggled to grapple with the aftermath of the war.

Isolated from the rest of the state by the Chesapeake Bay, the people of the Eastern Shore were independent minded in their politics and social activities. They were divided by local interests which, during the Civil War, made the area look more like a patchwork quilt of loyalties than one united front. That division was due to the varied economy and the population mix of the area.

In the 19th century the Eastern Shore's economy was based on fishing and oystering, lumbering, ship building, and wheat and corn production. The ports of Chestertown and Cambridge did a substantial business in exporting across the bay. The traditional large slave-based plantations were giving way to small farms and business operations. The large wealthy landowners were becoming fewer and were being replaced by wealthy lumbermen, ship builders and absentee landlords.

As in Baltimore there was a large free black population on the Eastern Shore. From the beginning of the 19th century, the black population had grown more than five times that of the white population, and only 20% of those were slaves at the time of the Civil War. Those free Blacks worked side by side with small farmers and fishermen of that region.

The Eastern Shore remained relatively quiet during the Civil War. The most notable incident there during the war was the May, 1862 forcible arrest, from his bench while he was holding court in Easton, of Judge Richard Bennett Carmichael, a state circuit judge who had spoken out against the suspension of *habeas corpus* in Maryland.

The Eastern Shore contributed about an equal number of Confederate and Union soldiers to the war, many of the Union volunteers forming black units, as there was a training base for black soldiers on the Eastern Shore. Eastern Shore men usually joined the army in localized, county-based groups. So you may find a Union monument in one county while in the neighboring county a Confederate monument.

CHIEF JUSTICE TANEY

Dedication Date: December 10, 1872
Location: front of State House, Annapolis
Medium: bronze, 6'3", w/6' granite pedestal
Donor: Maryland
Sculptor: William H. Rhinehart

Inscription:

> *Roger Brooke Taney*
> *Chief Justice of the United States*
> *of America*
> *Born March 17, 1777*
> *Commissioned March 15, 1836*
> *Died October 12, 1864*

Directions: From Rt. 50 take Rowe Boulevard into Annapolis and follow until it ends at the State House. The statue is on the other side of the State House. Alternative: At the second traffic light on Rowe Boulevard after exiting from Rt. 50, turn right and then right again into the stadium parking lot. Park there for a fee and take a shuttle bus to the State House.

This impressive monument is a testimonial to the changing political atmosphere of the period immediately after the Civil War. The money for the monument was appropriated by the Maryland General Assembly in 1868, soon after that austere body became dominated by Democrats and conservative Unionists. This shift occurred after the political maneuvering of Governor Thomas Swann allowed the Southern sympathizers and Confederates of Maryland to once again vote.

As Attorney General, Roger Brooke Taney was well known for his defense of President Jackson's withdrawal of government deposits from the United States Bank. The Senate refused to confirm Taney's appointment by Jackson as Secretary of the Treasury and also refused to confirm him as an associate justice of the Supreme Court. In 1836, however, the Senate majority changed and Taney was confirmed as chief justice of the U.S. Supreme Court.

As chief justice his most memorable case was the Dred Scott decision in which he declared that a slave could not escape his condition by moving into free territory. This decision dismissed the Missouri Compromise as unconstitutional and was one of the major arguments that precipitated the Civil War.

In May, 1861, in his capacity as judge on the federal circuit court of Maryland, he issued a writ of *habeas corpus* on behalf of John Merryman, arrested by federal authorities for his part in burning the railroad bridges to Baltimore after the April riot. By that act Taney challenged the authority of Lincoln to impose martial law on Maryland and suspend the rights of citizens, an authority vested not in the president, but in the Congress. Lincoln made no reply to Taney's suit. The arrests without charges or trial continued throughout the war.

At the unveiling of the monument Severn Teackle Wallis was the orator of the day. Wallis had been arrested himself as a representative to the meeting of the Maryland legislature on the question of secession, but defended the Union after his release. He delivered an eloquent and glowing tribute to the chief justice and also said that "in the 250 years of her history, this was the first time that Maryland had erected a statue to any of her distinguished sons in civil or military service." Whether Wallis knew it or not, this statement was not accurate because a statue of Governor Hicks had been appropriated by the General Assembly in 1865 and had been placed over his grave. (See Hicks monument, 6.4.)

The statue, heroic in size, was placed in front of the main entrance to the State House. It represents the Chief Justice, seated, in his robes of office, with his left hand resting upon the Constitution and his right hand holding a scroll. It was executed by the well-known Baltimore artist, William Rhinehart, who had studied in Europe and had previously made the bronze doors for the Capitol in Washington, D.C. the statue on the clock at the House of Representatives, and the statue for the fountain at the General Post Office, among others. The statue was cast at the royal foundry in Munich, and the artist was present for the unveiling, having recently returned from Rome to oversee the erection of the monument.

ANNAPOLIS STATE HOUSE PLAQUE

Dedication Date: October 5, 1964
Location: State House lobby
Medium: bronze plaque
Donor: Maryland

Inscription:

MARYLAND REMEMBERS
By the dedication of this plaque, she leaves
for posterity evidence of her remembrance of
her nearly 63,000 native sons who served
in the Union forces and the more than
22,000 in those of the Confederacy in the
War Between the States.

In commemorating the centennial of that great
struggle between the citizens of the tempo-
rarily divided nation in the 1860's, the
Maryland Civil War Centennial Commission
did not attempt to decide who was right
and who was wrong, or to make decisions
on other controversial issues.

On the contrary, its objective was solely to
commemorate important events of the war
within the state and to collect and
preserve documents and information
associated with her involvement.

By so doing it seeks to pay tribute to those
who fought and died, as well as to the citizens
who, during the Civil War, tried to do
their duty as they saw it.

Erected and dedicated October 5, 1964
by The Maryland Civil War Centennial
Commission

Honorable Millard J. Tawes
Honorary Chairman
Honorable George L. Radcliffe
Commission Chairman

Though not a monument in the literal sense, this plaque is important because it puts into words, made permanent for posterity, the intentions of the Maryland Civil War Centennial Commission, portrays the state's involvement in both sides of the conflict, and honors not only those who fought for either side, but also the citizens who "tried to do their duty as they saw it." It is the first memorial to so honor the citizens as well as the soldiers, except those to the women.

The dedication of this plaque was the last act of the Maryland Civil War Centennial Commission, which began its work of commemorating the Civil War in Maryland in 1960 with a grant from the state of $315,000, and ended by returning $80,000 of that appropriation to the state after sponsoring many celebrations, publications, reenactments, monuments and historical markers around the state.

The dedication ceremony took place on the north portico of the historic State House and was attended by more than 250 people. At the ceremony Governor Tawes said: "It is my hope and my prayer that all who see it will be reminded that a war that caused so much suffering and so much despair was not fought in vain, for out of the struggle we gained a strength and unity that has made us the greatest nation on the face of this earth."

The U.S. Naval Academy

There is a museum at the Naval Academy in Annapolis with many artifacts from the Civil War, including memorabilia of Admiral Franklin Buchanan, CSA, who was the first superintendent of the Academy.

EASTON

Dedication Date: June 5, 1916
Location: Courthouse green, Easton
Medium: bronze statue, 6', on 8 1/2' granite
    pedestal with bronze plaques on the
    sides
Donor: local monument committee

Inscription:

> *"To the Talbot Boys, 1861-1865, CSA"*
> (85 soldiers' names and 11 civilians are listed)*

Directions: Cross the Chesapeake Bay Bridge onto the Eastern Shore. From the Rt. 50/Rt. 301 split take Rt. 50, south. After 18 miles exit right onto the Easton Parkway (Rt. 322). At the traffic light turn left onto Bay Street and then right at the "T" intersection onto Washington Street. The courthouse is in the next block on the right.

In July of 1913 a committee was established in Easton to raise funds for a monument to the Confederate soldiers from Talbot County. Gen. Joseph B. Stein headed the committee which included Col. Oswald Tilghman, Levin Dawson, J. H. K. Shannahan, William Lowe and Henry Holliday. At first they wanted to make the statue of native son Admiral Franklin Buchanan because "what Robert E. Lee was to the army, Buchanan was to the navy." But there were some who disagreed and wanted the monument to be a tribute to "all the Boys in gray." The base for the statue, with the 85 names in bronze, was put in place on the courthouse green in July, 1914, but in February, 1915, the argument about the form of the statue was still going on. Finally, the committee made a decision and the statue, which was dedicated in June, 1916, is a

---

* See Appendix G.

figure representing youthful courage and enthusiasm as portrayed in Longfellow's poem "Excelsior." Like the Union monument at Federalsburg, this statue is of a standard commercial type, and the same one stands atop a tall column in front of the courthouse at Lake Charles, Louisiana.

On the other side, there were 334 Talbot County men who fought for the Union. It is one of the coincidences of the war that Trappe's Company H, of the Eastern Shore Home Guard, made up of Talbot County men, fought its only battle at Culp's Hill, Gettysburg, where they faced the 1st Maryland Confederate regiment, also with many men from the area. Confederate color sergeant P. M. Moore of Trappe faced Union color sergeant Robert Ross of Trappe, his cousin; and many of the other warriors fighting each other had been childhood friends.

There was a movement to erect a Union monument in 1914, but not enough funds could be raised.

SPRING HILL CEMETERY

Aurora Street and Cherry Street

Directions: From the Confederate Monument go north 1½ block, and take a right on Goldsborough Street. Go 5 blocks to Aurora Street. Go left and travel 2 blocks to the cemetery.

This small cemetery contains a Civil War cannon and commemorative plaque dedicated to both sides of the conflict.

5.a   Col. Oswald Tilghman, CSA (1841-1932)

A local hero, Col. Tilghman fought with the Texas Rangers and the Virginia Light Artillery of Norfolk during the war. After the war he represented Talbot County in the State legislature and was Secretary of State under Governor Warfield. He was the great-grandson of Lt. Col. Tench Tilghman, hero of the Revolutionary War.

WYE CEMETERY

Directions: The cemetery is about 4 miles northwest of Easton on Rt. 370, on the east side of the road.

5.b   Admiral Franklin Buchanan, CSA (1800-1874)

Baltimorean Franklin Buchanan entered the U.S. Navy at the age of 14. He was co-founder and first superintendent of the Naval Academy in Annapolis. He served in the Mexican War and was captain of the Navy Yard when the Civil War broke out. He joined the Confederacy and was assigned as chief of the Bureau of Orders and Details. He was wounded while commanding the Virginia (Merrimac) at Hampton Roads.

Promoted to admiral in 1862, he took command of the Mobile defenses where he was again wounded and captured. After the war he served as a college president and was in the insurance business.

5.c   Gen. Charles Sidney Winder, CSA (1829-1862)

Winder was born in Talbot County on October 18, 1829. He graduated from the U.S. Military Academy in 1850 and was promoted captain in 1855. He joined the Confederacy in April, 1861 and was appointed a major of artillery. In July of the same year he was commissioned a colonel of the 6th South Carolina Infantry. He became a brigadier general in command of the "Stonewall Brigade" in Jackson's division in March, 1862. After participating in several campaigns he was mortally wounded at Cedar Mountain on August 9, 1862.

GOVERNOR HICKS

Dedication Date: 1868
Location: Cambridge Cemetery, Cambridge
Medium: marble, 6', on 8' granite base, with
     bronze plaque attached to front
Donor: Maryland
Sculptor: H. D. A. Henning, Baltimore (1867)

Inscription (plaque):

*"This monument erected by the State in 1868,
honors Thom. Holl. Hicks, a native and life
resident of Dorchester Co. Late in 1860 and
early 1861 as Md.'s first Civil War governor
he opposed the doctrine of secession and of
coercion. In furtherance of his policy and
resisting great pressure he refused for five
months to call the legislature in special session. During the War he supported the Union."*

Md. Civil War Centennial Commission

Directions: From Easton go back to the parkway west of town and go south to rejoin Rt. 50. Travel 14 miles south to Cambridge. Take the Maryland Avenue exit from Rt. 50 into Cambridge. After crossing the bridge take the first left on Academy Street and then the second left on Cemetery Avenue and a right into the cemetery. The monument is near the center of the cemetery, east (left) of the entrance.

Though out of the way and difficult to locate, this monument, a life size portrait statue of Governor Hicks, has momentous political implications and is politically linked to the monument to Chief Justice Taney in Annapolis. These two monuments demonstrate the divisiveness during the funereal stage of monument building.

Thomas Holliday Hicks (1789-1865) was governor of Maryland from 1858 to 1862. Soon after the election of Lincoln, Governor Hicks began to receive petitions to call a special session of the General Assembly to decide whether Maryland should secede from the Union. Hicks, who was elected to office on the Know-Nothing ticket, was pro-slavery and a strong states-rights man, but he knew the dangers of secession for a middle state like Maryland which depended on the west and foreign shipping to supply its growing industries. He refused to call the General Assembly into special session and, even though they met anyway, he went down in history as a Union supporter for that non-action.

Hick's ambivalent feelings over states' rights is evident in the fact that he conspired with the mayor of Baltimore to burn the railroad bridges north of Baltimore to prevent Union troops from entering the city after the Baltimore riots in 1861. He also conspired with the mayor of Annapolis in denying supplies to Butler when he led his army into Maryland soon after the Baltimore riot. After his term Hicks became a United States senator and aligned himself with the conservative Unionists.

The erection of this monument was one of the last acts of the unconditional or radical Unionist party, in control of Maryland politics during the war. An appropriation of $5,000 was made in March, 1865, soon after the death of Hicks, for both a portrait at the state house of him and a monument over his grave (Laws of Maryland 1865, Chapter 185). In 1867, the Maryland legislature became domi-nated by the Union-Democrat, and then by the Democratic party. In 1868, this new legislature appropriated money for the erection of a monument to Chief Justice Taney, who was much hated by abolitionists, on the lawn of the State House in Annapolis.

The portrait statue is by the sculptor Herman Henning (1843-1893) of Baltimore and shows Hicks leaning on the "staff of law." Henning immigrated to Baltimore from Elberfeld, Germany, as a child and had risen to be known as "Baltimore's First Sculptor" at the time he made this monument. He also sculpted the four "Lady Baltimore" statues which used to be on the old Paul Street bridge (two now in Clyburn Park, one in Mt. Royal Terrace, and one in Baile Tighe Mor, Ireland), and the lions on the old Calvert Street bridge (now in the Baltimore Zoo) in Baltimore, as well as a portrait statue of Johns Hopkins.

OTHER STOPS OF INTEREST

5.d *Anna Ella Carroll (1815-1893)*
Old Trinity Church Cemetery,
Church Creek, south of Cambridge

Directions: Take Church Creek Road (Rt. 16) south from Cambridge 5.3 miles to the town of Church Creek. Turn left on Rt. 335. Go about one mile and turn left onto Old Field Road. The cemetery is on the left.

Anna Ella Carroll was known as an advisor to President Lincoln. She wrote several treatises defending Lincoln's war-making powers and advising on military strategy as well as a series of legally well-grounded papers on issues raised by the war. Her outrageous trespassing into matters formerly the exclusive territory of men made her a dynamic symbol for the women's movement.

5.e *Dr. Isaac D. Costen (1832-1931)*
Pitts Creek Presbyterian Cemetery,
Pocomoke City

Directions: From Rt. 13 south, left at "Winter Quarters" in Pocomoke City, then left on Greenwood Avenue to the cemetery.

Isaac Costen was born locally and went to Penn Medical School (now Penn State) for his medical degree. He returned to Pocomoke City (then known as Newtown) to practice medicine. At the beginning of the Civil War he served at the local Union army hospitals while at the same time operating a blockade running operation delivering medical supplies and money to the Confederacy by boat. After escaping from a chase he sought refuge in the South where he became a contract surgeon for the CSA. Upon returning to the area after the war he was elected as Pocomoke City's first mayor. His home, The Costen House, is open to the public.

FEDERALSBURG

Dedication Date: between 1903 and 1910
Location: Hillcrest Cemetery, Federalsburg
    center of cemetery at the top of the
    main hill
Medium: marble, 6', on 3' granite base
Donor: local G.A.R. post

Inscription:

front:
*In memory
of the soldiers of the Civil
War buried in this cemetery*

left & right:
G.A.R.

Courtesy of Jean Kelly

Directions: From Cambridge take Rt. 50 north back to Easton and turn right on Rt. 331. Go east 11 miles to Preston, and then take Rt. 318 another 9 miles to Federalsburg. The cemetery is on the left just before the intersection with Denton Road.

Not much is known about this Union statue which, at the time of this writing, is undergoing repairs after vandalism. Judge Marvin H. Smith, a local historian, believes that the statue was erected before 1910. Smith also believes that Caroline County was strongly pro-Union because of the influence of the many Quakers who lived in the area. He is 76 years old and says, "I knew many Union veterans, but never knew a Confederate veteran from this area." The local Grand Army of the Republic group was named The Federal Post, after the town, which adopted its name after the Constitution debates of the 1780s.

The marble statue is of a private soldier at parade rest. It is a stock commercial statue seen in many other towns in the North, this particular one being distinguished by the figure's short coat and straight, balanced stance.

CHESTERTOWN

Dedication Date: June, 1917
Location: High St. Memorial Park,
 Chestertown
Medium: granite
Donor: Judge James Alfred Pearce

Inscriptions:

 south:
 Erected by James A. Pearce
 June 1917
 In commemoration of the patriotism and valor
 of a once divided but now reunited country.
 To the soldiers of Kent in the Confederate army
 1861-1865
 (37 names)*
 Under the sod the Blue and the Gray
 Waiting alike the Judgement Day

 north:
 To the soldiers of Kent in the Federal army
 1861-1865
 (22 names)*
 and 130 other privates
 (same verse)

Directions: Return to Rt. 50 and travel north 13 miles to Rt. 213 and then 25 miles to Chestertown. From Rt. 213 turn left on Spring Street just after entering Chestertown, then left again after two blocks onto High Street. The Memorial Park is a traffic island in the second block on the left, running the length of the block. The Civil War monument is in the center.

This monument was erected by an individual, but in a public space and with public fanfare. It is emblematic of the reconciliation stage of memorialization after the war because it honors both the soldiers who fought for the Union and those who fought for the Confederacy on the same rough-cut granite stone.

Judge James Alfred Pearce, who designed and financed the monument, did not fight in the war, but he was the son of the Honorable James Pearce, who was a U.S. senator from 1843 until his death in December, 1862. The senator was much loved and honored by his constituents. Senator Pearce had been an

---

* See Appendix G.

outspoken critic of the Union policy toward Maryland.

At the grand dedication ceremony for the monument Pearce said that his motive in erecting the monument was "to pay just tribute to men whose convictions of right and duty in a great crisis of our country's history led them to devote their lives, their fortunes, and their sacred honor to the cause each believed to be just and righteous." He hoped to "draw together the minds and hearts of our reunited people." He alluded to the then present conflict (World War I), saying that our great nation, united in the blood of that past struggle, is stronger than before, and is answering the call now to defend country and democracy with the same unquestioning sense of loyalty and duty.

Not all of the soldiers from Kent County are listed on the monument. Pearce's method of selecting the names to adorn the monument is not known.

CHESTER CEMETERY

Directions: From the Memorial Park, drive west on High Street to the outskirts of the old town, just past the railroad tracks on the right.

5.f   *Gen. George Vickers, USA (1801-1879)*

George Vickers was admitted to the Maryland bar in 1832 and practiced law in Chestertown. He served as a delegate to the Whig National Convention in 1852. During the Civil War he was a general of the Maryland militia. After the war he was a member of the Maryland Senate from 1866 to 1868 when he was elected to fill the vacant Maryland seat in the U.S. Senate.

5.g   *Col. Edward D. Wilkins, USA (1813-1878)*

Wilkins was commander of the 2nd Eastern Shore Volunteer Infantry consisting of eight companies organized in Chestertown from October to December, 1861. Companies A, B, C, D and E were from Kent County; Company F from Baltimore; Company G and H were from Harford County. They served on the Eastern Shore and in the Shenandoah Valley campaign.

CHAPTER 6

WASHINGTON AREA, SOUTHERN MARYLAND, NORTHEASTERN MARYLAND, AND WESTERN MARYLAND

WASHINGTON AREA

At the outbreak of the Civil War Washington, D.C., the capital of the Union, lay unprotected along the muddy banks of the Potomac River. As the Confederate forces grew in strength it became apparent that Washington needed a formal system of forts to protect it from invasion and capture. The first defenses were built across the Potomac in Virginia, as that was the border with the enemy. In August, 1861, after the Confederates had proved their strength at Manassas, a plan of 48 forts and batteries surrounding the perimeter of the capital was approved by General McClellan, commander of the Army of the Potomac. When it was finished it presented a formidable barrier which withstood Jubal Early's test in July, 1864.

All that is left today, in Maryland, of that massive engineering feat is one fort and the remains of several scattered batteries. Although those remains cannot be considered monuments, their locations are noted here because they are related to the two monuments in Maryland connected to that defense system.

This tour will begin on the west side of Washington, D.C. and move to the east around the beltway.

6.a   *Battery Bailey*

Directions: From the District line at Westmoreland Circle go two blocks west on Massachusetts Avenue and turn left onto Jamestown Drive. Take the first right onto Elliott Road and follow until it ends in Little Falls Park. The battery remains are beyond the end of the parking area.

Battery Bailey was an arm of Fort Mansfield to the west of the city and overlooked the Powder Mill Branch valley. There were platforms for six siege guns, but the battery was never armed. It was named for Capt. Guilford D. Bailey of the 2nd U.S. Artillery who was killed at Seven Pines (Fair Oaks), Virginia, May 31, 1862.

---

* For Civil War Monuments within Washington, D.C. see: James M. Goode, *Outdoor Sculpture of Washington, D.C.*

SILVER SPRING

Dedication Date: November, 1896
Location: Grace Episcopal Church cemetery,
    Georgia Ave.
Medium: granite, 9'
Donor: Confederate Veterans Association

Inscription:

> *To the memory of*
> *seventeen*
> *Unknown*
> *Confederate dead*
> *who fell in front of*
> *Washington*
> *July 12, 1864*
> *by their*
> *comrades*

Directions: From the Washington Beltway (Rt. 495) take the Georgia Avenue, south exit (#31). After five blocks 16th Street will branch off to the right. Go two more blocks and turn left onto Grace Church Drive. The monument is on the north corner of Grace Church Drive and Georgia Avenue.

There were two ceremonies involved in the establishment of this monument, and a comparison of these two ceremonies clearly demonstrates the movement from the funereal stage to the reconciliation stage of monument building.

The remains of Confederate soldiers killed when Early led his army in an advance on Washington, D. C. in the summer of 1864 were reinterred ten years later in the Grace Episcopal Church's graveyard, not by a memorial association, but by a clergyman and "friends of the lost cause." Reverend James Battle Avirett, pastor of Grace Episcopal Church in Woodside (now a part of Silver Spring) and former chaplain of Ashby's Cavalry, CSA, was moved to action by the knowledge that those bodies lay in shallow graves on a local farm and had not been blessed by Christian burial. Some of the remains could not be located, but on December 15, 1874, seventeen bodies were laid to rest in six coffins in a grave in the church's graveyard, in a lot donated by the Honorable Montgomery Blair, a member of the church. All were unknown except Pvt. James B. Bland of Highland County, Virginia.

About 300 people attended the ceremony which was religious in character, beginning in the church with the "service for the burial of the dead" and then proceeding to the yard for the lowering of the coffins. The assemblage then proceeded to the nearby parsonage where the oration was delivered from the porch by Dr. A. Y. P. Garnett of Washington, D. C. According to the *Sentinel* (July 25, 1902) and *Evening Star* (November 14, 1874) newspapers:

> He congratulated those present that the time had come when they could do justice to the memories of their friends, and perform such services unmolested. He alluded to the causes of the war, and justified the south for their actions. He once alluded to the willingness of the south to take up arms to defend their homes from invasion, when a voice in the crowd said, "And we're still willing to do it Doctor." He alluded to the south as "our people" and Jeff Davis as "our president."

At the end of the speech an original poem was read by its author, Reverend William Pinkney, Bishop of Maryland.

A monument was not placed over these graves until 1896 when two Confederate veterans associations, one from Rockville and one from Washington, D. C., raised funds for that commemoration. About 500 people attended the unveiling ceremony on November 14, as described in the *Evening Star* (November 14, 1896). A parade began at the Woodside train station, where the delegation from Washington arrived, and proceeded to the church accompanied by a local band. The ceremony was opened with a prayer by Rev. Mead of Montgomery County. A member of the veterans group gave a history of the reinterment and the monument, then there was a reading of Robert E. Lee's farewell address at the end of the war, followed by a reading of the poem "The Bivouac of the Dead" by three young ladies. A letter from Gen. William Cox, who had commanded the brigade to which the dead soldiers belonged, was read, and then the monument was unveiled by a young lady, Miss Dollie Young. The orator of the day was Judge Samuel Blackwell of Alabama, who spoke of "the almost total obliteration of sectional lines" and the unity of North and South in "standing for the perpetuation of the nation and the flag." According to the *Sentinel* (November 20, 1896) newspaper, a well-known Washington citizen, Paul Jones, son of a man who had died fighting for the Union, then rose and "claimed the privilege of recognizing the valor of the Confederate soldiers" by laying a bunch of white chrysanthemums at the foot of the monument.

Battleground National Cemetery

Inside the District line, west of Georgia Avenue two blocks south of the Walter Reed Army Medical Center, portions of Fort Stevens have been preserved. The Battleground National Cemetery, which contains the bodies of 40 of the 49 Union soldiers killed in the battle as well as several unit monuments, is at 6625 Georgia Avenue.

FORT LINCOLN CEMETERY

Directions: From the beltway (Rt. 495) take the Baltimore-Washington Parkway, south, exit. Follow the parkway to Annapolis Road (Rt. 450), west. Follow this road to the intersection with Landover Road and continue west to the Peace Cross Circle. Turn left onto Bladensburg Road. Go about a mile to the entrance of the cemetery on the left. Inside the entrance turn right to the floral clock circle, taking the first right out of the circle on Chapel Drive. Continue on Chapel Drive to the fork, taking the left fork onto Fort Lincoln Drive. Battery Jamison of Fort Lincoln is on the right and the statue of Lincoln will be at the next intersection.

Fort Lincoln Cemetery officially began in 1912 when, as the Capitol Cemetery, it received a charter from the State of Maryland, although there had been a cemetery on the property for many years before. The cemetery was expanded in 1931 to 176 acres, which included parts of the old Fort Lincoln, and was formally designed as a lawn-park cemetery. This natural type of design allowed for the preservation of Battery Jamison.

6.b   *Battery Jamison*

This battery was part of Fort Lincoln, built during the summer of 1861 as part of the defenses of Washington. It was named Fort Lincoln in honor of the president by General Order #18, September 30, 1861. The Civil War cannons, commemorating the brigade of Gen. Hooker, the first to occupy the fort, were put in place by the Department of Defense.

FORT LINCOLN CEMETERY LINCOLN STATUE

Dedication Date: April 18, 1947
Location: Fort Lincoln Cemetery
Medium: bronze
Sculptor: Andrew O'Connor
Donor: Fort Lincoln Cemetery

This monument was erected in 1947, after the cemetery corporation hired Horace Peasley, architect and landscape designer, to redesign the cemetery in a lawn-park fashion.

The Rhode Island Sons of Veterans Association commissioned the statue in 1930 but was only able to raise $9,500 of the $20,000 cost. After the death of the sculptor in 1941, the Gorham Company surveyed cemetery corporations around the country and found a buyer, the Fort Lincoln Cemetery.

The sculptor, Andrew O'Connor, created the sculpture in 1930, and it was cast by the Gorham Manufacturing Company of Providence, Rhode Island. It shows a war-worn president in deep meditation, and is executed in an impressionistic style reminis-

cent of Rodin. O'Connor, a native of Massachusetts, was a student of D. C. French, and also did the Lincoln statue in front of the State House in Springfield, Illinois, as well as "Meditation" at the Art Institute of Illinois. His marble "Adam and Eve" can be seen at the Corcoran Gallery in Washington, D.C.

6.c   *Fort Foote*

Directions: From the Washington Beltway (Rt. 495) take the Indian Head Highway exit #7 and then take the first right onto Oxen Hill Road and follow to Fort Foote Road.

This Civil War fort, named for Rear Admiral Andrew Hull Foote, was constructed between 1863 and 1865 as part of the defenses of Washington. It overlooks the Potomac River and has been preserved by the National Park Service and remounted with cannons.

SOUTHERN MARYLAND

Directions: As you travel into southern Maryland on Rt. 5, you will be following part of the route taken by John Wilkes Booth after he assassinated President Lincoln. From the Washington Beltway take Rt. 5 (Branch Avenue South.)

The Surratt House
To stop at the Surratt House, turn right on Rt. 223W (Woodyard Road), and after one mile turn left on Brandywine Road to the museum/house on the left. It is open March through December.

Dr. Samuel Mudd's House
Continue south on Rt. 5. At Bryantown, approximately 18 miles south of Clinton, to take a visit to Dr. Samuel Mudd's House, turn left, east, off Rt. 5 at Bryantown and following the signs for about 6 miles. The house is open to the public April through October.

6.d   *Dr. Samuel A. Mudd (1833-1883)*
St. Mary's Church Cemetery

Directions: From Rt. 5 at Bryantown turn right, west, and go two miles to the church and cemetery on the left.

The case of Dr. Mudd's involvement in the Lincoln assassination plot is still a subject of debate. Not having practiced medicine for years, Dr. Mudd was approached, on his farm near Bryantown, by the escaping John Wilkes Booth to repair his leg, which he did. Convicted by a military court of conspiracy, Mudd was sent to Fort Jefferson prison in Dry Tortugas, Florida, where he voluntarily treated sick prisoners and guards. He was released by President Andrew Johnson and spent the rest of his life on his farm.

TULIP

Dedication Date: October 19, 1940
Rededicated: 1958
Location: Cross Manor, St. Inigoes
Medium: white marble
Contractor: U.S. Navy Yard
Donor: U.S.A.

Inscriptions:

front:
> *In memory of*
> *Those who perished*
> *In the Explosion*
> *of the U.S.S. Tulip*
> *Nov. 11, 1864*

rear:
> *Sacrifice*
> *Of lives in*
> *Discharge of*
> *Duty and in*
> *The interest*
> *Of achieving*
> *Peace and*
> *Scientific*
> *Advance*

Directions: From Rt. 5 take Rt. 235 south to Lexington Park. Six miles south of Lexington Park turn right on Mattapany Road to St. Mary's City and turn left onto Rt. 5. About four miles past the city turn right on Villa Road. Go about one mile and turn right on Grayson Road. At the end of this road (.6 mile) turn left on the unpaved Cross Manor Road. Proceed to the gate of the manor and stop. The monument is about 100 yards to the right.

This smallest (.53 acres) National Cemetery recounts a foolhardy act by a green officer which cost him his life as well as the lives of 48 others.

The *Tulip* was a small steamship built in New York for a Chinese merchant. The aging vessel was purchased by the United States government for use as a lighthouse tender. During the Civil War she was rigged as a gunboat and used to patrol the lower Potomac River and defend Point Lookout Prisoner of War Camp. One of her two steam boilers was condemned and she was ordered to Washington for repairs in November, 1864. The Master of the ship was Lt. William H. Smith from Pennsylvania. He dined with the Ellicotts, who lived nearby, the evening before sailing. Mr. Ellicott recalled that Smith had said that "as soon as he was out of signal distance he was going to get up steam on the condemned boiler as he did not intend to go creeping up the Potomac under the fire of Confederate batteries."

And so he did soon after he was out of port. Smith assembled the men not on watch in the mess room, which was right above the boiler room. One survivor related that when the engineer came up to report that the boiler had steam forming on it he became frightened and went outside to the rear of the ship. The explosion came a few minutes later and the ship was torn to fragments, only part of the bow being recovered later. There were 57 enlisted men and two officers on the ship. Ten survived the blast, but two later died of their wounds. About eight of the bodies recovered were so mangled that they could not be identified. Those were buried at the site, along with parts of bodies found in the river. The identified were buried elsewhere.

In 1937, Congress appropriated $2,000 for purchase of the tiny plot of ground and the erection of a monument. The monument, made at the Navy Yard in Washington, cost $520. The dedication ceremony was arranged by H. E. Riebe, Commandant of the Navy Yard. The main speaker was Representative Lansdale G. Sasscer of Maryland's 5th District, and the ceremony was accompanied by the Navy School of Music Band which played Taps and the national anthem at the conclusion. This was followed by a firing of three volleys by the Navy firing squad.

About twenty years later Admiral A. M. Pride, of the Patuxent River Naval Air Test Center, came across the monument, seemingly deserted, and arranged for an additional plaque, with a more detailed description of the incident, which was placed at the site in 1958.

ADMIRAL PRIDE'S PLAQUE

POINT LOOKOUT MARYLAND

Dedication Date: July 4, 1876
Location: Scotland, Rt. 5
Medium: marble, 20'
Donor: Maryland

Inscriptions:

south:
*At the call of Patriotism and duty
they encountered the perils of the field
endured the trials of a Prison; and were
faithful, even unto death*

north:
*Colonel Wm. Elliott
General Wm. C. Oates
and Gov. James H. Berry
Being U.S. Commissioners to mark
Confederate graves. The State of Maryland
having ceded to the federal government the
cemetery to which the bodies of the Confederates who died prisoners of war at Point Lookout Military Prison had been removed the War
Department granted permission to have the
state monument removed and re-erected at
this the original prison burying ground.
A.D. 1910-1911
dulce et decorum est pro patria mori*
(this inscription was added when the monument
was moved and no longer applies since it has
been moved back)

west:
*1876
Erected
by the
State of Maryland
in memory of
The Confederate soldiers
who died prisoners of war
at Point Lookout, from
March 1, 1864 to June 30, 1865.*

east:	
Virginia	*640*
North Carolina	*962*
South Carolina	*248*
Georgia	*249*
Alabama	*75*
Tennessee	*63*
Louisiana	*38*
Mississippi	*42*
Florida	*31*
Kentucky	*18*
Texas	*6*
Maryland	*6*
Arkansas	*4*
Missouri	*4*
	2386
Confederate States not designated	*618*
	3004

Directions: From the Tulip Monument go back to Rt. 5 and turn right. Continue south on Rt. 5 for 8 miles. The monuments are on the right.

Early in 1863, a prisoner of war camp, Camp Hoffman, was established by the Union at Point Lookout, the southernmost point of Maryland, a triangle of marsh and sand at the confluence of the Potomac River with the Chesapeake Bay. Over 50,000 prisoners passed through the camp during the two years it was in operation, and, by the end of the war, 3,384 Confederate prisoners had died and were buried in a cemetery outside the camp.

In 1870, the Maryland legislature appropriated money for the purchase of land and the reburial of the dead to prevent them from being washed away by flooding. A Board of Trustees of local men was established to oversee the work. The dead had originally been buried individually, but a fire had destroyed the wooden grave markers; so when the state government moved the bodies they were reburied in a mass grave. After the dead were reburied, the Maryland legislature in 1874 appropriated $3,000 to ornament the cemetery. This money was used to purchase the monument and surround the cemetery with a wrought-iron fence.

The monument was dedicated as a part of St. Mary's County's participation in the national centennial celebration on July 4th, 1876. Even though the site was more than 20 miles from any town, the ceremony was attended by hundreds, some arriving by boat. Speakers for the occasion included Capt. Joseph Forrest, CSA, a local member of the Board of Trustees; the Honorable John K. Tarbox of Massachusetts; the Honorable Charles E. Hooker, CSA, of Mississippi, who spoke on the Civil War and the southern prisoners of war; Dr. Henkle, local member of Congress; and Randolph Jones, a local staunch supporter of the Union during the war, who expounded at great length on the history of the United States. Texts of those rather verbose speeches can be found in the *St. Mary's Beacon* (July 6-Aug. 3, 1876).

In 1910, when the new federal monument was being built, the Maryland monument was moved to the original site of the burial ground. In May, 1938, the Maryland monument was moved next to the federal monument because the government had sold the land of the original cemetery. Both monuments now exist on the same site.

POINT LOOKOUT FEDERAL

Dedication Date: completed 1911
    (no unveiling)
Location: Scotland, Rt. 5
Sculptor: Van Amridge Granite Company
Medium: granite obelisk, 80'
Donor: U.S.A.

Inscriptions:

> *Federal Monument*
> *Erected by*
> *The United States*
> *to mark the burial place*
> *of Confederate*
> *soldiers and sailors*
> *who died at Point Lookout, Md.*
> *while prisoners of war and were there*
> *buried to the number of 3384, but whose*
> *remains were subsequently removed*
> *either to their respective homes*
> *or to this cemetery where the individual*
> *graves cannot be now identified*

(names, ranks and companies of 3,389 dead,
some of which are listed as "unkown")*

The federal government's patronage of Confederate monuments began in June, 1900, when the United States Congress, after being petitioned by the U.D.C. for many years, authorized the setting aside of a section of Arlington National Cemetery for Confederate dead. There were a small number of Confederates buried in the cemetery who had died in federal hospitals and prisons nearby during the war. Formerly, relatives of the Confederate dead in this cemetery were not allowed to decorate their graves, and sometimes were not even allowed on the cemetery grounds. A description of an 1869 Decoration

---

* For the list of those buried here contact the National Archives or see: *Point Lookout Prison Camp for Confederates* by Edwin W. Beitzell.

Day ceremony in Frederick, Maryland, includes the sentence "No armed minions of power and fanaticism were here – as they were in Arlington a few weeks ago – to drive away, with brutal indignity, the gentle footsteps that had approached with their memorial offerings!"

When a Confederate section was finally established at Arlington National Cemetery and the decorating of graves with flowers allowed on Memorial Day, it demonstrated a turning point in the federal government's attitude toward respect for the South – a necessary step for reconciliation. Another, more encompassing step came next.

In December, 1902, a bill was introduced on the floor of the U.S. Senate by Senator Joseph B. Foraker of Ohio to provide for the appropriate marking of the graves of Confederate soldiers and sailors who died in federal prisons during the Civil War. After being reintroduced several times, the bill was passed by the Senate in January, 1906. The house changed the bill to read that individual markers would be placed over the graves only "where practicable," and passed on March 5, 1906. President Theodore Roosevelt signed the bill into law on March 9, 1906. This bill, sometimes referred to as the Foraker Act, required the marking, with a white marble headstone, "similar to those placed over the graves in the Confederate section of the National Cemetery in Arlington," of the grave of every Confederate soldier or sailor who died in a federal prison or hospital. The sum of $200,000 was appropriated for the purpose.

The act had to be changed for the Point Lookout Cemetery because it was impossible to mark the graves of the dead individually since they were buried in a mass grave. Congress subsequently, on December 3, 1910, passed a Joint Resolution which allowed the erection of a monument on which bronze tablets would be placed containing the names of those buried.

The federal monument at Point Lookout is an impressive 85-foot-tall granite obelisk that was completed in October, 1911. Four bronze tablets on the sides of the base list the names of 3,383 soldiers and 44 civilians. The monument sits on 1.03 acres of ground belonging to the U.S. government beneath which are the remains of the soldiers. There is no record of any unveiling ceremony for the monument.*

6.e   *Annie Olivia Flood*
St. Ignatius Catholic Church
Cemetry, Port Tobacco (on Rt. 427)

Annie Flood was an agent in the Confederate underground mail service.

---

* For more information on the Point Lookout monuments see *Point Lookout Prison Camp for Confederates* by Edwin W. Beitzell, which includes a list of those buried there, or *The Chronicles of St. Mary's*, Vol. 27, #12, December, 1979.

NORTHEASTERN MARYLAND

JOHN RODGERS POST, G.A.R.

Dedication Date: July 4, 1900
Location: Angel Hill Cemetery, Havre de
  Grace
Medium: granite, 10'
Donor: John Rodgers Post, G.A.R.

Inscription:

front:

> Erected
> June 30, 1900
> by Admiral
> John Rodgers
> Post No. 28
> Department
> of Maryland
> Grand Army
> of the Republic
> to
> Honorably discharged
> Soldiers and Sailors
> of the Civil War
> 1861-1865

right:

> [G.A.R. badge]

rear:

> Dedicated
> by the members of
> Admiral John Rodgers
> Post No. 28
> G.A.R.
> 1861-1865

Directions: From I-95 take Rt. 155 east into Havre de Grace. Just past the railroad tracks turn right onto Ohio Street, and then take the first right into the cemetery. The monument is at the top of the hill near the railroad tracks.

The dedication of this monument was the highlight of the Havre de Grace Fourth of July celebration in 1900, described in the *Havre de Grace Republican* (July 7, 1900). Old soldiers led a parade from the center of town up the hill to the cemetery, marching to the music of the Aberdeen Fire Department band. At their head was Maj. John R. King, commander of the Maryland Department of the G.A.R., and they were followed by contingents from neighboring G.A.R. posts and the people of the town. Commander King accepted the monument on behalf of "the comrades of the Grand Army of the Republic, representing the soldiers and sailors who defended the integrity and the authority of the nation." He said that the monument, standing as silent sentinel, "assures that our dead are held in remembrance, and gives encouragement for the future."

The local newspaper described the ceremony: "The guard of honor then took its place; an anchor, emblematic of the navy; and a musket, haversack and canteen, emblematic of the army, were placed in position, and a sailor armed with a cutlass, and a soldier armed with a musket, were stationed to guard them; the commander and others of those taking part repeating the appropriate ritual service."

The ritual was followed by a recitation of "Hooker on Lookout Mountain" by Miss Sitzler and the singing of "Salute the Flag" by Miss Mary Bartol of Baltimore. The orator of the day was Capt. William H. Potter, of George B. Meade Post, G.A.R., formerly captain of Company A, 9th Pennsylvania, of which many of the veterans from Harford County had been members.

6.f   *Cecil County Union Plaque Cecil County Courthouse, Elkton, interior wall*

Inscription:

> *This plaque commemorates the patriotism and courage of approximately 1500 men from Cecil County who fought for preservation of the Federal union in the Civil War 1861-1865*

Directions: From Rt. 40 take Rt. 213 into Elkton, turn right on Howard Street after crossing the bridge over the creek, and take the second left on Church Street; then take the first left onto Main Street, which is one-way going west. The courthouse is in the second block on the right.

Cecil County was one of the few counties in Maryland which was almost unanimously for the Union. At a large mass meeting in Elkton on April 23, 1861, a resolution was adopted declaring that "Cecil County will stand by the Union if the rest of the State secedes." An estimated 1,500 Cecil County men joined the Union army, proportionately more than any other county in the state, and it is thought less than 25 went over to the Confederate army (one of those was Brig. Gen. W. W. Mackall of the army of Tennessee.) Units raised almost entirely in Cecil County were: Companies A and I of the 5th Maryland Regiment; Companies B, E, and G of the 6th Maryland Regiment; Company A of the 8th Maryland Regiment; Companies E and H of the Purnell Legion; Company B of the 1st Maryland Light Artillery (Snow's Battery); and Company C of the 2nd Delaware. Among the officers in the Union army from Cecil County were Brig. Gen. Andrew Wallace Evans, Col. George Howard, and Col. Joseph Hill, as well as 11 surgeons.

The veterans of the county erected a monument on Antietam Battlefield to Companies A and I of the 5th Maryland in 1890 (see 5th Regiment Monument, 4.8).

April 9, 1965 was chosen for the dedication of the Centennial plaque because, according to Ernest Howard, president of the Cecil County Historical Society, it was the 100th anniversary of the surrender of General Lee at Appomattox Courthouse. The dedication ceremony was opened with an invocation, then there was a reading of the "Gettysburg Address" followed by a short presentation by Howard on the history of Cecil County men in the Civil War. The *Cecil Whig* carried photographs of the ceremony.

ELKTON PRESBYTERIAN CEMETERY

Just two blocks east of the courthouse is the Elkton Presbyterian Church with a lovely small cemetery in the rear. This cemetery contains the graves of two people prominent in the effort to preserve the Union.

6.g *John Creswell (1828-1891) (lot #79 — 8' long, 5' tall marble bench)*

John Creswell was Adjutant General of Maryland during the Civil War, in charge of raising troops to meet the state's quotas. After the war he was prominent in Maryland politics, being elected to the U.S. House of Representatives and the Senate, and was Postmaster General under President Grant. The lengthy inscription on his tombstone tells his life story and is a wonderful example of Victorian sentiment in describing the "perfect gentleman" – "Faithful to every trust, loyal to every friend, generous to every cause, a wise counselor and an able advocate.... He was dignified in demeanor, commanding in person, courtly in manner, fearless in defense of the right, upright in his dealings with his fellow man, exemplary in his domestic life, pure in morals, faithful in religious duties, generous but not ostentatious in charity."

6.h *General Andrew Wallace Evans, USA (1829-1906) (lot #50 — coffin type marble stone with a cross on top)*

General Evans was an Elkton native who graduated from West Point in 1852 and spent his entire military career – before, during, and after the Civil War – in the West. He retired to Elkton in 1883.

CHERRY HILL

Dedication Date: May 30, 1965
Location: Cherry Hill Cemetery
Medium: 2 bronze plaques, $1^1/_2$ x 3'
Donor: local committee

Inscription:

(lists the names of 48 Union soldiers from Cecil County)*

Directions: From the center of Elkton take Rt. 213 north about 6 miles to Cherry Hill. Turn right on Elk Mills Road and the cemetery is at the top of the hill on the right.

Not satisfied with the plaque in the court-house at Elkton, two local history minded men, Lyman A. Spence and Joseph E. McFadden, raised funds for a monument which actually listed the names of the men from the local area who fought for the Union. The monument, in the form of two bronze plaques, was erected in the Cherry Hill Cemetery on Memorial Day, 1965. According to

the author's research, it is the most recent monument in Maryland to have been erected to the Civil War.

There was a small ceremony attended by about 50 people. The "Gettysburg Address" was read, as well as the order of General Logan, founder of the G.A.R., establishing Memorial Day.

---

* See Appendix G.

NORTH EAST

Dedication Date: May 30, 1928
Location: North East Methodist Cemetery
    gates
Medium: 2 bronze plaques
Donor: Isaac Henry Ford and John Ford
Contractor: John S. Norman

Inscription:

1928
Erected to
the memory of
the men of Cecil
County, Maryland
Many of whom
sleep here who
fought for the
Union of this nation
1861-1865
presented by
Isaac Henry Ford
and John Ford

"Lest We Forget"
Their heroism
sacrifice, and
Service to God
and country

Victorious in
life — immortal
in death

Directions: From Rt. 40 take Rt. 272 into North East. Turn left at the post office and go two blocks to the cemetery on the left.

This is the only monument in the state which takes the form of gates to a cemetery. The idea began after Miss Sarah M. Ford donated land for an addition to the Methodist-Episcopal Cemetery in North East. Miss Ford's brother, I. Henry Ford, of Washington, bequested $300 in his will to a fund for the memorial gates to the addition to honor the men from the area who fought for the Union in the Civil War, many of whom are buried in the cemetery. But the fund never materialized, and several years later, when the bequest had grown through interest to the amount of $425, Henry's brother, John Ford, applied to the trustees of the cemetery for the erection of the gates and agreed to pay any amount in excess of the bequest. The trustees approved the monument and it was built by a local contractor, John S. Norman.

The pillars for the gates are of Port Deposit granite and are 7 feet high and 24 inches square. The gates are of extra heavy iron, and the bronze plaques, with the dedication inscriptions, are affixed to the pillars.

The dedication ceremony for this monument was a part of the annual Memorial Day celebration in North East. According to the *Cecil Whig* (June 2, 1928) newspaper a parade of Boy Scouts, veterans, members of patriotic orders, and Daughters of the American Revolution, marched from the center of town, led by the local band. They first went to St. Mary's Cemetery where there were

speeches, prayers, and the laying of flowers on the graves. The procession then advanced to the Methodist-Episcopal Cemetery where the graves were decorated and the Memorial Gates unveiled. The address was given by the local pastor, Reverend E. M. Shockley. Local Civil War veterans Samuel Wingate and J. T. Kenney were the special guests of honor.

This is the only Union monument in Maryland with the inscription "Lest We Forget," which is more often found on Confederate monuments (see Monocacy Chapel 3.2, and "Recessional" in Appendix E).

WESTERN MARYLAND

CUMBERLAND UNION

Dedication Date: May 30, 1895
Location: Rose Hill Cemetery, Cumberland
Medium: 6' copper bronze statue, 6' granite
    base
Donor: Cumberland Women's Relief Corps
Sculptor: unknown

Inscriptions:

> front (base):
> *Infantry, Cavalry, Artillery, Navy*

> front (bronze plaque):
> *Erected with contributions of citizens*
> *to honor the men of our country*
> *who fought for the Union 1861-65*
> *by the Cumberland Woman's Relief Corps*
> *May 30, 1895*

Directions: From I-68/Rt. 40 take the Baltimore Avenue exit (#44). Turn left on Baltimore Street which becomes Washington Street after crossing the bridge over the railroad. After passing the library and courthouse on the right and the Historical Society on the left go six blocks and turn right on Allegany Street. Go one block and turn left on Fayette Street. The entrance to the cemetery is one block on the right. (Not navigable by oversize vehicles.)

There is a Civil War Room at the Allegany County Historical Society, 218 Washington Street.

The unveiling of this monument was preceded by the city's Memorial Day parade, which was led by the Cumberland Concert Band followed by more than 70 veterans of the G.A.R. in uniform, carriages with the speakers of the day, women of the Relief Corps, and ending with the three volunteer fire companies of Cumberland vying with each other for the brightest, most flashing, uniforms. The parade marched to the cemetery where the more than 3,000 spectators were regaled with hymns, the reading of locally composed poems, and long speeches about the heroism of the common soldier and the rightness of the victory. The prayer was read by Mary Hadra, Relief Corps Chaplain, and the dedication speech was given by Emma Wolfe, Corps Vice-President. This is one of the few monument ceremonies in which women had a prominent public part. Usually, even though the women raised the money for the monument, they let the men make the speeches on dedication day.

The monument is a bronze statue of a private soldier. It is one of the stock variety of statues which were ordered from foundries. The same statue can be found at Hopkinton, New Hampshire; Monson, Massachusetts; and Union, Maine.

6.i *Col. William Wallace McKaig, Jr., CSA*
Rose Hill Cemetery, Cumberland

Born in Cumberland May 5, 1842, McKaig was the son of the first mayor of that city, prominent lawyer William McKaig. He was a 1st Lieutenant in Co. A, 2nd Maryland Cavalry. After the war he became a colonel in the Maryland National Guard. He was an industrialist and a member of the Cumberland City Council.

WOMEN'S RELIEF CORPS BADGE

CUMBERLAND CONFEDERATE

Dedication Date: June 6, 1912
Location: Rose Hill Cemetery, Cumberland
Medium: granite obelisk, 25'
Donor: Ladies of Cumberland Memorial
　　　　Association

Inscriptions:

> front:
> *To the Unknown Confederate Dead*
>
> east:
> *Erected by the Ladies of Cumberland, Md.*
> *in 1912 to the heroes who died*
> *fighting for the Lost Cause*
>
> west:
> *This tablet was placed on this monument by*
> *the United States to mark the burial place of*
> *six Confederate soldiers who died at*
> *Clarysville, Maryland, while prisoners of war,*
> *and whose remains were buried but subse-*
> *quently removed to this lot where the indi-*
> *vidual graves cannot now be identified. And*
> *the names of the dead are:*

	Co.	Regiment
Brown, Allen	*C*	*37 N.C.*
Fuldenwider, H.W., 2nd Lt.	*E*	*23 N.C.*
Gilbert, Nicholas A., Sgt.	*F*	*58 VA*
Ramsey, Watson M.	*F*	*23 VA*
Smith, John A.	*E*	*52 VA*
Stow, Joel R.	*A*	*8 TN Cav*

The monument was erected about the same time as the federal government was marking all the graves of Confederate prisoners of war. Because the money for the monument had already been raised, the federal government added a bronze plaque listing the names of the six Confederates who died in the Union hospital nearby and whose remains had been brought here for reinterment by the James Breathed Camp, United Confederate Veterans. There are three others, not listed on the plaque who are buried here: Charles Wagner, killed at Pollock's farm; and James O. Choen, and an unknown soldier, killed at Folck's Mill.

The services for this reinterment took place on October 23, 1900. Grey-bearded veterans gathered around to pay tribute to their fallen comrades. The poem by J. Ratigan, "To The Unknown" was read.

The Ladies Auxiliary of the UCV next organized a movement to raise money for a monument to erect over the graves. It took them more than 10 years to raise the funds, but they persevered. Unveiled on June 6, 1912, to the oratory of Col. Robert E. Lee, grandson of the famous general, the granite monument is of the obelisk type, common at the time and produced commercially.

CAPTURE OF GENERALS KELLEY AND CROOK

Dedication date: probably 1910s
Location: intersection of Baltimore St. and
George St., Cumberland
Medium: raised bronze plaque on 4' granite
block
Donor: Henry Mullaney

Inscriptions:

*Capture of Generals
B. F. Kelly and George Crook
Nights, February 21-22, 1865*

*A company of Confederates, young men
from Cumberland, Maryland,
Hampshire and Hardy Counties,
West Virginia,
captured several picket posts,
obtained the countersign "Bulls Gap,"
rode into the city,
captured the two commanding Union generals,
Kelly and Crook,
and Adj. General Thayer Melvin,
and sent them to Richmond, Virginia,
as prisoners of war, without firing a shot.*

*Generals Kelly and Melvin
were taken from this building
then the "Barnum House."
(now Windsor Hotel)
General Crook was captured in the
"Revere House."
(now the Kenneweg Co. — Wholesale Grocers)*

*The generals were asleep when taken
from their respective beds.*

*General Lew Wallace was stationed here
in command of a large body
of Indiana Zouaves.
Also, Brig. General Hayes,
later President of the United States.*

*This most daring episode of the Civil War
created a great sensation
all over the country,
as at the time
several thousand Union troops
were stationed in Cumberland.
Henry Mullaney*

Inscription on aluminum plate below plaque:

*The Windsor Hotel — Formerly
Barnum House — was located on this site.
Razed in 1959*

*Displayed with permission of
Matthew J. Mullaney
and
Lt. Col. G.L. Morissey*

This monument is situated on the City Mall of Cumberland in front of a modern bank building. The plaque featured on the monument was originally placed on the front of the Windsor Hotel (formerly Barnum House), which was owned by Matthew J. Mullaney beginning in 1901. Matthew Mullaney never married. The plaque was removed from the Windsor Hotel when it was torn down in 1959, but appears not to have been placed in its current position until the bank was built in 1975.

The plaque commemorates a remarkable escapade that occurred near the end of the war. In the early morning hours of February 21, 1865, a group of about thirty Confederates, volunteers from McNeill's Partisan Rangers, formed from the 18th Virginia Cavalry, and from Company F of the 7th Virginia Cavalry and Company E of the 11th Virginia Cavalry, were led by Lt. Jesse McNeill to capture Brig. Gen. Benjamin Franklin Kelley, general of West Virginia volunteers, and Maj. Gen. George Crook, commander of the Department of West Virginia, from their beds in their hotel rooms in the midst of about 8,000 Union troops.*

Jesse McNeill had taken over command of the Rangers after the death of his father, the former commander, John Hanson McNeill, in the fall of 1864. Both father and son had a grudge against Kelley for arresting members of their family. The scheme to capture Kelley was apparently formulated by Jesse and his men convinced him to also capture Gen. Crook who was staying at the Revere House, a nearby hotel.

The entrance into the well-guarded city, the capture of the generals, and the escape of the captors with their quarry was carried out almost flawlessly. The adjutant general, Capt. Melvin, had to be taken along because he was inadvertently awakened by the invaders trying to locate Kelley in the Barnum House. The captured generals were taken to Richmond and later exchanged. McNeill and his party were given commendations by Lee, and Jesse McNeill was promoted to captain.

Gen. Kelley returned to Cumberland to marry Mary Clare Bruce, and Gen. Crook also later returned and married the daughter of the owner of the Revere House, Mary Daily, who was the sister of one of his captors, Charles Daily.

---

* The details of this operation can be found in the *History of Allegany County* by Thomas and Williams (1923).

SUMNER CEMETERY U.S.C.T.

Dedication date: 1991
Location: Yale Street on the east side of Cumberland
Medium: 4' granite block and a raised bronze plaque on a second block flush to the ground. A 30 ft. flag pole stands in front of the monument.
Contractor: Frostburg Memorials
Donor: Cumberland Historic Cemetery Organization, Inc.

Inscriptions:

Volunteers from southern and eastern Maryland formed Feb. 1864 The 30th participated in the Wilderness Campaign and saw action against Petersburg, Va.
It was faded out Dec., 1865
(30th Regiment Infantry U.S.C.T.)

Buried here are Frank Tyler, Abraham Craig, Thomas Lindsey, Thomas Simpson, David Kinner, Sam Parry.

base of flag pole:
Flag flies in honor of the holy souls of the U.S.C.T.

Directions: Heading west on Rt. 68 take the first Cumberland exit, Baltimore Avenue, turn right on the second street, Hamilton, which becomes Yale Street. There will be a large cemetery on either side of the street. Sumner Cemetery is at the east end of the cemetery on the left, just before the road turns to the right.

This is the oldest known black cemetery in Allegany County. Long before the Civil War this was the site of many slave burials, so it seemed the natural final resting place for six veterans of that war who had fought valiantly for their freedom as members of the United States Colored Troops.

Unfortunately, as so often happens with old unused cemeteries, Sumner Cemetery had fallen into sad disrepair. The honeysuckle and sumac had taken over and the few gravestones that existed in the small plot were either broken and sunk into the ground or totally overgrown with the vegetation.

In January, 1991, the Cumberland Historic Cemetery Organization made this cemetery its project. It was joined by the Ebenezer Baptist Church, the Metropolitan AME Church, the McKendree United Methodist Church, and the Sons of Union Veterans

(Harpers Ferry Camp 6), in cleaning up the cemetery and erecting the monument and flag pole to the USCT. Members of the 1991 Board of Directors of the CHCO were: Edward W. Taylor, Jr., president; Priscilla Collinson, vice-president; Florence Finan, Secretary; Florence Meade, treasurer; Daniel Whetzel, research; and Katherine Wolford.

The Cumberland Historic Cemetery Organization was founded in 1983 by Katherine Wolford and Edward Taylor, Jr. (who provided information on this monument) and is now an affiliate of the Coalition to Protect Historic Maryland Burial Sites. This state-wide coalition was formed in 1991 to preserve burial sites because of their importance as cultural resources. Many family grave plots, old church graveyards and even community cemeteries have fallen into neglect and even disappeared when the family or church is no longer in possession of the property, or the community becomes engulfed in suburbia.

For more information on this organization write to: Coalition to Protect Maryland Burial Sites, Inc., P.O. Box 1533, Ellicott City, MD 21041.

Sumner Cemetery, Memorial Day, 1993
Cumberland Historic Cemetery Organization
Courtesy of Ed Taylor

Appendix A

MARYLAND MONUMENTS
IN OTHER STATES

Virginia
Winchester, Stonewall Cemetery — Confederate, 1880
Fredericksburg — Confederate

Pennsylvania – Gettysburg National Battlefield Park
1st Maryland Artillery (Rigby's Battery A), USA
1st Maryland Artillery (Dement's Battery), USA
1st Maryland Cavalry, USA
1st (Later 2nd) Maryland Infantry, CSA
1st Maryland Infantry, Eastern Shore Volunteers, USA
1st Maryland Infantry, Potomac Home Brigade, USA
3rd Maryland Infantry, USA
Chesapeake Artillery (Brown's), CSA
Gregg Cavalry Shaft, USA & CSA
Maryland Monument to Maryland Union and Confederate Regiments
Purnell Legion Maryland Cavalry (Co. A), USA

Mississippi — Vicksburg National Battlefield Park
Third Confederate Battery, Stevenson's Division
Equestrian statue of Gen. Lloyd Tilghman

Tennessee – Chickamauga National Battlefield Park
Union and Confederate

Martha's Vineyard, Massachusetts
In August, 1891, the statue of a soldier was unveiled on Martha's Vineyard in Massachusetts, dedicated to the soldiers who fought for the Union by the Henry Wade Post of the G.A.R.

What makes this monument special to Marylanders is that it was erected by a native son of Maryland who fought for the Confederacy. Charles S. Strahan was born in Baltimore and enlisted in the 21st Virginia Regiment, Company B (the Maryland Guard). After being wounded at Fair Oaks he was commissioned a lieutenant. After the war he moved to Martha's Vineyard and became editor of the local newspaper, *The Herald*.

Strahan, wanting to "blot out the prejudice of war, and close the bloody chasm," raised the money for the monument to his former enemies. After the unveiling he wrote in his newspaper: "It will be remarked that the tablets on three sides are filled and one left blank. Who knows but that, as the Grand Army of the Republic becomes smaller, and the passions of war are lost in forgetfulness, these few remaining veterans may yet inscribe on the tablet a token of their respect to their old foes in the field 'who have passed over to the other side of the river and are resting under the shade of the trees [from Stonewall Jackson's last words], thus lifting up and keeping the American name and nation the brightest and most magnanimous in the galaxy of nations."

That final step occurred in 1925, while Strahan was still alive. The G.A.R. veterans inscribed the fourth tablet: "' The Chasm is Closed' In memory of the restored Union this tablet is dedicated by Union veterans of the Civil War and patriotic citizens of Martha's Vineyard."

Appendix B

MARYLAND CIVIL WAR MONUMENT STAGES

FUNEREAL STAGE (6 Union, 5 Confederate, 1 Other)

2.13	Gleeson, Union, New Cathedral Cem., 1866
5.4	Governor Hicks, Cambridge, 1868
2.2	Loudon Park Confederate Statue, Loudon Park Cem., 1870
4.4	Antietam National Cemetery Statue, Union, 1880
3.6	Mt. Olivet Cem. Confederate Statue, 1881
2.4	Lt. Col. Gilmor, Loudon Park Cem., Confederate, 1883
2.8	Union Obelisk, Loudon Park National Cem., 1884
2.3	Murray Association, Loudon Park Cem., Confederate, est. 1890's
4.8	5th Regiment, Union, Antietam Battlefield, 1890
6.9	Cumberland, Union, 1895
2.9	Unknown Soldier, Union, Loudon Park Nat. Cem., 1895
2.5	Jane Claudia and Gen. Johnson, Loudon Park Cem., Confederate, 1901

RECONCILIATION STAGE (16 Union, 19 Confederate, 2 Both, 2 Other)

5.1	Chief Justice Taney, Annapolis, 1872
6.4	Point Lookout Maryland Monument to Confederate POWs, 1876
4.9	Washington Cem., Confederate, Hagerstown, 1877
4.2	Gen. Reno, Union, South Mountain, 1889
2.10	U.S. Navy, Loudon Park National Cem., 1896
6.1	Silver Spring, Confederate, 1896
4.1	War Correspondents Arch, South Mountain, 1896
2.11	Dodge Post, G.A.R., Loudon Park National Cem., 1898
4.5	Maryland Monument, Antietam Battlefield, 1900
4.6	Maryland Markers, Antietam Battlefield (6 USA, 2 CSA), 1900
6.6	John Rodgers Post, GAR, Havre de Grace, 1900
5.5	Federalsburg, Union, est. 1910

1.5	Confederate Soldiers and Sailors, Baltimore, 1903
2.6	Confederate Mothers & Widows, Loudon Park Cem., 1906
1.2	Union Soldiers and Sailors, Baltimore, 1909
6.11	Capture of Generals, Cumberland, Confederate, 1910s
3.3	Monocacy Cemetery Names Tablet, Beallsville, Confederate, 1911/1975
6.5	Point Lookout Federal Monument to Confederate POWs, 1911
2.12	Confederate POWs, Loudon Park National Cem., 1912
6.10	Cumberland, Confederate, 1912
2.7	Loudon Park Confederate Women, Loudon Park Cem., 1913
3.1	Rockville, Confederate, 1913
3.4	Monocacy Battlefield Confederate, 1914
3.8	Barbara Fritchie, Mt. Olivet Cem., Union, 1914
3.2	Monocacy Chapel, Beallsville, Confederate, 1915
5.3	Easton, Confederate, 1916
5.6	Chestertown, Confederate and Union, 1917
1.4	Confederate Women, Baltimore, 1918
6.8	North East, Cemetery Gates, Union, 1928
3.7	Mt. Olivet Cemetery Names Tablet, Confederate, 1933
2.1	Ellicott City, Confederate, 1948
3.11	Winfield, Union, est. 1880-1910

COMMEMORATIVE STAGE (4 Union, 3 Confederate, 2 Both, 4 Other)

3.10	Gen. Meade, Union, Frederick, 1930
3.9	Chief Justice Taney Bust, Frederick, 1931
6.3	Tulip, Union, St. Inigoes, 1940
1.3	Sidney Lanier, Baltimore, 1942
6.2	Fort Lincoln Cem. Lincoln Statue, 1947
1.1	Lee/Jackson, Confederate, Baltimore, 1948
1.6	Frederick Douglass Statue, Baltimore, 1956
4.7	Clara Barton, Antietam Battlefield, 1962
3.5	Monocacy Battlefield, Maryland, 1964
5.2	Annapolis Plaque, 1964
6.7	Cherry Hill, Union, 1965
6.12	Sumner Cem., U.S.C.T., Union, 1991
4.3	Gen. Garland, Confederate, 1993

Appendix C

MARYLAND CIVIL WAR MONUMENT SITES

I. Cemetery Monuments

Confederate

Loudon Park Cemetery, Baltimore
1. Confederate Statue (1870)
2. Murray Association
3. Confederate Mothers and Widows (1906)
4. Confederate Women (1913)
5. Jane Claudia and Gen. Johnson (1901 & 1903)
6. Lt. Col. Gilmor (1883)

Loudon Park National Cemetery, Baltimore
7. Confederate POWs (1912)

Monocacy Cemetery, Beallsville
8. Monocacy Chapel (1915)
9. Confederate Names Tablet (1911/1975)

Mount Olivet Cemetery, Frederick
10. Soldier Statue (1881)
11. Confederate Names Tablet (1933)

Point Lookout National Cemetery, Scotland
12. Federal Monument to Confederate POWs (1911)
13. Maryland Monument to Confederate POWs (1876)

Washington Cemetery (Rose Hill), Hagerstown
14. Statue of Hope (1877)

Silver Spring, Grace Episcopal Church
16. Obelisk Monument (1896)

Rose Hill Cemetery, Cumberland
17. Shaft monument (1912)

Union

New Cathedral Cemetery, Baltimore
1.   Gleeson Union (1866)

Loudon Park Cemetery National Cemetery, Baltimore
2.   Obelisk – by daughters of the GAR (1884)
3.   U.S. Navy (1896)
4.   Reclining Statue to Unknown Soldier (1895)
5.   Dodge Post Statue (1898)

Mt. Olivet Cemetery, Frederick
6.   Barbara Fritchie (1914)

Antietam National Cemetery, Sharpsburg
7.   Soldier Statue (1880)

Fort Lincoln Cemetery, Brentwood
8.   Statue of Lincoln (1947)

Hillcrest Cemetery, Federalsburg
9.   Soldier Statue (est. 1910)

Angel Hill Cemetery, Havre de Grace
10.   Admiral John Rodgers Post GAR (1900)

Cherry Hill Cemetery, Cherry Hill
11.   Union Names plaque (1965)

Methodist Cemetery, North East
12.   Gates (1928)

St. Inigoes
13.   *Tulip* Disaster (1940)

Rose Hill Cemetery, Cumberland
14.   Statue of soldier (1895)

Ebenezer Methodist Cemetery, Winfield
15.   Winfield Union (1890s)
16.   Sumner Cemetery, Cumberland U.S.C.T. (1991)

Other

Cambridge Cemetery, Cambridge
1.   Statue of Governor Hicks (1868)

II. Town Square Monuments

Both Sides
1. Centennial Plaque, Annapolis (1964)
2. Kent County Soldiers, Chestertown (1917)

Confederate
1. Confederate Women, Baltimore (1918)
2. Confederate Soldiers & Sailors, Baltimore (1903)
3. Lee/Jackson Statue, Baltimore (1948)
4. Sidney Lanier, Baltimore (1942)
5. Slab Monument, Courthouse, Ellicott City (1948)
6. Soldier Statue, Courthouse, Rockville (1913)
7. Soldier Statue, Courthouse, Easton (1916)
8. Capture of Generals, Cumberland (1910s)

Union
1. Union Soldiers and Sailors, Baltimore (1909)

Other
1. Frederick Douglass, Baltimore (1956)
2. Chief Justice Taney Bust, Frederick (1931)
3. Chief Justice Taney, Annapolis (1872)

III. Battlefield Monuments

Both Sides
1. Maryland Monument, Antietam (Sharpsburg) (1900)
2. Maryland Monument at Monocacy (1964)

Confederate
1. Baltimore Battery, Antietam (1900)
2. 1st Maryland Artillery (Dement's), Antietam (1900)
3. UDC Monument at Monocacy (1914)
4. Gen. Garland, Confederate (1993)

Union
1. 2nd Maryland Infantry, Antietam (1900)
2. 3rd Maryland Infantry, Antietam (1900)
3. Purnell Legion Infantry, Antietam (1900)
4. 1st Light Artillery (Battery A), Antietam (1900)
5. 1st Light Artillery (Battery B), Antietam (1900)
6. 5th Maryland Infantry (Co.s A & I), Antietam (1890)
7. 5th Maryland Infantry, Antietam (1900)
8. Gen. Reno Monument, South Mountain (1889)
9. Gen. Meade Monument, Frederick (1930)

Other
1. War Correspondents Monument, South Mountain (1896)
2. Clara Barton Monument, Antietam (1962)

Appendix D

MONUMENTS BY DATE

2.13	Gleeson, Union, New Cathedral Cem., 1866
5.4	Governor Hicks, Cambridge, 1868
2.2	Loudon Park Confederate, Loudon Park Cem., 1870
5.1	Chief Justice Taney, Annapolis, 1872
6.4	Point Lookout Maryland Mon. to Confederate POWs, 1876
4.9	Washington Cemetery, Confederate, Hagerstown, 1877
4.4	Antietam National Cemetery Statue, Union, 1880
3.6	Mt. Olivet Cemetery Confederate Statue, Mt. Olivet Cem., 1881
2.4	Lt. Col. Gilmor, Loudon Park Cem., Confederate, 1883
2.8	Union Obelisk, Loudon Park National Cem., 1884
4.2	Gen. Reno, Union, South Mountain, 1889
4.8	5th Maryland, Union, Antietam Battlefield, 1890
2.3	Murray Association, Loudon Park Cem., Confederate, est. 1890's
3.11	Winfield, Union, est. 1890s
2.9	Union Unknown Soldier, Loudon Park Nat. Cem., 1895
6.9	Cumberland, Union, 1895
6.1	Silver Spring, Confederate, 1896
2.11	Dodge Post, G.A.R., Loudon Park Nat. Cem., 1898
4.1	War Correspondents Arch, South Mountain, 1896
2.10	U.S. Navy, Loudon Park National Cem., 1896
4.4	Maryland Monument, Antietam Battlefield, 1900
4.6	Maryland Markers, Antietam Battlefield (6 USA, 2 CSA), 1900
6.6	John Rodgers Post, GAR, Havre de Grace, 1900
5.5	Federalsburg, Union, est. 1910
2.5	Jane Claudia and Gen. Johnson, Loudon Park Cem., Confederate, 1901
1.5	Confederate Soldiers and Sailors, Baltimore, 1903
2.6	Confederate Mothers, Loudon Park Cem., 1906
1.2	Union Soldiers and Sailors, Baltimore, 1909
6.11	Capture of Gens. Kelley and Crook, 1910s
6.5	Point Lookout Federal Mon. to Confederate POWs, 1911
3.3	Monocacy Cemetery Names Tablet, Beallsville, Confederate, 1911
6.10	Cumberland, Confederate, 1912

2.12	Confederate POW, Loudon Park National Cem., 1912
3.1	Rockville, Confederate, 1913
2.7	Confederate Women, Loudon Park Cem., 1913
3.8	Barbara Fritchie, Mt. Olivet Cem., 1914
3.4	Monocacy Battlefield, Confederate, 1914
3.2	Monocacy Chapel, Beallsville, Confederate, 1915
5.3	Easton, Confederate, 1916
5.6	Chestertown, 1917
1.4	Baltimore, Confederate Women, 1918
6.8	North East Cemetery Gates, Union, 1928
3.10	Gen. Meade, Union, Frederick, 1930
3.9	Chief Justice Taney, Frederick, 1931
3.7	Mt. Olivet Cemetery Names Tablet, Confederate, 1933
6.3	Tulip, Union, St. Inigoes, 1937
1.3	Sidney Lanier, Baltimore, 1942
6.2	Fort Lincoln Cemetery, Statue of Lincoln, 1947
1.1	Lee/Jackson, Confederate, Baltimore, 1948
2.1	Ellicott City, Confederate, 1948
1.6	Frederick Douglass Statue, Baltimore, 1956
4.7	Clara Barton, Antietam Battlefield, 1962
3.5	Monocacy Battlefield, Maryland, 1964
5.2	Annapolis Plaque, 1964
6.7	Cherry Hill, Union, 1965
6.12	Sumner Cemetery U.S.C.T., 1991
4.3	Gen. Garland, Confederate, 1993

Appendix E

POEMS AND SONGS

"MARYLAND, MY MARYLAND!"
(the poem) *James Ryder Randall 1861*

'The despot's heel is on thy shore,
    Maryland!
His torch is at thy temple door,
    Maryland!
Avenge the patriotic gore
That flecked the streets of Baltimore,
And be the battle queen of yore,
    Maryland! My Maryland!

'Hark to an exiled son's appeal,
    Maryland!
My mother State! to thee I kneel,
    Maryland!
For life and death, for woe and weal,
Thy peerless chivalry reveal,
And gird thy beauteous limbs with steel,
    Maryland! My Maryland!

'Thou wilt not cower in the dust,
    Maryland!
Thy beaming sword shall never rust,
    Maryland!
Remember Carroll's sacred trust,
Remember Howard's warlike thrust, –
And all thy slumberers with the just,
    Maryland! My Maryland!

'Come! 'tis the red dawn of the day,
    Maryland!
Come with thy panoplied array,
    Maryland!
With Ringgold's spirit for the fray,
With Watson's blood at Monterey,
With fearless Loew and dashing May,
    Maryland! My Maryland!

'Come for thy shield is bright and strong,
    Maryland!
Come! for thy dalliance does thee wrong,
    Maryland!
Come to thy own heroic throng,
Stalking with Liberty along,
And chaunt thy deathless slogan song,
    Maryland! My Maryland!

'Dear Mother! burst the tyrant's chain,
    Maryland!
Virginia should not call in vain,
    Maryland!
She meets her sisters on the plain –
'Sic semper!' 'tis the proud refrain
That baffles minions back again,
    Maryland! My Maryland!

'I see the blush upon thy cheek,
    Maryland!
For thou wast ever bravely meek,
    Maryland!
But lo! there surges forth a shriek
From hill to hill, from creek to creek –
Potomac calls to Chesapeake,
    Maryland! My Maryland!

'Thou wilt not yield the Vandal toll,
    Maryland!
Thou wilt not crook to his control,
    Maryland!
Better the fire upon thee roll,
Better the blade, the shot, the bowl,
Than crucifixion of the soul,
    Maryland! My Maryland!

'I hear the distant thunder-hum,
  Maryland!
The Old Line bugle, fife and drum,
  Maryland!
She is not dead, nor deaf, nor dumb –
Huzza! she spurns the Northern scum!
She breaths! she burns! she'll come! she'll come!
  Maryland! My Maryland!

*Adopted as Maryland's state song in 1939,
"Maryland, My Maryland!" was written by a
Louisianian in response to Baltimore's 1861 riots.*

THE STAR-SPANGLED BANNER
Francis Scott Key 1814

Oh! say, can you see, by the dawn's early light,
What so proudly we hailed at the twilight's last
  gleaming?
Whose broad stripes and bright stars, thro' the
  perilous fight,
O'er the ramparts we watched were so gallantly
  streaming?
And the rockets' red glare, the bombs bursting in
  air,
Gave proof thro' the night that our flag was still
  there.
Oh! say, does that star-spangled banner yet wave
O'er the land of the free and the home of the
  brave?

On the shore, dimly seen thro' the mist of the
  deep,
Where the foe's haughty host in dread silence
  reposes,
What is that which the breeze, o'er the towering
  steep,
As it fitfully blows, half conceals, half discloses?
Now it catches the gleam of the morning's first
  beam,
In full glory reflected, now shines on the stream.
'Tis the star-spangled banner. Oh! long may it
  wave
O'er the land of the free and the home of the
  brave!

And where is that band who so vauntingly swore
That the havoc of war and the battle's confusion
A home and a country should leave us no more?
Their blood has washed out their foul footstep's
  pollution.
No refuge could save the hireling and slave

From the terror of flight or the gloom of the grave,
And the star-spangled banner in triumph doth
  wave
O'er the land of the free and the home of the
  brave.

Oh! thus be it ever when free men shall stand
Between their loved home and the war's
  desolation,
Blest with vict'ry and peace, may the Heav'n-
  rescued land
Praise the Pow'r that hath made and preserved us
  a nation.
Then conquer we must, when our cause it is just,
And this be our motto, "In God is our trust."
And the star-spangled banner in triumph shall
  wave
O'er the land of the free and the home of the
  brave.

BATTLE-HYMN OF
THE REPUBLIC
Julia Ward Howe 1861

Mine eyes have seen the glory of the coming of the
  Lord:
He is trampling out the vintage where the grapes
  of wrath are stored;
He hath loosed the fateful lightning of his terrible
  swift sword:
His truth is marching on.

I have seen Him in the watch-fires of a hundred
  circling camps;
They have builded Him an altar in the evening
  dews and damps;
I can read His righteous sentence by the dim and
  flaring lamps.
His day is marching on.

I have read a fiery gospel, writ in burnished rows
  of steel:
"As ye deal with my contemners, so with you my
  grace shall deal;
Let the Hero, born of woman, crush the serpent
  with his heel,
Since God is marching on."

He has sounded forth the trumpet that shall
  never call retreat;
He is sifting out the hearts of men before his
  judgment-seat:

Oh! be swift, my soul, to answer Him! be jubilant,
    my feet!
Our God is marching on.

In the beauty of the lilies Christ was born across
    the sea,
With a glory in his bosom that transfigures you
    and me:
As He died to make men holy, let us die to make
    men free,
While God is marching on.

He is coming like the glory of the morning on the
    wave,
He is wisdom to the mighty, he is honor to the
    brave,
So the world shall be his footstool, and the soul of
    wrong his slave,
Our God is marching on!

DIXIE
Dan Emmet 1859

The original version

I wish I was in de land ob cotton,
Old times dar am not forgotten;
Look away, look away, look away,
    Dixie Land.
In Dixie Land whar I was born in,
Early on one frosty mornin',
Look away, look away, look away, Dixie Land.

Chorus–
Den I wish I was in Dixie,
    Hooray! Hooray!
In Dixie'Land, I'll took my stand,
To lib and die in Dixie:
Away, away, away, down South in Dixie
Away, away, away, down South in Dixie.

TENTING ON THE
OLD CAMP GROUND
Walter Kittridge (date unknown)

We're tenting tonight on the old camp ground,
    Give us a song to cheer
Our weary hearts, a song of home,
    And friends we love so dear.

Chorus–
Many are the hearts that are weary tonight,
    Wishing for the war to cease;
Many are the hearts that are looking for the right,
    To see the dawn of peace.
Tenting tonight, tenting tonight,
    Tenting on the old camp ground.

We've been tenting tonight on the old camp ground,
    Thinking of days gone by,
Of the loved ones at home that gave us the hand,
    And the tear that said "Good-bye!"

We are tired of war on the old camp ground,
    Many are dead and gone,
Of the brave and true who've left their homes;
    Others been wounded long.

We've been fighting today on the old camp ground,
    Many are lying near,
Some are dead and some are dying,
    Many are in tears.

CAMP SONG OF THE
MARYLAND LINE
(date unknown)

We are the boys, so gay and happy,
    Where e'er we chance to be,
If at home, or on camp duty,
    'Tis the same, we're always free;
So let the war guns roar as they will,
    We'll be gay and happy still;
Gay and happy, gay and happy,
    We'll be gay and happy still.

We've left our homes and all we cherish,
    In our loved old Maryland,
Rather than wear chains, we'll perish,
    Side by side, and sword in hand.
So let the war guns roar as they will,
    We'll be gay and happy still;
Gay and happy, gay and happy,
    We'll be gay and happy still.

Old Virginia needs assistance,
    Northern hordes invade her soil;
We'll present a firm resistance,
    Courting danger, death and toil;
So let the war guns roar as they will,
    We'll be gay and happy still;
Gay and happy, gay and happy,
    We'll be gay and happy still.

Then let drums and muskets rattle,
    Fearless as our sires of yore;
We'll not leave the field of battle,
    'Till we ransom Baltimore;
So let the war guns roar as they will,
    We'll be gay and happy still;
Gay and happy, gay and happy,
    We'll be gay and happy still.

DEDICATION DIRGE SUNG AT THE UNVEILING OF THE MONUMENT AT WASHINGTON CEMETERY, HAGERSTOWN, 15 JUNE 1877
words by Kyd Douglas, music by F. J. Halm

Their banners furled – their cannons hushed;
These graves their camping ground:
Their bones are dust – their swords are rust –
Their souls are with God we trust.

Green fields now hide the wounds they felt,
Where met the Blue and Gray:
The Blue now rests on hills they pressed;
With flowers and tears the Gray are blessed.

To consecrate this hallowed spot,
Help us, O Lord of Hosts;
Unknown to fame – unknown in name –
These tears and flowers our love proclaim.

Bless thou these dead! and speed the day
When Blue and Gray unite;
And on each tomb his foe shall write,
God only knows which one was right!
They both shall write with words of light,
God only knows which one was right!

RECESSIONAL
Rudyard Kipling 1897

God of our fathers, known of old,
    Lord of our far-flung battle-line,
Beneath whose awful Hand we hold
    Dominion over palm and pine –
Lord God of Hosts, be with us yet,
Lest we forget – lest we forget!

The tumult and the shouting dies;
    The Captains and the Kings depart:

Still stands Thine ancient sacrifice,
    An humble and contrite heart.
Lord God of Hosts, be with us yet,
Lest we forget – lest we forget!

Far-called, our navies melt away;
    On dune and headland sinks the fire:
Lo, all our pomp of yesterday
    Is one with Nineveh and Tyre!
Judge of the Nations, spare us yet,
Lest we forget – lest we forget!

If, drunk with sight of power, we loose
    Wild tongues that have not Thee in awe
Such boastings as the Gentiles use,
    Or lesser breeds without the Law–
Lord God of Hosts, be with us yet,
Lest we forget – lest we forget!

For heathen heart that puts her trust
    In reeking tube and iron shard,
All valiant dust that builds on dust,
    And guarding, calls not Thee to guard,
For frantic boast and foolish word –
Thy mercy on Thy people, Lord!

BARBARA FRITCHIE
John Greenleaf Whittier 1864

Up from the meadows rich with corn,
Clear in the cool September morn,
The clustered spires of Frederick stand
Green-walled by the hills of Maryland.
Round about them orchards sweep,
Apple and peach-tree fruited deep,
Fair as a garden of the Lord
To the eyes of the famished rebel horde,
On that pleasant morn of early Fall
When Lee marched over the mountain wall,
Over the mountains winding down,
Horse and foot, into Frederick Town.
Forty flags with their silver stars,
Forty flags with their crimson bars,
Flapped in the morning wind; the sun
Of noon looked down, and saw not one,
Up rose old Barbara Fritchie then,
Bowed with her fourscore years and ten;
Bravest of all in Frederick Town.
She took up the flag the men hauled down;
In her attic-window the staff she set,
To show that one heart was loyal yet.
Up the street came the rebel tread,
Stonewall Jackson riding ahead.

Under his slouched hat left and right
He glanced; the old flag met his sight.
"Halt!" – the dust-brown ranks stood fast.
"Fire!" – out blazed the rifle-blast.

It shivered the window, pane and sash;
It rent the banner with seam and gash,
Quick as it fell, from the broken staff
Dame Barbara snatched the silken scarf;
She leaned out far on the window sill,
And shook it forth with a royal will.
"Shoot, if you must, this old gray head,
But spare your country's flag," she said.
A shade of sadness, a blush of shame,
Over the face of the leader came;
The nobler nature within him stirred
To life that woman's deed and word;
"Who touches a hair of yon gray head
Dies like a dog! March on!" he said.
All day long through Frederick street
Sounded the tread of marching feet;
All day long that free flag tost
Over the heads of the rebel host.
Ever its torn folds rose and fell
On the loyal winds that loved it well;
And through the hill-gaps, sunset light
Shone over it with a warm good-night
Barbara Fritchie's work is o'er,
And the Rebel rides on his raids no more.
Honor to her! and let a tear
Fall, for her sake, on Stonewall's bier.
Over Barbara Fritchie's grave
Flag of Freedom and Union, wave!
Peace and order and beauty draw
Round thy symbol of light and law;
And ever the stars above look down
On thy stars below in Frederick Town!

"THE BIVOUAC OF THE DEAD"
Theodore O'hara 1847

The muffled drum's sad roll has beat
    The soldier's last tattoo;
No more on life's parade shall meet
    That brave and fallen few.
On Fame's eternal camping ground
    Their silent tents are spread,
And glory guards, with solemn round,
    The bivouac of the dead.

No rumour of the foe's advance
    Now swells upon the wind;
No troubled thought at midnight haunts
    Of loved ones left behind;

No vision of the morrow's strife
    The warrior's dream alarms;
No braying horn, nor screaming fife,
    At dawn shall call to arms.

The neighboring troop, the flashing blade,
    The bugle's stirring blast,
The charge, the dreadful cannonade,
    The din and shout are past;
Now war's wild note nor glory's peal
    Shall thrill with fierce delight
Those breasts that never more may feel
    The rapture of the fight.

Like the fierce northern hurricane
    That sweeps his great plateau
Flushed with the triumph yet to gain,
    Came down the serried foe.
Who heard the thunder of the fray
    Break o'er the field beneath,
Knew well the watchword of that day
    Was "Victory or death."

Long had the doubtful conflict raged
    O'er all that stricken plain,
For never fiercer fight had waged
    The vengeful blood of Spain;
And still the storm of battle blew,
    Still swelled the glory tide;
Not long, our stout chieftain knew,
    Such odds his strength could bide.

'Twas in that hour his stern command
    Called to a martyr's grave
The flower of his beloved land
    The nation's flag to save.
By the rivers of their fathers' gore
    His first-born laurels grew,
And well he deemed the sons would pour
    Their lives for glory too.

Sons of the Dark and Bloody Ground,
    Ye must not slumber there,
Where stranger steps and tongues resounds
    Along the heedless air;
Your own proud land's heroic soil
    Shall be your fitter grave;
She claims from war his richest spoil
    The ashes of her brave.

Rest on, embalmed and sainted dead,
    Dear as the blood ye gave;
No impious footstep here shall tread
    The herbage of your grave;

Nor shall your glory be forgot
    While Fame her record keeps,
On Honour points the hallowed spot
    Where Valour proudly sleeps.

You marble minstrel's voiceless stone,
    In deathless song shall tell,
When many a vanished age hath flown,
    The story how ye fell;
Nor wreck, nor change, nor winter's blight,
    Nor Time's remorseless doom,
Shall dim on ray of glory's light
    Tha gilds your deathless tomb.

Written in memory of the Americans slain in the Mexican War battle at Buena Vista, Feb. 22-23, 1847.

UNTITLED ODE
William Collins 1746

How sleep the brave who sink to rest
    By all their country's wishes blest!
When Spring, with dewy fingers cold,
    Returns to deck their hallowed mold,
She there shall dress a sweeter sod
    Than Fancy's feet have ever trod.

By fairy hands their knell is rung,
    By forms unseen their dirge is sung;
There Honor comes, a pilgrim gray,
    To bless the turf that wraps their clay,
And Freedom shall awhile repair,
    To dwell a weeping hermit there!

THE CONQUERED BANNER
Abram Joseph Ryan 1865

Furl that Banner, for 'tis weary;
Round its staff 'tis drooping dreary;
    Furl it, fold it – it is best;
For there's not a man to wave it,
And there's not a sword to save it,
And there's not one left to lave it
In the blood which heroes gave it;
And its foes now scorn and brave it;
    Furl it, hide it – let it rest!

Take that Banner down! 'tis tattered;
Broken is its staff and shattered;
And the valiant hosts are scattered,
    Over whom it floated high.

Oh, 'tis hard for us to fold it,
Hard to think there's none to hold it,
Hard that those who once unrolled it
    Now must furl it with a sigh!

Furl that Banner – furl it sadly;
Once ten thousands hailed it gladly,
And ten thousands wildly, madly,
    Swore it should forever wave –
Swore that foeman's sword should never
Hearts like theirs entwined dissever,
Till that flag should float forever
    O'er their freedom or their grave!

Furl it! for the hands that grasped it,
And the hearts that fondly clasped it,
    Cold and dead are lying low;
And that Banner – it is trailing,
While around it sounds the wailing
    Of its people in their woe.

For, though conquered, they adore it –
Love the cold, dead hands that bore it!
Weep for those who fell before it!
Pardon those who trailed and tore it!
But, oh, wildly they deplore it,
    Now who furl and fold it so!

Furl that Banner! True, 'tis glory,
Yet 'tis wreathed around with glory,
And 'twill live in song and story
    Though its folds are in the dust!
For its fame on brightest pages,
Penned by poets and by sages,
Shall go sounding down the ages –
    Furl its folds though now we must.

Furl that Banner, softly, slowly;
Treat it gently – it is holy,
    For it droops above the dead;
Touch it not – unfold it never;
Let it droop there, furled forever, –
    For its people's hopes are fled.

THE DYING WORDS OF STONEWALL JACKSON
Sidney Lanier (Jackson died May 10, 1863)

"Order A. P. Hill to prepare for battle."
"Tell Major Hawks to advance the commissary train."
"Let us cross the river and rest in the shade."

The stars of Night contain the glittering Day
And rain his glory down with sweeter grace
Upon the dark World's grand, enchanted face –
    All loth to turn away.

And so the Day, about to yield his breath,
Utters the stars unto the listening Night,
To stand for burning fare-thee-wells of light
    Said on the verge of death.

O hero-life that lit us like the sun!
O hero-words that glittered like the stars
And stood and shone above the gloomy wars
    When the hero-life was done!

The phantoms of a battle came to dwell
I' the fitful vision of his dying eyes –
Yet even in battle-dreams, he sends supplies
    To those he loved so well.

His army stands in battle-line arrayed:
His couriers fly: all's done: now God decide!
– And not till then saw he the Other Side
    Or would accept the shade.

Thou land whose sun is gone, thy stars remain!
Still shine the words that miniature his deeds.
O thrice-beloved, where'er thy great heart bleeds,
    Solace hast thou for pain!

Appendix F

CIVIL WAR NOTABLES BURIED IN MARYLAND

Page numbers are listed in index.

Armistead, Brig. Gen. Lewis A., CSA — Old St. Paul's Cem., Baltimore

Bankhead, Brig. Gen. (brevet) Henry, USA — Green Mount Cem., Baltimore

Blumenberg, Gen. Leopold, USA — Har Sinai Cem., Baltimore

Bond, Capt. Frank, CSA — Loudon Park Cem., Catonsville

Booth, John Wilkes — Green Mount Cem., Baltimore

Bowerman, Brig. Gen. (brevet) Richard Neville, USA — Green Mount Cem., Baltimore

Bradford, Governor Augustus W. — Green Mount Cem., Baltimore

Breathed, Maj. James, CSA — St. Thomas Episcopal Church Cem., Hancock

Brent, Brig. Gen. Joseph Lancaster, CSA — Green Mount Cem., Baltimore

Brown, Col. Ridgley, CSA — family cemetery at Elton, near Unity

Buchanan, Admiral Franklin, CSA — Wye Cemetery, Talbot Co.

Carroll, Anna Ella — Old Trinity Church Cem., Cambridge

Chiswell, Capt. George — Monocacy Cem., Beallsville

Cooper, Brig. Gen. James, USA — Mt. Olivet Cem., Frederick

Costen, Dr. Isaac — Pocomoke City

Creswell, Adj. Gen. John, USA — Presbyterian Cem., Elkton

Deems, Brig. Gen. (brevet) James Monroe, USA — Green Mount Cem., Baltimore

Denison, Maj. Gen. (brevet) Andrew Woods, USA — Green Mount Cem., Baltimore

Dodd, Brig. Gen. (brevet) Levi Axrell, USA — Green Mount Cem., Baltimore

Elzy, Maj. Gen. Arnold, CSA — Green Mount Cem., Baltimore

Evans, Brig. Gen. Andrew Wallace, USA — Presbyterian Cem., Elkton

Field, Maj. Gen. Charles W., CSA — Loudon Park Cem., Catonsville

Freaner, Major George, CSA — Rose Hill Cem., Hagerstown

Fritchie, Barbara – Mt. Olivet Cem., Frederick

Gilmor, Col. Harry, CSA — Loudon Park Cem., Catonsville

Gleeson, Capt. John P., USA (war hero) — New Cathedral Cem., Baltimore

Herbert, Gen. James (Maj. in Civil War), CSA — Loudon Park Cem., Catonsville

Hicks, Gov. Thomas Holliday — Cambridge Cem., Cambridge

Hollins, Comm. George Nichols, CSA — Westminster Burying Grounds, Baltimore

Horn, Brig. Gen. (brevet) James Watt, USA — Loudon Park Cem., Catonsville

Huger, Maj. Gen. Benjamin, CSA — Green Mount Cem., Baltimore

Johnson, Brig. Gen. Bradley Tyler – Loudon Park Cem., Catonsville

Johnson, Jane Claudia – Loudon Park Cem., Catonsville

Johnston, Brig. Gen. Joseph E., CSA — Green Mount Cem., Baltimore

Kenly, Maj. Gen. John Reese, USA — Green Mount Cem., Baltimore

King, Brig. Gen. (brevet) Adam Eckfeldt, USA, Loudon Park Nat. Cem., Catonsville

Lanier, Sidney, poet — Green Mount Cem., Baltimore

Little, Brig. Gen. Lewis H., CSA — Green Mount Cem., Baltimore

McKaig, Col. William Wallace, Jr., CSA — Rose Hill Cem., Cumberland

Mudd, Dr. Samuel A. — St. Mary's Church Cemetery, Bryantown

Murray, Capt. William – Christ Episcopal Cem., Owings Mills

Norris, Col. William, CSA — All Saints Episcopal Cem., Reisterstown

Northrup, Brig. Gen. Lucius B., CSA — New Cathedral Cem., Baltimore

Phelps, Brig. Gen. (brevet) Charles Edward, USA — Woodlawn Cem., Baltimore

Ringgold, Admiral Cadwallader, USA — Green Mount Cem., Baltimore

Stanton, Brig. Gen. (brevet) David Leroy, USA — Loudon Park Nat. Cem., Catonsville

Steuart, Brig. Gen. George, CSA — Green Mount Cem., Baltimore

Surratt, John — New Cathedral Cem., Baltimore

Swann, Governor Thomas — Green Mount Cem., Baltimore

Taney, Chief Justice Roger Brooke — St. John's Catholic Cem., Frederick

Taylor, 2nd Lt. Wm. (Medal of Honor), USA — Loudon Park Nat. Cem., Catonsville

Tilghman, Col. Oswald, CSA — Easton Cem., Easton

Trimble, Maj. Gen. Isaac Ridgeway, CSA — Green Mount Cem., Baltimore

Tyler, Brig. Gen. Erastus Barnard, USA — Green Mount Cem., Baltimore

Vickers, Maj. Gen. George, USA — Chester Cem., Chestertown

Wallis, Severn Teackle, writer — Green Mount Cem., Baltimore

Wilkins, Col. Edward D., USA — Chester Cem., Chestertown

Winder, Brig. Gen. Charles Sidney, CSA — Wye Cemetery, Talbot Co.

Winder, Brig. Gen. John H., CSA — Green Mount Cem., Baltimore

APPENDIX G

NAMES OF CIVIL WAR SOLDIERS HONORED IN LISTS ON MONUMENTS

2.1 ELLICOTT CITY (CONFEDERATE)

Baker, Robert T.
Bond, William
Bond, Frank A.
Brown, John R.
Brown, Henry
Buckingham, George
Burgess, William
Carroll, Albert
Carroll, R. G. Harper
Cauthorn, Byron
Childs, N. Soper
Clark, Nicholas W.
Clark, Basil C.
Clark, David I.
Clark, James
Crawford, John T.
Debrow, John
Dorsey, Samuel W.
Dorsey, Upton W.
Dorsey, Samuel of B.
Dorsey, William
Dorsey, Charles R.
Dorsey, Charles W.
Dorsey, Pulaski
Dorsey, Hammond
Dorsey, Gustavus
Dorsey, John W.
Dorsey, Harry C.
Dorsey, John T. B.
Dorsey, John C.

Fahey, Alexander
Forsythe, William Henry
Gaither, Capt. George R.
Gaither, George W.
Gibbons, Charles
Griffin, Richard
Hammond, Charles
Harding, John
Henderson, Gaither
Herbert, Gen. James R.
Hewitt, Resin D.
Hill, John
Hobbes, Capt. Nathan Chew
Hobbs, Jarrett
Hobbs, Townsen
Howard, Capt. George
Hughes, Evan R.
Kenley, John R.
Leyman, Robert
Linthicum, Edwin
Linthicum, John W.
McNulty, Stephen
Mercer, George W.
Miller, William H.
O'Brien, John N.
Owings, L. I. G.
Owings, John H.
Peddicord, Bascum
Polk, Trusten
Pue, Lieut. Ventress

Pue, Ferdinand
Ridgely, Thomas
Ridgely, John T.
Ridgely, Charles H.
Scaggs, Robert
Scott, George
Shafer, Cornelius
Shakers, John
Shipley, Elmond
Shipley, Samuel C.
Thompson, Dorsey
Thompson, L. G.
Thompson, Tompkins
Treakle, Albert
Treakle, Emmett
Warfield, Albert G.
Warfield, Gassaway W.
Watkins, Louis J.
Webb, William A.
Whalen, John W.
Willis, Beale
Willis, Albert
Willis, Carver
Willis, William B.
Willis, Frank
Wooten, Henry E.
Wright, William
Zepp, Charles T.

2.3 MURRAY ASSOCIATION (CONFEDERATE)

CO. A 2ND MD INF. CSA

Baxley, W. G.
Blakistone, Sergt. W. T.
Bowly, William H.
Broddock, C. S.
Bruce, William
Chandler, W. S. T.
Davis, J. N.
Deale, T. N.
Denton, Cpl. George
Fulton, Alexander
Gill, Cpl. S. P.
Hammett, Thomas

Hardesty, J. W.
Hollyday, W. M.
Hubbard, W. H.
Iglehart, J. H.
Ives, L. W.
Kennedy, A.
Laird, Adjt. J. W.
Lake, Craig
Lloyd, C. T.
McCormack, H. A.
McIntyre, A.
Morrison, W.

Nicolai, H.
Owens, H. C.
Pindell, P.
Prentiss, W. S.
Sanderson, P. H.
Slartings, G. C.
Starlings, G. C.
Steele, C. H.
Treco, J. L.
Wagner, I.
Windolph, J. H.

CO. H 1ST MD INF. CSA

Burke, J. M.
Colston, W. E.
Costigan, D. J.
Farr, Joseph
Greenwell, T. W. H.
Harris, William

Hebb, T. A.
McKim, W. D.
Phillips, J. J.
Redmond, G. I.
Rice, F.
Rogers, S. B.

Russell, E.
Schleigh, L.
Sindall, S.
West, E. H.

2.11 DODGE POST GAR

PAST COMMANDERS

Barrett, John H., frigate Minnesota, USN
Bissel, Joseph, Sergt., Co. B, 3rd Md. Cav.
Bowers, John, gunboat Kinco USN; died 24 Nov 1909
Briscoe, Alexander M., 1st Lieut., Co. I, Cole's Cav.; died 9 Nov 1901
Brooks, Joseph, Pvt., Co. F, Cole's Cav.; died 15 Jun 1935
Donaldson, Walter A., Capt. & Act'g Maj., 71st NY; died 7 Feb 1903
Dulaney, Joseph, Cpl., Co. B, 1st Del. Cav.; died 27 Sep 1928
Fisher, George W., Pvt., Co. C, 11th Md. Inf., died 19 Dec 1926
Gibson, Andrew J., Batt. A, Balt. Light Art.; died 17 Oct 1918

Glazey, George W., Pvt., Co. H, 11th Md. Inf.
Goodmanson, John J., steamer Osceola, USN; died 20 Apr 1919
Harrison, Alexander, Pvt., Co. A, 11th Md. Inf.; died 3 Oct 1915
Houck, John A., Pvt., Co. B, 87th Pa. Vol. Inf.
Jones, Jerimiah, Sergt., Co. C, 1st Eastern Shore Inf.; died 12 Feb 1920
Keirle, William T., sloop of war Tuscarora USN
Knorr, Charles K., drummer, Co. C, 11th Md. Inf.; died 21 Sep 1921
Luber, John J., Cpl., Co. C, 13th Md. Inf.; died 23 Feb 1921

Marig, George W., Pvt., Co. A, 11th Md. Inf.; died 5 Apr 1911
McEvoy, John J., Pvt., Co. E, 11th Md. Inf.; died 12 Jan 1927
Meyers, Jacob W., gunboat Kinco, USN; died 11 Jan 1927
Pierreman, George E., USN
Rush, George H,. Pvt., Co. C, 1st Md. Cav.
Tagart, Samuel H., Sergt., Co. C, 13th Ohio Inf.; died 27 Mar 1884
Wheeler, James M., Pvt., Co. C, 11th Md. Inf.; died 11 Oct 1910
White, Alphonso, surgeon, 8th Md. Inf.; died 18 Dec 1904

ARTILLERY

Brown, Theodore
Clark, Thomas W.
Eaton, George W.
Hilleary, William H.

Irving, Henry
Lacy, Patrick
Meske, William
Mulligan, James

Sagle, Thos. W.
Schuerholz, Wm L.
Ward, William
Wittle, Jacob

CAVALRY

Bisser, Joseph
Booker, John
Bragg, William F.
Briscoe, Alex. M.
Bromley, Thomas I.
Brooks, Joseph
Devaney, John H.

Duncan, Charles V.
Ellis, Richard
Getz, Joseph
Hoffman, Charles T.
Kahl, George
Maynard, John G.
Montgomery, John

Rush, George H.
Otto, Christian
Sponcler, George D.
Sutton, Thomas
Weil, Samuel

NAVY

Albrecht, Fred'k
Barrett, John H.
Bowers, John
Boyle, Geo. W.
Burdett, Geo.
Dempster, Ja's T.
Gill, James
Givvings, Wm L.
Glenn, John H.
Goodmanson, J. J.
Hiker, John
Hughes, Jacob H.
Jory, Joseph H.
Keirle, Wm T.

Kendall, Geo.
Klessell, Chas.
Lanahan, Dennis
Malloy, James A.
Mills, Wm F.
Mullin, Patrick
Meyer, Jacob W.
Myers, John J.
McGee, John
McKenna, Hugh
Pierman, Geo. E.
Powers, Josiah
Reid, Peter
Riley, Peter

Rowan, John
Rudolph, Harm. F.
Ruark, John S.
Seipp, Fred. K.
Sherwood, J. R.
Skuhr, Charles
Sullivan, Geo.
Thompson, Chas.
Tracey, Thomas
Tufts, John
Warner, Geo. W.
Zimmerman, Wm H.

INFANTRY

Abendschoen, R.
Anderson, Jas. B.
Andrews, Benj. S.
Baker, Jacob
Baker, John
Baker, John G.
Baker, Robt. J.
Barnett, Jas. A.
Barr, Danl. L.
Beck, John G.
Bitter, Christin
Bradley, John C.
Brown, James H.
Bruce, Granville
Bull, John
Callander, Henry

Carrick, Andrew F.
Cash, John H.
Caswell, Robt. B.
Cavey, Thomas J.
Collins, Chas S.E.
Colwell, John
Craig, Thomas
Cummings, Wm P.
Cushing, Richard C.
DeFalco, Pasquale
Degrodt, Wm H.
Dehn, Lewis
Deitzell, Fred'k
Dennock, Levin T.
Donalson, Walter A.
Donnelly, Daniel J.

Dotson, Mansfield H.
Dougherty, Eman'l E.
Dwyer, Timothy
Darsch, Philip W.
Ensor, Thaddeus T. A.
Ernst, John
Eberline, Conrad
Fishback, George
Fisher, George W.
Flood, James
Ford, Augustus
Fox, Abner
Freberger, C. M.
Faid, John
Gaylor, John
Grines, Henry

Gonder, Mann C.
Gutt, Michael
Harig, Geo. W.
Harris, Theo. F.
Harrison, A. A.
Hartenstine, Jos.
Hersh, Fred'k
High, William
Himmell, Wolf'g
Holdhorst, Phil'p
Hutchens, John F.
Haddaway, J. S.
Jones, Henry
Jones, Jerimiah
Johnson, Joseph P.
Kaiser, John
Keister, Wm H.
Kingsmore, Geo.
Knorr, Charles J.
Leaming, Ruben H.
Lemmon, William T.
Lindner, Christ.
Long, Alex. R.
Long, Frank
Luber, John

Lyman, Chas. B.
March, Philip
McAllister, H. C.
McEvoy, John J.
McKeigle, Wm
McGee, Mich'l J.
Miller, William
Murphy, Thos. F.
Murr, Jacob
Neuschaefer, J.
Otto, Simon
O'Brien, Mich'l
Park, Conrad
Parley, Mich'l
Pensmith, J. W.
Potee, George A.
Rhein, Henry G.
Riegel, Jacob L.
Robinson, Lazerus
Rosenthal, Henry
Roy, Robert
Real, Joseph
Schleig, Adam
Schmidt, George
Sella, Fred'k K.

Shipley, George
Simon, Joseph
Slaughter, A. F.
Smith, William C.
Stanton, David L.
Stephens, J. H.
Strieb, Henry
Sturgeon, Wm B.
Tagart, Samuel H.
Thrush, Frank D.
Upton, William M.
Vogelsang, Philip
Von Hagle, George
Vose, George H.
Wahl, Conrad
Ward, William R.
Webb, Timon W.
Weyer, John
Wheeler, James H.
White, A.
Williams, John
Williams, John W.
Wilson, Henry
Wilson, James A.
Yater, John L.

3.3 MONOCACY CEMETERY CONFEDERATE NAMES TABLET

Bouic, John P.
Burch, Francis
Butler, Chas. M.
Butler, George W.
Chiswell, Lieut. Edward J.
Chiswell, Capt. Geo W.
Dade, Wm F.
Dickerson, Wm H.
Hays, Richard P.
Holland, John W.
Jones, Benjamin C.

Mason, Henry C.
Moulden, Elias
Munger, John B.
Price, Elias
Pyles, B. Franklin
Pyles, M. Thomas
Reed, James W.
Sellman, Alonzo
Sellman, John P.
Sellman, Wallace
Stallings, Richard S.

Veirs, Elijah
Veirs, Henry C.
Veirs, W. Seneca
Waesche, Wm H.
White, Maj. B. S.
White, L. Collinson
White, Samuel C.
White, Thomas H.
Williams, Francis T.
Wooton, Dr. Edward

3.7 MT. OLIVET CEMETERY CONFEDERATE NAMES TABLET

Baer, Dr. Caleb Dorsey
Baughman, Louis Victor,
    wounded
Beall, Thomas
Bell, Wiliam Cyrus, wounded

Bender, F. T.
Besant, Wm T.
Betts, Samuel
Biser, Chas. Tilghman,
    captured

Biser, Wm Doddrige, killed
Bitzer, George W.
Blummenaur, Michael
Boland, William F., captured
Boone, Daniel

Boteler, Dr. E. L.
Boyd, Hamilton
Brashear, Thomas Pitts, wounded
Bready, C. Edward
Bready, D. Calvin, wounded
Brien, Col. Luke Tiernan
Bromwell, Henry H.
Bromwell, Josiah R.
Bromwell, Thomas C. G.
Brookey, Peter
Burns, William, wounded
Butler, Cyrus
Carey, Timothy
Carlisle, Charles, killed
Carter, Crafton
Castle, James L.
Cecil, Columbus C.
Chiswell, William T.
Clagett, Thomas
Cockey, S. Sprigg
Cockrell, James Daniel
Cosgove, William
Crampton, Benjamin P., wounded
Cretin, Andrew
Cretin, Hilary
Cretin, John T.
Crist, Ephram, killed
Crouse, W. Frank
Crown, Frederick N.
Crown, John R., wounded
Crown, Joshua, wounded
Davis, Evan
Davis, Sergt. John Ignatius
Davis, Sergt. Phineas J.
Davis, Thomas S.
Delashmutt, John M.
Delashmutt, William G., wounded
Devitt, Edward
Dixon, James W.
Dorsey, Capt. Ignatius Waters
Dorsey, Harry Woodward
Dorsey, Lieut. William H. B.
Dorsey, Nicholas, wounded

Dorsey, Upton W.
Downey, Dr. Jesse W.
Dunlap, Henry, killed
Dunlap, John, wounded
Eader, Charles
Eader, Lewis
Ebert, Charles
England, Joseph R.
Fearhake, Adolphus
Fearhake, George
Fitzsimmons, Nicholas
Ford, Clement, wounded
Forman, Valentine
Fout, John
Gatton, William F.
Geasey, Charles H.
Gephart, Solomon A.
Gittings, Edward
Goldsboro, Lee
Grabrill, Abraham W.
Graham, Israel, wounded
Grayson, George M.
Groshon, John F.
Grove, Lewis
Hagan, Michael
Haller, John E.
Hammond, Denton
Hammond, Oliver B.
Harwood, Thomas
Hergesheimer, David J.
Hilleary, Clar. W., wounded
Hilleary, Thomas
Hitzilberger, Charles T.
Hubbard, Alexander
Jenkins, Samuel, killed
Johnson Dr. Wm Hilleary
Johnson, Dr. James T.
Johnson, Gen. Bradley T.
Johnson, Newman, killed
Johnson, Otis
Johnson, Richard Potts
Jones, Albert
Jones, Edward C.
Jones, John
Jones, Spencer C.
Keepers, Alexius
Kehne, Charles

Kennedy, McPherson
Kephart, Charles, killed
Kephart, George A., killed
Kessler, Windsor G.
King, Christian
Knott, Frank G., killed
Koester, Louis H.
Koester, William A., killed
Lamar, George Albert, wounded
Lawrence, Stephen D.
Lickle, John D.
Lowe, Enoch Louis
Marlow, Robert
Maxwell, John
Mayberry, James Polk
Maynard, Albert
Maynard, Thomas B.
McAleer, Joseph L.
McBride, Thomas
McDaniel, John
McDowell, Perry
McKnight, Robert
McLanahan, William H.
McMullen, Charles
McSherry, Dr. Edward Cole
Mercier, Elihu Washington
Miles, G. T.
Moberly, Bradley
Morrison, John
Motter, Jacob, wounded
Murdock, Augustus
Myers, Christopher P., killed
Myers, Mahlon
Myers, Thomas
Noonan, Robert, killed
Norris, Richard H.
O'Boyle, Charles M., wounded
O'Boyle, James O., wounded
O'Connell, Patrick
O'Leary, Jerome
Oates, Charles T.
Obenderfer, Augustus A.
Obenderfer, John
Oden, William, wounded
Ordeman, Charles, killed

Ordeman, John, wounded
Orrison, John W.
Ott, George M.
Peters, Thomas, wounded
Pettingall, D. Carlton, killed
Pettit, Henry M.
Philpott, Gowson B.,
　　wounded
Pope, William H.
Potts, Richard
Railing, George H.
Reid, James Henry, killed
Reid, Joseph Thomas, killed
Riddlemoser, Dr. Joseph
Ritter, William
Rogers, James P., wounded
Schaeffer, Luther
Schley, Capt. Tench
Sellman, Frank, wounded
Septer, John H.
Shearer, George
Shell, Horace
Shellman, George
Shipley, William H.,
　　wounded

Shriver, Charles S., killed
Simmons, John
Simpson, Corp. George R.
Smith, John C.
Smith, Nicholas, killed
Spittle, Lewis
Stalling, Richard
Steves, Christopher, killed
Stokes, Bradley T.
Swisher, John, killed
Tabler, John W.
Taylor, Charles T.
Thomas, Byron, wounded
Thomas, David O.
Thomas, Dr. Samuel Frank
Thomas, Edmond, wounded
Thomas, Eleven
Thomas, James H., killed
Thompson, John W.
Thrasher, Thaddeus, killed
Trail, Sergt. Lewis W.
Trapnell, Joseph H.
Trundle, Joseph H.
Trundle, Samuel
Tyler, George

Tyler, John E.
Tyler, Samuel Albert
Veit, Lewis H., killed
Wagner, Henry, killed
Welsh, Capt. Warner,
　　wounded
Welsh, Lieut. Milton
Welsh, Luther
Wentz, Lewis R., killed
West, Eugene, wounded
West, John P., wounded
Whalen, John W.
Whitter, George, killed
Wilcom, Casper
Willard, Peter F., captured
Williams, Henry
Wilson, C. P., wounded
Worthington, Joshua
Worthington, Sergt. Thomas G.
Yingling, David
Yingling, Zadoc
Young, Alexander H., killed
Zacharius, Granville
Zacharius, John F.

4.1 WAR CORRESPONDENTS ARCH

ARMY CORRESPONDENTS

Farley Anderson
J. N. Ashley
Adam Badean
T. Barnard
George W. Beaman
M. Bentley
W. D. Bickham
A. H. Bodman
George C. Bower
H. V. Boynton
J. H. Browne
S. T. Bulkley
A. H. Byington
S. Cadwallader
S. M. Carpenter
T. M. Cash
F. G. Chapman

F. P. Church
W. C. Church
G. W. Clarke
John A Cockerill
C. C. Coffin
R. T. Colburn
J. Cook
T. M. Cook
E. Crapsey
Creighton
L. L. Crounst
E. Cuthbert
N. Davidson
Dr. E. F. Nyst
J. P. Dunn
D. B. M. Eaton
C. H. Farrell

J. C. Fitzpatrick
R. D. Francis
T. B. Glover
T. C. Grey
C. H. Griffen
Charles G. Halpine
C. Hannem
B. Harding
G. H. Hart
J. Hasson
John Hay
S. Hayes
L. A. Hendricks
A. R. Henry
F. Henry
V. Hickox
A. S. Hill

G. H. Hosmer
E. H. House
A. Houston
W. P. Isham
B. B. Korm
W. H. Kent
Thos. W. Knox
F. C. Long
B. T. McAlpin
Rchd. C. McCormack
Jos. B. McCullagh
W. B. Mirriam
J. E. Norcross
C. S. Noyes
G. H. Osbon
B. E. Osborn
C. A. Page
Nathaniel Page

U. H. Painter
Count de Paris
A. Paul
E. A. Paul
E. Peters
Henry J. Raymond
Whiteton Reid
Albert D. Richardson
W. H. Runkle
O. G. Sawyer
W. F. C. Shanks
R. H. Shelly
George W. Smalley
Henry M. Stanley
Edmund C. Stedman
Jerome B. Stillson
W. H. Stiner
William Swinton

B. H. Sylvester
Benj. F. Taylor
Geo. Alfred Townsend
B. C. Truman
Henry Villard
J. H. Vosburg
E. W. Wallace
J. S. Ward
Sam Ward
F. Watson
E. D. Westfall
F. B. Wilkie
Sam Wilkeson
F. Wilkison
A. W. Williams
J. C. Wilson
T. C. Wilson
John Russell Young
W. Young

ARMY ARTISTS

A. A. Backer
E. Beard
H. Benson
A. Berghans
H. Bonuill
S. S. Davis
F. Dielman

G. Ellsbury
S. Fox
C. E. Hillen
E. B. Hough
J. E. Laycock
A. McCallum
W. R. McComas

E. F. Mullen
Fred. Shell
W. L. Sheppard
J. S. Trader
G. E. Williams
W. Waud

SOUTHERN CORRESPONDENTS

P. H. Alexander
Durent Duponte
T. G. DeFontaine

D. C. Jenkins
Geo. W. Olney
Geo. Perry

James B. Soner
W. Shepardson
Henry Watterson

SOUTHERN ARTISTS

M. B. Brady
W. T. Crane
E. O. C. Darley
Theo. R. Davis
Ed. Forbes

J. S. Jewett
Henry Lovi
Arthur Lumley
F. H. Mason
Larkin G. Mead

Henry Mosler
Frank Shell
Dan. H. Strother
Alfred Woud
H. Vizzitelly
A. E. Taylor

5.3 EASTON (CONFEDERATE)

Bennett, Capt. Jno. W.
Blunt, L. James
Bracco, Edw. L. L.
Buchanan, Adm. Franklin
Byus, Charles
Byus, Lieut. Wm R.
Byus, Stanley M.
Calvert, Seth
Cheezum, D. Richard
Clough, Robert H.
Covey, Sur. Gen. Edward N.
Cryer, Thomas E.
Dawson, Levin G.
Dawson, Robert M.
Dawson, Robert Alex.
Dickenson, W. Elveno
Eckhart, Charles H.
Edgar, Thomas J.
Ewing, Wm Thomas
Fairbank. Frank M.
Fletcher, Solomon
Gibson, Fayette
Gibson, Wm C.
Glenn, Samuel T.
Goldsborough, Edmund K.
Goldsborough, Lieut. Robert
   H.
Grace, William

Hambleton, James P.
Hambleton, William H.
Hardcastle, Col. A. B.
Hardcastle, Wm R.
Harper, James K.
Hopkins, Alexander Rigby
Jones, Robert C.
Lane, Benjamin F.
Lane, John N.
Lee, Robert
Lloyd, Charles T.
Lloyd, Daniel,
Lockerman, Theodore
Loveday, William T.
Lowe, William E.
Lowe, Wrightson L.
Lyons, William H.
Martin, John N. S.
McDaniel, John W.
McMahan, Wrightson
Moore, Augustus
Moore, Percolus M.
Murray, Alexander
Noble, Josiah
Oliver, Thomas H.
Plater, J. Rousby
Porter, William J.
Price, Alfred C.

Price, James H.
Quinn, Michael
Reddie, James
Redmond, George
Ridgeway, Jos.
Roberts, Edward
Ross, Anthony P.
Sears, Col. Chas. E.
Shannahan, John H. K.
Slaughter, Louis
Tharp, James M.
Thomas, John R.
Thompson, Maj. A. C. C.
Tilghman, Brig. Gen. Lloyd
Tilghman, Capt. Oswald
Tilghman, Lieut. John Leeds
Tilghman, Richard C.
Tilghman, Tench F.
Todd, George
Tunis, John O.
Tunis, Theophilus
Valliant, Edwin S.
Valliant, George E.
Valliant, Thomas Rigby
White, John G.
Willis, Charles N.
Willis, Thomas E.
Winder, Brig. Gen. Chas. S.
Winder, William S.

CITIZENS AFTER THE WAR

Berry, John P.
Bryan, James
Edmunds, George
George, Harmon K.

Henderson, Charles E.
Holliday, Henry
Lynch, Chris. C.
Michley, Burton S.

Stewart, Maj. W. E.
Trail, Louis W.
Wilson, Andrew

5.6 CHESTERTOWN (CONFEDERATE)

Baker, Fred K.
Beasten, Geo. M.
Blackiston, Lieut. H.C.
   killed, Bunker Hill, Va.
Blackiston, S. H.
Dulaney, Josiah L.

Everett, Rev. Wm B.
Gemmill, Thos. H.
   killed, Winchester, Va.
Gleaves, Samuel G.
Handy, Luther
Hollyday, Geo. T.

Hynson, Medford
Kelly, Samuel J.
   wounded, 1st Manassas
Kennard, Jas. A.
   killed, 1st Manassas
Kennard, John H.

Lassell, Dr. Wm H.
Lassell, Rev. Jas. T.
McCoy, Harry
McCoy, Robert H.
Perkins, Levi
  killed, Winchester, Va.
Price, Ferdinand B.
Price, James S.
  killed, Franklin, Tenn.

Price, Wm C.
  killed, Appomattox, Va.
Rasin, Capt. William
Rasin, Mackall M.
Rolph, Geo. W.
Spear, Edwin W.
Spear, Jas. J.
Spencer, B. H.
Spencer, C. Chapman
  killed, Greenland Gap, Va.

Sudler, John C.
Vickers, Benj. C.
  killed, Shiloh, Tenn.
Wallis, H. C.
Wallis, Hugh M.
Wallis, Wm T.
Willson, Henry
Wright, Sol.

(UNION)

Allen, Jacob, killed
Baker, Sorin S.
Benjamin, A. S.
Burchinal, Capt. Wm D.
Corey, Capt. Albert L.
Crane, Lieut. Stephen M.
Fiddis, Thornton A.
Gray, James Moat, killed

Greenwood, Lieut. W. I.
Hamilton, Wm H.
Hines, Capt. Jesse K.
Howard, John T.
Lambert, George E.
Massey, Lieut. Col. E. E.
McDaniel, John N.
Rasin, John W.

Redde, Lieut. John H.
Smythe, Capt. Robt. H.
Stanley, Lieut. Chas. A. A.
Vannort, Lieut. Wm J.
Wickes, Capt. Chas. H.
Wilkins, Col. Ed

6.7 CHERRY HILL (UNION-POST 10 GAR)

Alexander, Robert
Anderson, Martin, V. B.
Biddle, George C.
Brown, Rev. Joseph T.
Burnett, Joseph T.
Caleb, Vincent S.
Cantwell, Joseph T.
Carr, John
Cole, James T.
Davidson, William G.
Davis, John T.
Drummond, John H.
Drummond, William P.
Founds, Lewis H.
Goodyear, Luke

Grant, William J.
Haas, Charles E.
Hiner, Elijah
Kelly, James T.
Lee, Thomas E.
Lutton, James T.
Macinson, William A.
Mahan, James H.
McDonald, William
McGlory, John
McLane, Allen
McNeal, George W.
Miller, John W.
Pierson, William T.
Poore, John

Pryce, William H.
Ricketts, Benjamin
Roberson, William
Ross, Robert P.
Sampson, Charles
Sebold, Emley W.
Simonton, Marmaduke
Simpson, John
Smiley, James C.
Spence, George R.
Terrell, George C.
Tong, Robert J.
Yocum, Joseph T.
Zane, Hiram C.

GLOSSARY OF TERMS

allegorical sculpture – Symbolic representation of an idea or principle.

bas-relief – Low relief carving on a flat background with little depth or projection from background.

beaux-arts – An artistic movement originating in Paris about 1870, emphasizing Classical style with great exuberance of expression and eclectic form.

brevet – A military rank, usually of honor. It could be given after discharge or while still serving, and a person could hold more than one brevet commission.

bronze – An alloy of copper and tin, often containing other elements; used for durable statues and plaques.

carrara marble – A fine, white marble mined in the mountains of Italy, having a flat rather than glossy finish.

cemetery – From Greek "sleeping chamber." The movement towards erecting park-like cemeteries outside of the cities began in U.S. in mid 19th century.

cherub – A winged child angel, or only the head and wings, as often found on early American gravestones.

classical – Following the traditions, rules and styles of ancient Greece and Rome.

contropposto – Pose of a statuary figure with the weight on one foot with the other knee bent, giving the hips and shoulders a slant. Began in 5th century B.C. Greece.

escutcheon – A decorative shield carved in relief.

memorial – Something that is a reminder of a person or event. A memorial can include books, holidays, stained glass windows, poems, buildings, gravestones, etc., as well as monuments.

monument – From Latin "monumentum" and its root "monere," to remind. A structure, edifice, or construction intended to commemorate a notable person, action, or event.

neoclassical – An artistic movement, 1890-1930, reviving the classical art and architecture of ancient Greece and Rome.

obelisk – An upright four-sided pillar, gradually tapering as it rises and terminated by a pyramid.

patina – A film, often green, formed on copper or bronze sculpture exposed to the elements.

pedestal – The base for a sculpture.

public memory – A body of beliefs and ideas about the past that help a group or society understand its past and define its present identity. It represents a combination of official and vernacular culture.

stele – An upright slab of stone bearing an inscription and often bas-relief sculpture.

Victorian – Related to the period of the reign of Queen Victoria (1837-1901); having to do with sentimentality, conventionality, and romantic ideals.

SYMBOLS

acorn – rebirth, life

anchor – Navy, hope (with a female figure), regimental insignia

anemone – sorrow, death

angel – Eternal life (can also indicate victory or vengeance)

boots – cavalry

bugle – musician, regimental insignia

cannon – artillery (also see "inverted cannon")

crossed swords – military, cavalry

cross bottony – symbol of the Marylanders who fought for the Confederacy. From the Maryland State Seal, Crossland part of the Calvert Coat-of-Arms. Now on the state flag.

drum – drummer

eagle – eternal vigilance, liberty

fasces – a bundle of rods bound by leather cords. Used in ancient Rome to symbolize the authority of the law.

furled flag – defeat

goldenrod – loyalty

inverted cannon – marks the site of death of a general

ivy – memory

lamb – innocence

laurel wreath – used in ancient Greece to crown the victors of athletic games. Symbolizes victory or honor.

lily – purity

oak – immortality, faith and virtue

poppy – forgetfulness

rifle – infantry

rosebud – young woman

rose – prime of life

sheathed sword – end of conflict

ship's wheel – Navy

square and compass – Masons

trefoil – regimental insignia

violet – humility

BIBLIOGRAPHY

ARCHIVAL COLLECTIONS

Antietam National Battlefield Park
  Monument File

Cecil County Historical Society
  Civil War Files

Dorchester County Library
  Cambridge Files

Enoch Pratt Library, Baltimore
  Green Mount Cemetery File
  Loudon Park Cemetery File

Frederick Historical Society
  Delaplane Collection
  Mount Olivet Cemetery File
  Monocacy Battlefield File

Hagerstown County Library, Maryland Room
  Antietam National Cemetery File
  Washington Cemetery File

Hagerstown Historical Society
  Antietam File
  Washington Cemetery File
  Minutes of the Antietam Cemetery Commission

Howard County Historical Society
  Civil War Files

Library of Congress
  Congressional Record, 1899-1914

Loudon Park Cemetery
  File on Confederate Hill

Maryland Historical Society
  Confederate Monuments File
  Loudon Park Cemetery File
  Taylor Collection
  Union Monuments File
  United Daughters of the Confederacy Collection

Maryland State Archives
  Antietam Battlefield File
  Civil War Memorabilia Collection
  Laws of Maryland, 1864-1914
  Maryland Civil War Centennial Commission Files

Montgomery County Historical Society
  DeSellum Collection
  Records of the White Chapter, UDC
  Records of the Brown Camp, UCV

National Archives
  Antietam National Battlefield Files
  Point Lookout National Monument File
  Tulip Monument File

St. Mary's Historical Society
  Point Lookout File

Talbot County Free Library, Maryland Room
  Civil War Files

BOOKS AND PAMPHLETS

Barach, Mildred C., and Ellen J. Beckman. *Civil War Union Monuments*. Washington, D.C.: Daughters of Union Veterans of the Civil War, 1978.

Beath, Robert B. *History of the Grand Army of the Republic*. New York: Bryan, Taylor & Co., 1889.

Beirne, Francis F. *The Amiable Baltimoreans*. New York: E. P. Dutton and Co., 1951.

Beitzell, Edwin W. *Point Lookout Prison Camp for Confederates*. Abell, Maryland: self-published, 1972.

The Biographical Cyclopedia of Representative Men of Maryland and Baltimore. Baltimore, Md.: National Biographical Publishing Co., 1879.

Boatner, Mark Mayo III. *The Civil War Dictionary*. New York: David McKay Co., Inc., 1987.

Bodnar, John. *Remaking America: Public Memory, Commemoration, and Patriotism in the Twentieth Century*. Princeton: Princeton University Press, 1992.

Brugger, Robert J. *Maryland: A Middle Temperament*. Baltimore: Johns Hopkins University Press, 1988.

Cohen, Hennig and Tristram Potter Coffin, eds. *The Folklore of American Holidays*. Detroit: Gale Research Co., 1987.

Cooling, Benjamin Franklin III, and Walton H. Owen II. *Mr. Lincoln's Forts*. Shippensburg, Pa.: White Mane Publishing Co., 1988.

Curl, James Stevens. *A Celebration of Death*. London: Constable and Co., 1980.

Doezema, Marianne, and June Hargrave. *The Public Monument and Its Audience*. Cleveland: The Cleveland Museum of Art, 1977.

Evitts, William J. *A Matter of Allegiances: Maryland From 1850 to 1861*. Baltimore: The Johns Hopkins University Press, 1974.

Fielding, Mantle. *Dictionary of American Painters, Sculptors, and Engravers*. ed. Genevieve Doran, Green Farms, Conn.: Modern Books and Crafts, 1974.

Foner, Eric. *Reconstruction: America's Unfinished Revolution*. New York: Harper and Row, 1988.

Foster, Gaines M. *Ghosts of the Confederacy: Defeat, the Lost Cause, and the Emergence of the New South*. New York: Oxford University Press, 1987.

Fusco, Peter, and H. W. Janson, eds. *The Romantics to Rodin: French Nineteenth-Century Sculpture from North American Collections*. Los Angeles: Los Angeles County Museum of Art, 1980.

Goode, James M. *The Outdoor Sculpture of Washington, D.C.* Washington, D.C.: Smithsonian Press, 1974.

Governor's Commission on Protocol for the Maryland State Flag. *Protocol for the Maryland State Flag*. Annapolis: Maryland State Archives, 1990.

Governor Oden Bowie's Commission on Antietam Burials. *Description of the Burial Places of the Remains of Confederate Soldiers Who Fell in the Battles of Antietam, South Mountain, Monocacy and Others*. Hagerstown: Free Press, no date [1868].

Hartzler, Daniel D. *Marylanders in the Confederacy*. Silver Spring, Md.: Family Line Publications, 1986.

Hess, George. *History of the Antietam Cemetery*. Hagerstown, Md.: Globe Job Rooms Press, 1880.

Hiebert, Eldon, and Richard K. MacMaster. *A Grateful Remembrance: The Story of Montgomery County*. Rockville, Md.: Montgomery County Government, 1976.

Hill, Lois, ed. *Poems and Songs of the Civil War*. New York: The Fairfax Press.

Hobsbawm, Eric and Terence Ranger, eds. *The Invention of Tradition*. Cambridge, Massachusetts: Cambridge University Press, 1983.

Holt, Dean W. *American Military Cemeteries*. Jefferson, N.C.: McFarland & Co,. Inc., 1992.

Hunt, Roger D. and Jack R. Brown. *Brevet Brigadier Generals in Blue*. Gaithersburg, Md.: Old Soldiers Books, 1990.

Jackson, Elmer Martin, Jr. *Maryland Symbols.* Annapolis: Capital-Gazette Press, Inc. 1964.

Jackson, J. B. *Necessity for Ruins and Other Topics.* Amherst: University of Massachusetts Press, 1980.

Jacobs, Charles T. *Civil War Guide to Montgomery County.* Montgomery County Historical Society, 1983.

Kent, Frank Richardson. *The Story of Maryland Politics: 1864-1910.* Baltimore, Thomas & Evans Printing Co., 1911.

Manakee, Harold R. *Maryland in the Civil War.* Baltimore: Maryland Historical Society, 1961.

Maryland Civil War Centennial Commission. *Maryland Remembers: A Guide to Historic Places and People of the Civil War in Maryland.* Hagerstown, Md., 1961.

Mayo, James M. *War Memorials as Political Landscape.* New York: Praeger, 1988.

Mitchell, Mary. *Divided Town.* Barre, Massachusetts: Barre Press, 1968.

Moore, Sally F. and Barbara G. Myerhoff, eds. *Secular Ritual.* Amsterdam, The Netherlands: Van Gorcum Co., 1977.

Osterweiss, Rollin G. *The Myth of the Lost Cause, 1865-1900.* Hamden, Connecticut: The Shoe-String Press, 1973.

Peters, James Edward. *Arlington National Cemetery: Shrine to America's Heroes.* McLean, Va.: Woodbine House, 1986.

Rusk, William Sener. *Art in Baltimore: Monuments and Memorials.* Baltimore: Norman Remington Co., 1929.

Scharf, J. Thomas. *History of Baltimore City and County.* Baltimore: Regional Publishing Company, 1971 (reprint of 1881 edition).

Scharf, J. Thomas. *History of Western Maryland.* Baltimore: Regional Publishing Company, 1968 (reprint of 1882 edition).

Schildt, John W. *Monuments at Antietam.* Frederick, Md.: Great Southern Press, 1991.

Sifakis, Stewart. *Who Was Who in the Civil War.* New York: Facts on File Publications, 1988.

Sloane, David Charles. *The Last Great Necessity: Cemeteries in American History.* Baltimore: Johns Hopkins University Press, 1991.

Stotelmyer, Steven R. *The Bivouacs of the Dead.* Baltimore, Md. Toomey Press, 1992.

Thomas, James W. and T. J. C. Williams. *History of Allegany County.* Cumberland, Md.: L. R. Titsworth & Co., 1923.

Thompson, Mary Ellen. *Loudon Park: Celebrating 125 Years.* Baltimore: Schneidereth and Sons, 1979.

Turner, Victor W. *The Ritual Process.* Chicago: Aldine Publishing Co., 1969.

United Daughters of the Confederacy, Baltimore Chapter. "The Monumental City's Confederate Monuments." 1987.

United States. National Commission of Fine Arts. *Report on War Memorials.* 79th Congress, 2nd session. Senate Doc. 234. 1946.

Warner, Ezra J. *Generals in Blue.* Louisiana State, 1959.

Warner, Ezra J. *Generals in Gray.* Louisiana State, 1959.

Warner, W. Lloyd. *The Living and the Dead: A Study of The Symbolic Life of Americans.* New Haven: Yale University Press, 1959.

Who Was Who. Historical Volume. Chicago: A. N. Marquis Co., 1963.

Widener, Ralph W., Jr. *Confederate Monuments.* Washington, D.C.: Andromeda Associates, 1982.

Wiebe, Robert H. *The Search For Order 1877-1920.* New York: Hill and Wang, 1967.

Williams, Thomas J. C. *A History of Washington County.* Hagerstown: J. M. Runk and L. R. Titsworth, Pub., 1906.

Williams, Thomas J. C. *A History of Frederick County.* Hagerstown: L. R. Titsworth, Pub., 1910.

Wilson, Jane B. *The Very Quiet Baltimoreans: A Guide to the Historic Cemeteries and Burial Sites of Baltimore.* Shippensburg, Pa.: White Mane Publishing Co., Inc., 1991.

Worthington, Glenn H. *Fighting for Time: The Battle That Saved Washington.* Shippensburg, Pa.: White Mane Publishing Co., Inc., 1985.

Zelinsky, Wilbur. *Nation into State: the Shifting Symbolic Foundations of American Nationalism.* Chapel Hill: the University of North Carolina Press, 1988.

THESES AND DISSERTATIONS

Duncan, Richard R. "The Social Impact of the Civil War on Maryland." Diss., Ohio State, 1965.

Grimaldi, Anthony Eugene. "The Indian Soldiers' and Sailors' Monument and Its Dedication: A Study of a Nineteenth-Century American Monument and Its Allied Arts of Pageantry." Diss., Ohio University, 1982.

Panhorst, Michael Wilson. "Lest We Forget: Monuments and Memorial Sculpture in National Military Parks on Civil War Battlefields." Diss., University of Delaware, 1988.

Ruffner, Kevin. "Border State Warriors: Maryland's Junior Officers in the Union and Confederate Armies." Diss., George Washington University, 1992.

Savage, Kirk Eugene. "Race, Memory, and Identity: The National Monuments of the Union and Confederacy." Diss., University of California, Berkeley, 1990.

Siedenhans, Michael. "Their Deeds are Written on the Temple of Fame: Veterans Organizations in Baltimore 1866-1914." Thesis, Johns Hopkins University 1988.

Soderberg, Susan. "Lest We Forget: Confederate Monuments and Ceremonies in Maryland, 1870-1918." Thesis, George Washington University, 1992.

Williams, Lewis Walron, II. "Commercially Produced Forms of American Civil War Monuments." Thesis, University of Illinois, 1948.

ARTICLES

Albanese, Catherine. "Requiem for Memorial Day: Dissent in the Redeemer." *American Quarterly* 26 (Oct. 1974): 386-398.

Asper, Lewis D. "The Long and Unhappy History of Loyalty Testing in Maryland (1861-1867)." *Maryland Historical Magazine* 28 (1933): 309-328.

Barber, Bernard. "Place, Symbol, and Utilitarian Function in War Memorials." *Social Forces* 28 (1949): 64-68.

Bardsley, Virginia O., ed. "Frederick Diary: September 5-14, 1862." *Maryland Historical Magazine* 60 (1965): 132-138.

Bruchey, Eleanor. "The Industrialization of Maryland." *Maryland: A History.* Ed. Richard Walsh and William Lloyd Fox. Baltimore: Maryland Historical Society, 1983.

Clarke, Charles B. "Recruitment of Union Troops in Maryland, 1861-1865." *Maryland Historical Magazine* 53:2 (June, 1958): 153-176.

Cooper, Gordon F. "The Maryland Flag: Its Origin." *Chronicles of St. Mary's* 4:10 (Oct., 1956): 65-68.

Davis, Stephen. "Empty Eyes, Marble Hand: The Confederate Monument and the South." *Journal of Popular Culture* 16.3 (1982): 2-21.

Duncan, Richard R. "The Era of the Civil War." *Maryland: A History.* Ed. Richard Walsh and William Lloyd Fox. Baltimore: Maryland Historical Society, 1983.

Fusco, Peter. "Allegory," in *The Romantics to Rodin: French Nineteenth-Century Sculpture from North American Collections*. Peter Fusco, Peter and H. W. Janson, eds. Los Angeles: Los Angeles County Museum of Art, 1980.

Hargrove, June. "The Public Monument," in *The Romantics to Rodin: French Nineteenth-Century Sculpture from North American Collections*. Peter Fusco, Peter and H. W. Janson, eds. Los Angeles: Los Angeles County Museum of Art, 1980.

Howells, William Dean. "Question of Monuments." *Atlantic Monthly*. 18 (May 1866): 646-649.

Hubbard, William. "A Meaning For Monuments." *The Public Interest* 74 (Winter 1984): 17-31.

Lindberg, Tod. "Of Arms, Men and Monuments." *Commentary* 78.4 (1984): 51-56.

Lowenthal, David. "Age and Artifact: Dilemmas of Appreciation" in *The Interpretation of Ordinary Landscapes*," D. W. Meining, ed. N.Y.: Oxford University Press, 1979.

Moore, Virginia Campbell. "Remembrances of Life Along the Rockville Pike." *The Montgomery County Story*. 27.4, (Nov., 1984).

Nora, Pierre. "Between Memory and History: Les Lieux de Memoire." *Representations* 26 (Spring 1989): 7-25.

Russ, William A. "Disfranchisement in Maryland (1861-67)." *Maryland Historical Magazine* 53:2 (June, 1958).

Sanderlin, Walter S. "A House Divided: the Conflict of Loyalties on the C & O Canal." *Maryland Historical Magazine* 42 (1947): 206-213.

Soderberg, Susan C. "The Confederate Monument and Its Symbolism." *The Montgomery County Story* 36:3 (Aug., 1993).

Stiverson, Gregory A. "The Maryland Flag." *Protocol for the Maryland State Flag*. Annapolis: Maryland State Archives, 1990.

Stone, James. "War Music and War Psychology in the Civil War." *Journal of Abnormal and Social Psychology* 36: 543-60.

Sturken, Marita. "The Wall, the Screen, the Image: The Vietnam Veterans Memorial." *Representations* 35 (summer, 1991): 118-142.

Sword, Gerald J. "Confederate Cemetery at Point Lookout, Maryland." *Chronicles of St. Mary's* 27:12 (December, 1979): 121-129.

Thelan, David. Introduction to special issue on memory and American history. *Journal of American History* 75:4 (March, 1989): 1117-1129.

Tuan, Yi-Fu. "The Significance of the Artifact" *Geographical Review* 74:4 (1980): 462-472.

Wagandt, Charles L. "Redemption or Reaction? – Maryland in the Post-Civil War Years," in *Radicalism, Racism, and Party Realignment: The Border States During Reconstruction*, Richard O. Curry, ed. Baltimore: Johns Hopkins University Press, 1969.

Winberry, John J. "Symbols in the Landscape: The Confederate Memorial." *Pioneer America Society Transactions* 5 (1982): 9-15.

RECORDINGS

Mastrangelo, Coleen. "All Quiet Along the Potomac." Maryland, 1993. Available at Antietam National Battlefield Park.

Mormon Tabernacle Choir, Richard P. Condie conducting. "Songs of the North and South, 1861-1865." Columbia. LC #R61-1178.

National Geographic Society, "Songs of the Civil War." Washington, D.C., 1976.

UNPUBLISHED PAPERS, INTERVIEWS AND LECTURES

Cushing, Mrs. H. Stanley (Anita). Howard County Historical Society. Interview. November, 1992.

Elgin, Charles (President of the Monocacy Cemetery Association). Interview. 20 April, 1990.

Jacobs, Marian. "Montgomery County Confederate Veterans." unpublished book.

Hauck, Jeanne. "The Memorialization Process in Collective Culture" unfinished diss.

Legg, Joseph B. "The Burying Grounds of Baltimore."

Maryland Historical Trust, "Military Monuments Inventory," 1991.

Primer, Ben (Dir. Reference Services, Md. State Archives). "Was Maryland a Northern or a Southern State?" "Maryland and the Civil War" Conference. Annapolis, 20 April, 1991.

Pruett, Samuel (President of the Washington Cemetery Asssociation), interview. March, 1991.

Stiverson, Gregory A. "The Maryland Flag." unpublished lecture, 1991.

Walewajk, Joyce. "History of Woodside," unpublished, 1991.

Index